THE NEVILLE READER

OTHER BOOKS BY NEVILLE

Awakened Imagination

The Power of Awareness

Your Faith is Your Fortune

Immortal Man

And now, go,
write it before them
on a tablet,
and inscribe it in a book,
that it may be
for the time to come
as a witness for ever.

ISAIAH 30:8

THE
Neville
READER

The Law and the Promise

Prayer: The Art of Believing

Feeling is the Secret

Resurrection

Freedom for All

Out of This World

Seedtime and Harvest

DeVorss Publications
Camarillo, California

I want to express my sincere appreciation to the hundreds of men and women who have written me, telling me of their use of imagination to create a greater good for others as well as for themselves; that we may be mutually encouraged by each other's faith, a faith which was loyal to the unseen reality of their imaginal acts.

The limitation of space does not allow the publication of all the stories in this one volume. In the difficult task of selecting and organizing this material, Ruth Messenger and Juleene Brainard have been of invaluable assistance.

NEVILLE

TABLE OF CONTENTS

THE SUBSTANCE OF THINGS HOPED FOR
Searching for Neville Goddard

By Mitch Horowitz

The words of spiritual teacher Neville Goddard retain their power to electrify more than thirty years following his death. In a sonorous, clipped tone that is preserved and circulated on tapes made during his lifetime, Neville asserts with complete ease what many would find fantastic: Our thoughts create the world, and do so in the most literal sense.

Neville Goddard was among the last century's most articulate and charismatic purveyors of the philosophy generally called New Thought. He wrote ten books under the solitary penname Neville, and was a popular speaker on metaphysical themes from the late 1930s until his death in 1972. Possessed of a self-educated and uncommonly sharp intellect, Neville captured the sheer *logic* of creative-mind principles as perhaps no other figure of his era.

Neville's way of thought is extolled today by major-league pitcher Barry Zito, and some say it influenced the ideas of Carlos Castaneda, Aldous Huxley, and others. And yet little is known about this teacher who exerted so unusual a pull on the American spiritual scene of the mid-century.

A Philosopher Born

Details of Neville's early life are few—and are mostly self-proffered. But this much is evident: Neville Lancelot

Goddard was born in 1905 on the then British-protectorate of Barbados to an Anglican family of nine sons and one daughter. A 1950s gossip column described the young Neville as "enormously wealthy," his family possessing "a whole island in the West Indies." Other suggestions are far more modest. At various times Neville depicted his own English childhood home as comfortable, but hardly lavish.

He came to New York at the age of seventeen to study theater—a move that would lead to a successful career as a vaudeville dancer and stage actor. Yet Neville described himself as often living hand-to-mouth, working for a time as an elevator operator and a shipping clerk.

His ambition for the stage began to fade as he encountered a remarkable range of spiritual ideas—first with self-styled occult groups, and later with the help of a life-transforming mentor. In his lectures, Neville describes studying with an Ethiopian-born rabbi named Abdullah. Their initial meeting, Neville says, had an air of kismet:

> When I first met my friend Abdullah back in 1931 I entered a room where he was speaking and when the speech was ended he came over, extended his hand and said: "Neville, you are six months late." I had never seen the man before, so I said: "I am six months late? How do you know me?" and he replied: "The brothers told me that you were coming and you are six months late."

According to Neville, the two studied Hebrew, Scripture, and kabala together for five years—planting the seeds of the philosophy of mental creativity that Neville would develop.

Neville says his first encounter with creative thought came while he was living in a rented room on Manhattan's Upper West Side during the winter of 1933. The young man was depressed: his theatrical career had stalled and his pockets were empty. "After twelve years in America, I was a failure in my own eyes," he later said. "I was in the theatre and made money one year and spent it the next month." The 28-year-old Neville ached to spend Christmas with his family in Barbados; but he couldn't afford to travel.

"Live as though you are there," Abdullah told him, "and that you shall be." Wandering the streets of New York City, Neville *thought from his aim*—as he would later urge his listeners—and adopted the feeling that he was really and truly at home on his native island. "Abdullah taught me the importance of remaining faithful to an idea and not compromising," he later remembered. "I wavered, but he remained faithful to the assumption that I was in Barbados and had traveled first class."

One December morning before the last ship was to depart New York that year for Barbados, Neville received a letter from a long out-of-touch brother: In it was $50 and a ticket to sail. The experiment, it seemed, had worked.

Neville discovered what would eventually become the hallmark of his teaching: It was imperative to assume the feeling that one's goal has already been attained. "It is not what you want that you attract," he would later write; "you attract what you believe to be true."

Feeling is the Secret

Neville grew convinced that Scripture was rife with this idea that man had to *think from the end*. He called it the state of "I AM"—this being a mystical translation of the name of God. Man could attain any goal, he reasoned, provided he adopted the feeling of it in the present. Neville reinterpreted each episode in Scripture as a psychological parable of this truth. In a typical example from his first book, *Your Faith Is Your Fortune*, he took a fresh sounding of the tale of Lot's wife, who turns into a pillar of salt after looking back upon the city of Sodom: "Not knowing that consciousness is ever outpicturing itself in conditions round about you, like Lot's wife you continually look back upon your problem and again become hypnotized by its seeming naturalness."

In his eyes, all of Scripture was nothing other than a blueprint for man's development. "The Bible has no reference at all to any person who ever existed, or any event that ever occurred upon earth," Neville told his audiences. "All the stories of the Bible unfold in the minds of the individual man." Neville depicted Christ not as a living figure but, rather, as a mythical master psychologist whose miracles and parables demonstrated the power of creative thought.

While Neville could quote from Scripture with photographic ease, one is left with the impression that he sometimes strained to fit all of it within a psychological formula. But there is no questioning the power that Neville brought to Scriptural analysis: in his hands, Scripture became a living book, pulsating with relevance and purpose. "Today," he wrote, "those to whom this great treasure has been entrusted, namely the priesthoods of the world, have forgotten that the Bibles are psychological dramas representing consciousness in man; in their blind forgetfulness they now teach their followers to worship its characters as men and women who actually lived in time and space."

The Ethics of Creative Thought

Another innovative aspect of Neville's teaching is the ethical analysis he brought to mental science. In a powerfully rendered pamphlet called *Prayer*, which was later reissued in his 1966 book Resurrection, Neville takes measure of whether imagination can be used to harm another.

The subject has no power to resist your controlled subjective ideas of him unless the state affirmed by you to be true of him is a state he is incapable of wishing as true another. In that case, it returns to you, the sender and will realize itself in you ... A person who directs a malicious thought to another will be injured by its rebound if he fails to get subconscious acceptance of the other.

Hence,

Never accept as true of others what you would not want to be true of you.

A truth as old as time, perhaps, but one that Neville saw literally enacted by the power of thought.

It is uncommon, at least today, for New Thought or Religious Science writers to raise questions of ethics or consequence in connection with one's wish. In using the law, one might ask, what part of me is manifesting, and for what purpose? Am I conscious of my motives? To Neville, the law operates in a neutral, amoral way—but consequences befall those who harness it for ill:

One of the most prevalent misunderstandings is that this law works only for those have a devout or religious objective. This is a fallacy. It works just as impersonally as the law of electricity works. It can be used for greedy, selfish purposes as well as noble ones. But it should always be borne in mind that ignoble thoughts and actions inevitably result in unhappy consequences.

The Metaphysics of Creativity

Neville was not content to rest his teaching upon anecdote and parable alone. In some of his most elegant and convincing writing, he defined a metaphysical justification—an internal logic—for the workings of mental science. In Prayer, Neville spoke of the "universal law of reversibility:"

> Mechanical motion caused by speech was known for a long time before any one dreamed of the possibility of inverse transformation, that is, the reproduction of speech by mechanical motion (the phonograph). For a long time electricity was produced by friction without ever a thought that friction, in turn, could be produced by electricity. Whether or not man succeeds in reversing a force, he knows, nevertheless, that all transformations of force *are* reversible ... This law is of the highest importance, because it enables you to foresee the inverse transformation once the direct transformation is verified. If you knew how you would *feel* were you to realize your objective, then, inversely, you would know what state you could realize were you to awaken in yourself such feeling.

If one follows Neville's line of thought, what emerges seems almost too good to be true: Believe that you already possess your goal, and so you will. "Man moves in a world that is nothing more or less than his consciousness objectified," he concluded. If so, one might ask, why has this imperative been discovered by so relatively few?

Does it Work?

In a little-known book from 1946, the occult philosopher Israel Regardie took measure of the burgeoning creative-mind movements, including Unity, Christian Science, and Religious

Science. Regardie paid special attention to the case of Neville, whose teaching, he felt, reflected both the hopes and limits of New Thought philosophy. Regardie believed that Neville possessed profound and truthful ideas; yet he felt these ideas were proffered without sufficient attention to training or practice. Could the everyday person really control his thoughts and moods in the way Neville prescribed? In *The Romance of Metaphysics*, Regardie wrote:

> Neville's method is sound enough. But the difficulty is that few people are able to muster up this emotional exaltation or this intellectual concentration which are the royal approaches to the citadel of the Unconscious. As a result of this definite lack of training or technique, the mind wanders all over the place, and a thousand and one things totally unrelated to 'I AM' are ever before their attention.

Neville offered his listeners and readers meditative techniques, such as using the power of visualization before going to sleep. But Regardie reasons that, as a dancer and actor, Neville possessed a unique control over his body that his audience did not share: "Neville knows the art of relaxation instinctively. He is a dancer, and a dancer must, of necessity, relax. Hence I believe he does not fully and consciously realize that the average person in his audience does not know the mechanism of relaxation, does not know how to 'let go.'"

In experimenting with Neville's philosophy myself, I placed an empty bud vase on my dining-room table, and—for a period of days—imagined a rose in that vase. I set no parameters on how it would get there, but simply envisioned the texture, smell, and color of that rose. No rose appeared. And yet, when in a completely different feeling state, I envisioned winning a door prize that was offered in an auditorium filled with several hundred people. I won. My feeling state, Neville would argue, was the key. Perhaps I sincerely desired the second item and not the first. It may also be so that my emotions were randomly more open, my body by chance more relaxed in the latter episode. And herein lies one of the potential frustrations of Neville's philosophy: Few understand—or can manipulate - their emotions or sensations in the face of contrary truths or the vicissitudes of mood. Stick your finger with a pin, and try imagining the taste of an ice cream sundae.

"Of all the metaphysical systems with which I am acquainted," Regardie concluded, "Neville's is the most magical. But being the most magical, it requires for that very reason, a systematized training on the part of those who would approach and enter its portals." Absent this training, Regardie reasons, "His system is in reality strictly personal." It may work for him but not others.

Living in the Material World

Is Regardie's a fair criticism? Certainly evidence exists to the contrary—much of it offered by Neville himself. In his 1961 book *The Law and the Promise*, Neville provides a plethora of vividly rendered case studies of people who achieved success using his methods. As one reads these passages, however, another impression emerges. Student after student is concerned with ardently material goals: a new house, a new car, a new suit, cash in the pocket. Is this, one wonders, the aim of spiritual practice? Do these principles come down simply to get-rich methods? In an unpublished lecture from 1967, Neville draws an intriguing counterpoint:

What would be good for you? Tell me, because in the end every conflict will resolve itself as the world is simply mirroring the being you are assuming that you are. One day you will simply mirroring the being you are assuming that you are. One day you will be so saturated with wealth, so saturated with power in the world of Caesar, you will turn your back on it all and go in search of the word of God ... I do believe that one must completely saturate himself with the things of Caesar before he is hungry for the word of God.

This passage sounds a note that resonates through many of the spiritual traditions of the world: One cannot renounce what one has not attained. To move beyond the material world, or its wealth, one must know that wealth.

The Law—and the Legacy

Neville never achieved the fame or reputation of some of his contemporaries, such as Norman Vincent Peale and Ernest Holmes. Still, at the height of his career he reached many thousands of seekers. In New York, Los Angeles, and San Francisco, he addressed crowded church pews and packed auditoriums. He had a radio program and, for a short time, an inspirational television show broadcast from Los Angeles in the mid-1950s. His books and pamphlets were sold at lectures, and he freely allowed students to tape his addresses without charge—tapes that continue to informally spread his message today.

In the last twelve years of his life, he took his philosophy in a radical new direction—one that would cost him some of his popularity on the positive-thinking circuit. Neville spoke of a jarring mystical experience he had in 1959 in which he was reborn as a child from within his skull, which opened as a womb. (In the Bible, Golgotha translates as skull). In a complex interpretation of Scripture and personal experience, Neville told of "the Promise:" that each of us is Christ

In his lectures, Neville shifted his focus to this story of mystical rebirth. His audiences, however, seemed to prefer the earlier message of self-affirmation. They began to drift away. Urged by a speaking agent to abandon this theme, "or you'll have no audience at all," a student recalls Neville replying, "Then I'll tell it to the bare walls." His popularity would partly rebound as he settled into teaching a mixture of both the mystical and creative-mind aspects of his philosophy. Though when he died, reportedly of a brain aneurysm in 1972, there was no obituary to mark his passing, even in Los Angeles where he had made his home.

Whatever his mixed fortunes—and perhaps because of them—Neville was one the last century's most remarkable spiritual impresarios. He remained true to the principles on which he founded his career, yet dared to move beyond them without regard for convention or popular acceptance.

For all the recent talk of America being a faith-based nation, it was this iconoclastic foreigner who lived out the promise of religious freedom in a manner, perhaps, that a Benjamin Franklin or Thomas Paine would have smiled upon. Through the force of intellect and self-study, Neville developed a personal theology, and barnstormed through auditoriums and churches on both American coasts winning followers. Here was a man who stretched his wings in the winds of a nation that was open to religious innovation. It is in Neville that one finds a truly American spiritual figure: an innovator, a nonconformist, someone who dared to live by the inner light of his ideas.

MITCH HOROWITZ

A frequent contributor to *Science of Mind*, Mitch Horowitz is the Executive Editor of Tarcher/Penguin in New York, where he has published some of today's leading titles in world religion, esoterica, and the metaphysical.

"Neville Goddard was one of the last century's most unusual and convincing purveyors of mental science. His work seeks to explain the metaphysics behind 'the law' and to provide an ethical framework for its use. Anyone interested in New Thought or Religious Science who doesn't know Neville has a treasure to discover."

Feeling is the Secret: Neville in His Own Words

"The Lord of hosts will not respond to your wish until you have assumed the feeling of already being what you want to be, for acceptance is the channel of His action."

—from *The Power of Awareness*, 1952

"Leave the mirror and change your face. Leave the world alone and change your conceptions of yourself."

—from *Your Faith is Your Fortune*, 1941

"If a man look upon any other man and estimates that man as less than himself, then he is stealing from the other. He is stealing the other's birthright - that of equality."

—as quoted in the *Los Angeles Times*, 1951

"Do not try to change people; they are only messengers telling you who you are. Revalue yourself and they will confirm the change."

—from *Your Faith is Your Fortune*, 1941

"Fools exploit the world; the wise transfigure it."

—from *Prayer* as reprinted in *Resurrection*, 1966

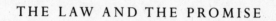

THE LAW AND THE PROMISE

CHAPTER 1

"THE LAW"
Imaging Creates Reality

Man is all Imagination. God is Man and exists in
us and we in Him . . . The Eternal Body of Man is
the Imagination, that is, God, Himself.
— Blake

The purpose of the first portion of this book is to show, through actual true stories, how imagining creates reality. Science progresses by way of hypotheses tentatively tested and afterwards accepted or rejected according to the facts of experience. The claim that imagining creates reality needs no more consideration than is allowed by science. It proves itself in performance.

The world in which we live is a world of imagination. In fact, life itself is an activity of imagining, "For Blake," wrote Professor Morrison of the University of St. Andrews, "the world originates in a divine activity identical with what we know ourselves as the activity of imagination;" his task being "to open the immortal eyes of man inward into the worlds of thought, into eternity, ever expanding in the bosom of God, the Human Imagination."

Nothing appears or continues in being by a power of its own. Events happen because comparatively stable imaginal activities created them, and they continue in being only as long as they receive such support. "The secret of imagining," writes Douglas Fawcett, "is the greatest of all problems to the solution of which the mystic aspires. Supreme power,

9

"The Law"

supreme wisdom, supreme delight lie in the far-off solution of this mystery"

When man solves the mystery of imagining, he will have discovered the secret of causation, and that is: Imagining creates reality. Therefore, the man who is aware of what he is imagining knows what he is creating; realizes more and more that the drama of life is imaginal not physical. All activity is at bottom imaginal. An awakened Imagination works with a purpose. It creates and conserves the desirable, and transforms or destroys the undesirable.

Divine imagining and human imagining are not two powers at all, rather one. The valid distinction which exists between the seeming two lies not in the substance with which they operate but in the degree of intensity of the operant power itself. Acting at high tension, an imaginal act is an *immediate* objective fact. Keyed low, an imaginal act is realized in a time process. But whether imagination is keyed high or low, it is the "ultimate, essentially nonobjective Reality from which objects are poured forth like sudden fancies." No object is independent of imagining on some level or levels. Everything in the world owes its character to imagination on one of its various levels. "Objective reality," writes Fichte, "is solely produced through imagination." Objects seem so independent of our perception of them that we incline to forget that they owe their origin to imagination. The world in which we live is a world of imagination, and man—through his imaginal activities—creates the realities and the circumstances of life; this he does either knowingly or unknowingly.

Men pay too little attention to this priceless gift—The Human Imagination—and a gift is practically nonexistent unless there is a conscious possession of it and a readiness to use it. All men possess the power to create reality, but

10

this power sleeps as though dead, when not consciously exercised. Men live in the very heart of creation—The Human Imagination—yet are no wiser for what takes place therein. The future will not be fundamentally different from the imaginal activities of man; therefore, the individual who can summon at will whatever imaginal activity he pleases and to whom the visions of his imagination are as real as the forms of nature, is master of his fate.

The future is the imaginal activity of man in its creative march. Imagining is the creative power not only of the poet, the artist, the actor and orator, but of the scientist, the inventor, the merchant and the artisan. Its abuse in unrestrained unlovely image-making is obvious; but its abuse in undue repression breeds a sterility which robs man of actual wealth of experience.

Imagining novel solutions to ever more complex problems is far more noble than to run from problems. Life is the continual solution of a continuously synthetic problem. Imagining creates events. The world, created out of men's imagining, comprises un-numbered warring beliefs; therefore, there can never be a perfectly stable or static state. Today's events are bound to disturb yesterday's established order. Imaginative men and women invariably unsettle a pre-existing peace of mind.

Do not bow before the dictate of facts and accept life on the basis of the world without. Assert the supremacy of your Imaginal acts over facts and put all things in subjection to them. Hold fast to your ideal in your imagination. Nothing can take it from you but your failure to persist in imagining the ideal realized. Imagine only such states that are of value or promise well.

"The Law"

To attempt to change circumstances before you change your imaginal activity, is to struggle against the very nature of things. There can be no outer change until there is first an imaginal change. Everything you do, unaccompanied by an imaginal change, is but futile readjustment of surfaces. Imagining the wish fulfilled brings about a union with that state, and during that union you behave in keeping with your imaginal change. This shows you that an imaginal change will result in a change of behavior. However, your ordinary imaginal alterations as you pass from one state to another are not transformations because each of them is so rapidly succeeded by another in the reverse direction. But whenever one state grows so stable as to become your constant mood, your habitual attitude, then that habitual state defines your character and is a true transformation.

How do you do it? Self-abandonment! That is the secret. You must abandon yourself mentally to your wish fulfilled in your love for that state, and in so doing, live in the new state and no more in the old state. You can't commit yourself to what you do not love, so the secret of self-commission is faith—plus love. Faith is believing what is unbelievable. Commit yourself to the feeling of the wish fulfilled, in faith that this act of self-commission will become a reality. And it must become a reality because imagining creates reality.

Imagination is both conservative and transformative. It is conservative when it builds its world from images supplied by memory and the evidence of the senses. It is creatively transformative when it imagines things as they ought to be, building its world out of the generous dreams of fancy. In the procession of images, the ones that take precedence (naturally) are those of the senses. Nevertheless, a present sense impression is only an image. It does not differ in nature from a memory image or the image of a wish. What makes a present sense impression so objectively real is the individual's imagination functioning in it and thinking from it; whereas, in a memory image or a wish, the individual's imagination is not functioning *in* it and thinking *from* it, but is functioning out of it and thinking of it.

If you would enter *into* the image in your imagination, then would you know what it is to be creatively transformative: then would you realize your wish; and then you would be happy. Every image can be embodied. But unless you, yourself, enter the image and think from it, it is incapable of birth. Therefore, it is the height of folly to expect the wish to be realized by the mere passage of time. That which requires imaginative occupancy to produce its effect, obviously cannot be affected without such occupancy. You cannot be in one image and not suffer the consequences of *not* being in another.

Imagination is spiritual sensation. Enter the image of the wish fulfilled, then give it sensory vividness and tones of reality by mentally acting as you would act were it a physical fact. Now, this is what I mean by spiritual sensation. Imagine that you are holding a rose in your hand. Smell it. Do you detect the odor of roses? Well, if the rose is not there, why is its fragrance in the air? Through spiritual sensation—that is— through imaginal sight, sound, scent, taste and touch, you can give to the image sensory vividness. If you do this, all things will conspire to aid your harvesting and upon reflection you will see how subtle were the threads that led to your goal. You could never have devised the means which your imaginal activity employed to fulfill itself.

"The Law"

If you long to escape from your present sense fixation, to transform your present life into a dream of what might well be, you need but imagine that you are already what you want to be and to feel the way you would expect to feel under such circumstances. Like the make—believe of a child who is remaking the world after its own heart, create your world out of pure dreams of fancy. Mentally enter into your dream; mentally do what you would actually do, were it physically true. You will discover that dreams are realized not by the rich, but by the imaginative. Nothing stands between you and the fulfillment of your dreams but facts and facts are the creations of imagining. If you change your imagining, you will change the facts.

Man and his past are one continuous structure. This structure contains all of the facts which have been conserved and still operate below the threshold of his surface mind. For him it is merely history. For him it seems unalterable—a dead and firmly fixed past. But for itself, it is living-it is part of the living age. He cannot leave behind him the mistakes of the past, for nothing disappears. Everything that has been is still in existence. The past still exists, and it gives—and still gives—its results. Man must go back in memory, seek for and destroy the causes of evil, however far back they lie. This going into the past and replaying a scene of the past in imagination as it ought to have been played the first time, I call revision and revision results in repeal.

Changing your life means changing the past. The causes of any present evil are the unrevised scenes of the past. The past and the present form the whole structure of man; they are carrying all of its contents with it. Any alteration of content will result in an alteration in the present and future.

"The Law"

Live nobly—so that mind can store a past well worthy of recall. Should you fail to do so, remember, the first act of correction or cure is always— *"revise."* If the past is recreated into the present, so will the *revised* past be recreated into the present, or else the claim . . . though your sins are like scarlet, they shall be as white as snow . . . is a lie. And it is no lie.

The purpose of the story-to-story Commentary that follows is to link up as briefly as possible the distinct but never disconnected themes of the fourteen chapters into which I have divided the first part of this book. It will serve, I hope, as a thread of coherent thought that binds the whole into proof of its claim! Imagining Creates Reality.

To make such a claim is easily done. To prove it in the experience of others is far sterner. To stir you to use the "Law" constructively in your own life—that is the aim of this book.

CHAPTER 2

"DWELL THEREIN"

My God, I heard this day,
That none doth build a stately habitation,
But he that means to dwell therein.
What house more stately hath there been,
Or can be, than is Man? to whose creation
All things are in decay.
　　　　　　　　　　—George Herbert

I wish it were true of man's noble dreams, but unfortunately-perpetual construction, deferred occupancy—is the common fault of man. Why "build a stately habitation," unless you intend to "dwell therein?" Why build a dream house and not "dwell therein?"

This is the secret of those who lie in bed awake while they dream things true. They know how to live in their dream until, in fact, they do just that. Man, through the medium of a controlled, waking dream, can predetermine his future. That imaginal activity, of living in the feeling of the wish fulfilled, leads man across a bridge of incident to the fulfillment of the dream. If we live in the dream-thinking from it, and not of it—then the creative power of imagining will answer our adventurous fancy, and the wish fulfilled will break in upon us and take us unawares.

Man is all imagination; therefore, man must be where he is in imagination, for his imagination is himself. To realize that imagination is not something tied to the senses or enclosed within the spatial boundary of the body is most important.

"Dwell Therein"

Although man moves about in space by movement of his physical body, he need not be so restricted. He can move by a change in what he is aware of. However real the scene on which sight rests, man can gaze on one never before witnessed. He can always remove the mountain if it upsets his concept of what life ought to be. This ability to mentally move from things as they are to things as they ought to be, is one of the most important discoveries that man can make. It reveals man as a center of imagining with powers of intervention which enable him to alter the course of observed events, moving from success to success through a series of mental transformations of nature, of others, and himself.

For many years a doctor and his wife "dreamed" about their "stately habitation," but not until they imaginatively lived in it, did they manifest it. Here is their story:

"Some fifteen years ago, Mrs. M. and I purchased a lot on which we built a two-story building housing our office and living area. We left ample space on the lot for an apartment building—if and when our finances would permit. All those years we were busy paying off our mortgage, and at the end of that time had no money for the additional building we still desired so much. It was true that we had an ample savings account which meant security for our business, but to use any part of it for a new building would be to jeopardize that security.

"But now your teaching awakened a new concept, boldly telling us we could have what we most desired through the controlled use of our imagination and that realizing a desire was made more convincing 'without money.' We decided to put it to a test to forget about 'money' and concentrate our attention on the thing we desired most in this world—the new apartment building.

"Dwell Therein"

"With this principle in mind, we mentally constructed the new building as we wanted it, actually drawing physical plans so we could better formulate our mental picture of the completed structure. Never forgetting to think from the end (in our case, the completed, occupied building,) we took many imaginative trips through our apartment house, renting the units to imaginary tenants, examining in detail every room and enjoying the feeling of pride as friends offered congratulations on the unique planning. We brought into our imaginal scene one friend in particular (I shall call her Mrs. X) a lady we had not seen for some time as she had 'given us up' socially, believing us a bit peculiar in our new way of thinking. In our imaginal scene we took her through the building and asked how she liked it. Hearing her voice distinctly, we had her reply, 'Doctor, I think it is beautiful.'

"One day while talking together of our building, my wife mentioned a contractor who had constructed several apartment houses in our neighborhood. We knew of him only by the name that appeared on signs adjacent to buildings under construction. But realizing that if we were living in the end, we would not be looking for a contractor, we promptly forgot this angle. Continuing these periods of daily imagining for several weeks, we both felt we were now 'fused' with our desire and had successfully been living in the end.

"One day a stranger entered our office and identified himself as the contractor whose name my wife had mentioned weeks before. In an apologetic manner, he said, 'I don't know why I stopped here. I normally don't go to see people, but rather, people come to see me.' He explained that he passed our office often and had

18

"Dwell Therein"

wondered why there wasn't an apartment building on the corner lot. We assured him we would like very much to have such a building there but that we had no money to put into the project, not even the few hundred dollars it would take for plans.

"Our negative response did not faze him and seemingly compelled, he began to figure and devise ways and means to carry out the job, unasked and unencouraged by us. Forgetting the incident, we were quite startled when a few days later this man called, informing us that plans were completed and that the proposed building would cost us thirty thousand dollars! We thanked him politely and did absolutely nothing. We knew we had been 'living imaginatively in the end' of a completed building and that Imagination would assemble that building perfectly with out any 'outside' assistance from us. So, we were not surprised when the contractor called again the next day to say he had found a set of blueprints in his files that fitted our needs perfectly with few alterations. This, we were informed, would save us the architect's fee for new plans. We thanked him again and still did nothing.

"Logical thinkers would insist that such negative response from prospective customers would completely end the matter. Instead, two days later the contractor again called with the news that he had located a finance company willing to cover the necessary loan with the exception of a few thousand dollars. It sounds incredible, but we still did nothing. For—remember—to us this building was completed and rented, and in our imagination we had not put one penny into its construction.

"The balance of this tale reads like a sequel to Alice

"Dwell Therein"

In Wonderland, for the contractor came to our office the next day and said, as though presenting us with a gift, 'You people are going to have that new building anyway. I've decided to finance the balance of the loan myself. If this is agreeable, I'll have my lawyer draw up the papers, and you can pay me back out of net profits from rentals.'

"This time we did do something! We signed the papers, and construction began immediately. Most of the apartment units were rented before final completion, and all but one occupied the day of completion. We were so thrilled by the seemingly miraculous events of the past few months that for a while we didn't understand this seeming 'flaw' in our imaginal picture. But knowing what we had already accomplished through the power of imagining, we immediately conceived another imaginal scene and in it, this time, instead of showing the party through the unit and hearing the words 'we'll take it,' we ourselves in imagination visited tenants who had already moved in that apartment. We allowed them to show us through the rooms and heard their pleased and satisfied comments. Three days later that apartment was rented.

"Our original imaginary drama had objectified itself in every detail save one, and that one became a reality when one month later our friend, Mrs. X, surprised us with a long overdue visit, expressing her desire to see our new building. Gladly we took her through, and at the end of the tour heard her speak the line we had heard in our imagination so many weeks before, as with emphasis on each word, she said, 'Doctor, I think it is beautiful.'

"Our dream of fifteen years was realized. And we know, now, that it could have been realized any time with

"Dwell Therein"

in those fifteen years if we had known the secret of imagining and how to 'live in the end' of desire. But now it was realized-our one big desire was objectified. And we did not put one penny of our own money into it."

—Dr. M.

Through the medium of a dream—a controlled, waking dream-the Doctor and his wife created reality. They learned how to live in their dream house as, in fact, now they do. Although help seemingly came from without, the course of events was ultimately determined by the imaginal activity of the Doctor and his wife. The participants were drawn into their imaginal drama because it was dramatically necessary that they should be. Their imaginal structure demanded it.

"All things by a law divine In one another's being mingle."

The following story illustrates the way in which a lady prepared her "stately habitation" by imaginatively sleeping in it—or "dwelling therein."

"A few months ago my husband decided to place our home on the market. The main object for the move which we had discussed many times was to find a home large enough for the two of us, my mother and my aunt, in addition to ten cats, three dogs and one parakeet. Believe it or not, the contemplated move was my husband's idea as he loved my mother and aunt and said I was at their house most of the time anyway, so 'why not live together and pay one tax bill?' I liked the idea tremendously, but I knew that this new home would have to be something

21

"Dwell Therein"

very special in size, location and arrangement as I insist
ed on privacy for all concerned.

"So at the moment I was undecided whether to sell
our present home or not, but I didn't argue as I knew
quite well from past experience with imagining that our
house would never sell until I stopped 'sleeping' in it.
Two months and four or five real estate brokers later, my
hus band had 'given up' on the sale of our house and so
had the brokers. At this point I had convinced myself I
now wanted the change, so for four nights in my
imagination I went to sleep in the kind of home I would
like to own. On the fifth day, my husband had an
appointment at a friend's home and while there, met a
stranger who 'just happened' to be looking for a house in
the hills. He was, of course, brought swiftly back to see
our house which he walked through once and said, 'I'll
buy it.' This didn't make us very popular with the
brokers, but that was all right with me as I was happy to
keep the broker's commission in the family! We moved
within ten days and stayed with my mother while looking
for our new home.

"We listed our requirements with every agent on the
Sunset Strip only (because I wouldn't move out of the
area) and each one of them without exception informed
us we were both mad. It was entirely impossible, they
said, to find an older home of English style with two
separate living rooms, separate apartments, a library, and
built on a flat knoll with enough ground space to fence
for large dogs—and located in one particular area. When
we told them the price we would pay for this house they
just looked sad.

22

"Dwell Therein"

"I said that wasn't all we wanted. We wanted wood paneling all through the house, a huge fireplace, a magnificent view and seclusion—no close neighbors, please. At this point the lady agent would giggle and remind me that there was no such house, but if there were they would realize five times what we were willing to pay. But I knew there was such a house-because my imagination had been sleeping in it, and if I am my imagination, then I had been sleeping in it.

"By the second week we had exhausted five real estate offices, and the gentleman in the sixth office was looking a little wild when one of his partners who had not spoken until then said, 'Why don't you show them the place up Kings Road?' A third partner in the office laughed sourly and said, 'That property isn't even listed. And besides—the old lady would throw you off the property. She's got two acres up there and you know she wouldn't split.'

"Well, I didn't know what she wouldn't split, but my interest had been aroused by the street name for I liked that particular area best of all. So I asked why not just take a look anyway, for laughs. As we drove up the street and turned off onto a private road, we approached a large two-story house built of redwood and brick, English in appearance, surrounded by tall trees and sitting alone and aloof on its own knoll, viewing the city below from all of its many windows. I felt a peculiar excitement as we walked to the front door and were greeted by a lovely woman who graciously asked us in.

"I do not think I breathed for the next minute or two, for I had walked into the most exquisite room I had ever seen. The solid redwood walls and the brick of a great

23

"Dwell Therein"

fireplace rose to a height of twenty-eight feet terminating in an arched ceiling joined together by huge redwood beams. The room was straight out of Dickens, and I could almost hear Christmas carolers singing on the balcony of the upstairs dining room which looked out over the living room. A great cathedral window gave a view of sky, mountains and city far below, and the beautiful old red wood walls glowed in the sunlight. We were shown through a spacious apartment on the lower floor with connecting library, separate entrance and separate patio. Two staircases led upward to a long hail opening into two separated bedrooms and baths, and at the end of the hail was—yes—a second living room, opening out onto a second patio screened by trees and redwood fencing.

"Built on two acres of beautifully landscaped grounds, I began to understand what the agent had meant by saying, 'she wouldn't split' for on one acre stood a large swimming pool and poolhouse completely separated from the main house but undoubtedly belonging to it. It did, indeed, seem to be an impossible situation as we did not want two acres of highly taxable property plus a swimming pool a block away from the house.

"Before we left, I walked through that magnificent living room, once more going up the stairs to the dining room balcony. I turned, and looking down saw my hus band standing by the fireplace, pipe in hand, with an expression of perfect satisfaction on his face. I placed my hands on the balcony railing and watched him for a moment.

"When we were back in the real estate office, the three agents were ready to close for the day, but my husband detained them saying, 'Let's make her an

24

"Dwell Therein"

offer anyway. Maybe she will split the property. What can we lose?' One agent left the office without a word.

Another said, 'The idea is ridiculous.' The agent we had originally talked to said, 'Forget it. It's a pipe dream.' My husband is not easily annoyed but when he is, there is no more stubborn creature on earth. He was now annoyed. He sat down, slammed his hand on a desk and roared, 'It's your business to submit offers, isn't it?' They agreed that this was so and finally promised to submit our offer on the property.

"We left, and that night—in my imagination—I stood on that dining room balcony and looked down at my husband standing by the fireplace. He looked up at me and said, 'Well, honey, how do you like our new home?' I said, 'I love it.' I continued to see that beautiful room and my husband in it and 'felt' the balcony railing gripped in my hands until I fell asleep.

"The next day as we were having dinner in my mother's house, the telephone rang and the agent, in an unbelieving voice, informed me that we had just purchased a house. The owner had split the property right down the middle, giving us the house and the acre it stood on for the price we offered."— J.R.B.

". . . dreamers often lie in bed awake, while they do dream things true."

One must adopt either the way of imagination or the way of sense. No compromise or neutrality is possible. "He who is not for me is against me." When man finally identifies

"Dwell Therein"

himself with his Imagination rather than his senses, he has at long last discovered the core of reality.

I have often been warned by self-styled "realists" that man will never realize his dream by simply imagining that it is already here. Yet, man can realize his dream by simply imagining that it is already here. That is exactly what this collection of stories proves; if only men were prepared to live imaginatively in the feeling of the wish fulfilled, advancing confidently in their controlled waking dream, then the power of imagining would answer their adventurous fancy and the wish fulfilled would break in upon them and take them unawares.

Nothing is more continuously wonderful than the things that happen every day to the man with imagination sufficiently awake to realize their wonder. Observe your imaginal activities. Imagine better than the best you know, and create a better world for yourself and others. Live as though the wish had come, even though it is yet to come, and you will shorten the period of waiting. The world is imaginal, not mechanistic. Imaginal acts—not blind fate—determine the course of history.

CHAPTER 3

TURN THE WHEEL BACKWARD

*"Oh, let your strong imagination turn the
great wheel backward, until Troy unburn.
All life is, throughout the ages nothing but
the continuing solution of a continuous
synthetic problem."*

—H. G. Wells

The perfectly stable or static state is always unattainable.
The end attained objectively always realizes more than the end
the individual originally had in view. This, in turn, creates a new
situation of inner conflict, needing novel solutions to force man
along the path of creative evolution. "His touch is infinite and
lends a yonder to all ends." Today's events are bound to disturb
yesterday's established order. The creatively active imagination
invariably unsettles a pre-existing peace of mind.

The question may arise as to how, by representing others
to ourselves as better than they really were, or mentally
rewriting a letter to make it conform to our wish, or by
revising the scene of an accident, the interview with the
employer, and so on-could change what seems to be the unalterable facts of the past, but remember my claims for imagining: Imagining Creates Reality. What it makes, it can unmake.

It is not only conservative, building a life from images
supplied by memory"— it is also creatively transformative,
altering a theme already in being.

Turn The Wheel Backward

The parable of the unjust steward gives the answer to this question. We can alter our world by means of a certain "illegal" imaginal practice, by means of a mental falsification of the facts that is, by means of a certain intentional imaginal alteration of that which we have experienced. All this is done in one's own imagination. This is a form of falsehood which not only is not condemned, but is actually approved in the gospel teaching. By means of such a falsehood, a man destroys the causes of evil and acquires friends and on the strength of this revision proves, judging by the high praise the unjust steward received from his master, that he is deserving of confidence.

Because imagining creates reality, we can carry revision to the extreme and revise a scene that would be otherwise unforgivable. We learn to distinguish between man"— who is all imagination"— and those states into which he may enter. An unjust steward, looking at another's distress, will represent the other to himself as he ought to be seen. Were he, himself, in need"— he would enter his dream in his imagination and imagine what he would see and how things would seem and how people would act 'after these things should be.' Then, in this state he would fall asleep, feeling the way he would expect to feel, under such circumstances.

Would that all the Lord's people were unjust stewards - mentally falsifying the facts of life to deliver individuals forevermore. For the imaginal change goes forward, until at length the altered pattern is realized on the heights of attainment. Our future is our imaginal activity in its creative march. Imagine better than the best you know.

To revise the past is to re-construct it with new content. Man should daily relive the day as he wished he had lived it, revising the scenes to make them conform to his ideals. For

28

Turn The Wheel Backward

instance, suppose today's mail brought disappointing news. Revise the letter. Mentally rewrite it and make it conform to the news you wish you had received. Then, in imagination, read the revised letter over and over again and this will arouse the feeling of naturalness; and imaginal acts become facts as soon as we feel natural in the act. This is the essence of revision and revision results in repeal. This is exactly what F.B. did:

"Late in July I wrote to a real estate agent of my desire to sell a piece of land which had been a financial burden to me. His negative reply listed all the reasons why sales were at a standstill in that area, and he forecast a bleak period of waiting until after the first of the year.

"I received his letter on a Tuesday, and"—in my imagination"—I rewrote it with words indicating that the agent was eager to take my listing. I read this revised letter over and over, and I extended my imaginal drama using your theme of the Four Mighty Ones of our Imagination"—rom your book 'Seedtime and Harvest." —the Producer, the Author, the Director, and the Actor.

"In my imaginal scene as Producer, I suggested the theme, 'The lot is sold for a profit.' As the Author, I wrote this simple scene which, to me, implied fulfillment: Standing in the real estate office, I extended my hand to the agent and said, 'Thank you, sir,' and he replied, 'It was a pleasure doing business with you.' As Director, I rehearsed myself as Actor until that scene was vividly real and I felt the relief which would be mine if the burden were really lifted.

"Three days later, the agent I had originally written phoned me saying he had a deposit for my lot at the price I had specified. I signed the papers in his office the next

Turn The Wheel Backward

day, extended my hand and said, 'Thank you, sir.' The
agent replied, 'It was a pleasure doing business with you.'

"Five days after I had constructed and enacted an
imaginal scene, it became a physical reality and was
played word for word just as I had heard it in my imagi
nation. The feeling of relief and joy came"—not
so much from selling the property"— but from the
incontrovertible proof that my imagined drama worked."

— F.B.

If the thing accomplished were all, how futile! But F.B.
discovered a power within himself that can consciously create
circumstances.

By mentally falsifying the facts of life, man moves from
passive reaction to active creation; this breaks the wheel of
recurrence and builds a cumulatively enlarging future. If man
does not always create in the full sense of the word, it is
because he is not faithful to his vision, or else he thinks of
what he wants rather than from his wish fulfilled.

Man is such an extraordinary synthesis, partly tied by his
senses, and partly free to dream that his internal conflicts are
perennial. The state of conflict in the individual is expressed
in society.

Life is a romantic adventure. To live creatively, imagining
novel solutions to ever more complex problems is far nobler
than to restrain or kill out desire. All that is desired can be
imagined into existence.

"Wouldst thou be in a Dream, and yet not sleep?" Try to
revise your day every night before falling asleep. Try to visualize clearly and enter into the revised scene which would be
the imaginal solution of your problem. The revised imaginal

Turn The Wheel Backward

structure may have a great influence on others, but that is not your concern. The "other" influenced in the following story is profoundly grateful for that influence. L. S. E. writes:

"Last August, while on a 'blind date' I met the man I wanted to marry. This happens sometimes, and it happened to me. He was everything I had ever thought of as desirable in a husband. Two days after this enchanted evening, it was necessary for me to change my place of residence because of my work, and that same week the mutual friend who had introduced me to this man, moved away from the city. I realized that the man I had met probably did not know of my new address, and frankly, I was not sure he knew my name.

"After your last lecture, I spoke to you of this situation. Although I had plenty of other 'dates' I could not forget this one man. Your lecture was based on revising our day; and after speaking to you, I determined to revise my day, every day. Before going to sleep that night, I felt I was in a different bed, in my own home, as a married woman"— and not as a single working girl, sharing an apartment with three other girls. I twisted an imaginary wedding band on my imaginary left hand, saying over and over to myself, 'This is wonderful! I really am Mrs. J.E.!' and I fell asleep in what was"—a moment before"— a waking dream.

"I repeated this imaginary scene for one month, night after night. The first week in October he 'found' me. On our second date, I knew my dreams were rightly placed. Your teaching tells us to live in the end of our desire until that desire becomes 'fact' so although I did not know how

Turn The Wheel Backward

he felt toward me, I continued, night after night, living in the feeling of my dream realized.

"The results? In November he proposed. In January we announced our engagement; and the following May we were married. The loveliest part of it all, however, is that I am happier than I ever dreamed possible; and I know in my heart, he is too."

—Mrs. J.E.

By using her imagination radically, instead of conservatively,—by building her, world out of pure dreams of fancy-rather than using images supplied by memory, she brought about the fulfillment of her dream. Common sense would have used images supplied by her memory, and thereby perpetuated the fact of lack in her life. Imagination created what she desired out of a dream of fancy. Everyone must live wholly on the level of imagination, and it must be consciously and deliberately undertaken.

". . . Lovers and madmen have such seething brains, such shaping fantasies, that apprehend more than cool reason over comprehends."

If our time of revision be well spent, we need not worry about results—our fondest hopes will be realized.

"Art thou real, Earth? Am I?
In whose dream do we exist? . . ."

32

Turn The Wheel Backward

There is no inevitable permanence in anything. Both past and present continue to exist only because they are sustained by "Imagining" on some level or other; and a radical transformation of life is always possible by man revising the undesirable part of it.

In his letter, Mr. R.S. questions this subject of influence:

"During your current series of lectures, trouble developed with collections on one of my Trust Deeds. The security, a house and lot, was neglected and run down. The owners were apparently spending their money in bars while their two little girls, aged nine and eleven, were noticeably uncared for. However, forgetting appearances, I began to revise the situation. In my imagination I drove my wife past the property and said to her, 'Isn't the yard beautiful? It's so neat and well cared for. Those people really show their love for their home. This is one Trust Deed we will never have to worry about.' I would 'see' the house and lot as I wanted to see it—a place so lovely, it gave me a warm glow of pleasure. Every time the thought of this property came to me, I repeated my imaginal scene.

"After I had been practicing this revision for some time, the woman who lived in the house had an automobile accident; while she was in the hospital her husband disappeared. The children were cared for by neighbors; and I was tempted to visit the mother in the hospital to reassure her of assistance, if necessary. But how could I, when my imaginary scene implied that she and her family were happy, successful and obviously contented? So I did nothing but my daily revision. A short while after leaving the hospital, the woman and her two

33

daughters disappeared also. Payments were sent in on the property and a few months later she reappeared with a wedding certificate and a new husband. At this writing, all payments are right up to date. The two little girls are obviously happy and well cared for, and a room has been added to the property by the owners giving our Trust Deed additional security.

"It was mighty nice to solve my problem without threats, unkind words, eviction, or worry about the little girls; but was there something in my imagining that sent that woman to the hospital?"

—R.S.

Any imaginal activity acquiring intensity through our concentrated attention to clarity of the end desired tends to overflow into regions beyond where we are; but we must leave it to take care of such imaginal activity itself. It is marvelously resourceful in adapting and adjusting means to realize itself. Once we think in terms of influence rather than of clarity of the end desired, the effort of imagination becomes an effort of will and the great art of imagining is perverted into tyranny.

The buried past usually lies deeper than our surface mind can plumb. But fortunately, for this lady, she remembered and proved that the "made" past can also be "unmade" through revision.

"For thirty-nine years I had suffered from a weak back. The pain would increase and decrease but would never leave completely. The condition had progressed to the point where I used medical treatment almost

Turn The Wheel Backward

constantly; the doctor would put the hip right for the moment but the pain simply would not go away. One night I heard you speak of revision and wondered to myself if a condition of almost forty years could be revised. I had remembered that at the age of three or four years I had fallen backward from a very high swing and had been quite ill at that time because of a serious hip injury. From that time on I had never been completely free from pain and had paid many a dollar to alleviate the condition, to no avail.

"This year during the month of August the pain had become more intense and one night I decided to test myself and attempt to revise that 'ancient' accident which had been the cause of so much distress in pain and costly medical fees most of my adult life. Many nights passed before I could 'feel' myself back to the age of childhood play. But I succeeded. One night I actually 'felt' myself on that swing feeling the rush of wind as the swing rose higher and higher. As the swing slowed down, I jumped forward landing solidly and easily on my feet. In the imaginal action I ran to my mother and insisted that she come watch what I could do. I did it again, jumping down from the swing and landing safely on my two feet. I repeated this imaginal act over and over until I fell asleep in the doing of it.

"Within two days the pain in my back and hip began to recede and within two months pain no longer existed for me. A condition that had plagued me for more than thirty-nine years, that had cost a small fortune in attempted cure—was no more . . ." —L.H.

It is to the pruning shears of revision that we owe our

prime fruit. Man and his past are one continuous structure. This structure contains all of the past which has been conserved and still operates below the threshold of his senses to influence the present and the future of his life. The whole is carrying all of its contents with it; any alteration of content will result in an alteration in the present and the future. The first act of correction or cure is always "Revise." If the past can be recreated into the present, so can the revised past. And thus the Revised Past appears within the very heart of her present life; not Fate but a revised past brought her good fortune.

Make results and accomplishment the crucial test of true imagination and your confidence in the power of imagination to create reality will grow gradually from your experiments with revision confronted by experience. Only by this process of experiment can you realize the potential power of your awakened and controlled imagination.

"How much do you owe my master?" He said, "A hundred measures of oil." And he said to him, "Take your bill, and sit down quickly and write fifty!" This parable of the unjust steward urges us to mentally falsify the facts of life, to alter a theme already in being. By means of such imaginative falsehoods a man "acquires friends." As each day falls, mentally revise the facts of life and make them conform to events well worthy of recall; tomorrow will take up the altered pattern and go forward until at length it is realized on the heights of attainment.

The reader will find it worth while to follow these clues —imaginal construction of scenes implying the wish fulfilled, and imaginative participation in these scenes until tones of reality are reached. We are dealing with the secret of imagining, in which man is seen awakening into a world completely subject to his imaginative power.

Turn The Wheel Backward

Man can understand recurrence of events well enough (the building of a world from images supplied by memory)— things remaining as they are. This gives him a sense of security in the stability of things. However, the presence within him of a power which awakens and becomes what it wills, radically changing its form, its environment and the circumstances of life, inspires in him a feeling of insecurity, a dreadful fear of the future. Now, "it is high time to awake out of sleep" and put an end to all the unlovely creations of sleeping Man. Revise each day. "Let your strong imagination turn the great wheel backward until Troy unburn."

CHAPTER 4

THERE IS NO FICTION

"The distinction between what is real and what is imaginary is not one that can be finally maintained . . . all existing things are, in an intelligible sense, imaginary."
—John S. MacKenzie

There is no fiction. If an imaginal activity can produce a physical effect, our physical world must be essentially imaginal. To prove this would require merely that we observe our imaginal activities and watch to see whether or not they produce corresponding external effects. If they do, then we must conclude that there is no fiction. Today's imaginal drama—fiction —becomes tomorrow's fact.

If we had this wider view of causation—that causation is mental— not physical—that our mental states are causative of physical effects, then we would realize our responsibility as a creator and imagine only the best imaginable. Fable enacted as a sort of stage-play in the mind is what causes the physical facts of life. Man believes that reality resides in the solid objects he sees around him, that it is in this world that the drama of life originates, that events spring suddenly into existence, created moment by moment out of antecedent physical facts. But causation does not lie in the external world of facts. The drama of life originates in the imagination of man. The real act of becoming takes place within man's imagination and not without.

There Is No Fiction

The following stories could define "causation" as the assemblage of mental states, while occurring, creates that which the assemblage implies.

The foreword from Walter Lord's "*A Night to Remember*" illustrates my claim, "Imagining Creates Reality"

"In 1898 a struggling author, named Morgan Robertson, concocted a novel about a fabulous Atlantic liner, far larger than any that had ever been built. Robertson loaded his ship with rich and complacent people and then wrecked it one cold April night on an iceberg. This somehow showed the futility of everything, and in fact, the book was called 'FUTILITY' when it appeared that year, published by the firm of M. F. Mansfield.

"Fourteen years later a British shipping company, named the White Star Line, built a steamer remarkably like the one in Robertson's novel. The new liner was 66,000 tons displacement; Robertson's was 70,000 tons.

"The real ship was 882.5 feet long; the fictional one was 800 feet. Both could carry about 3,000 people, and both had enough lifeboats for only a fraction of this number. But, then this didn't seem to matter because both were labeled 'unsinkable!'

"On April 19, 1912, the real ship left Southampton on her maiden voyage to New York. Her cargo included a priceless copy of the Rubaiyat of Omar Khayyam and a list of passengers collectively worth $250 million dollars. On her way over she, too, struck an iceberg and went down on a cold April night.

"Robertson called his ship the Titan; the White Star Line called its ship the Titanic."

There Is No Fiction

Had Morgan Robertson known that Imagining Creates Reality, that today's fiction is tomorrow's fact, would he have written the novel Futility? "In the moment of the tragic catastrophe," writes Schopenhauer, "the conviction becomes more distinct to us than ever that life is a bad dream from which we have to awake." And the bad dream is caused by the imaginal activity of sleeping humanity.

Imaginal activities may be remote from their manifestation and unobserved: events are only appearance. Causation as seen in this tragedy is elsewhere in space-time. Far off from the scene of action, invisible to all, was Robertson's imaginal activity, like a scientist in a control room directing his guided missile through Space-Time.

> "Who paints a picture, writes a play or book
> Which others read while he's asleep in bed
> O' the other side of the world-when they o'erlook
> His page the sleeper might as well be dead;
> What knows he of his distant unfelt life?
> What knows he of the thoughts his thoughts are raising,
> The life his life is giving, or the strife
> Concerning him-some cavilling, some praising?
> Yet which is most alive, he who's asleep
> Or his quick spirit in some other place,
> Or score of other places, that doth keep
> Attention fixed and sleep from others chase?
> Which is the "he"—the "he" that sleeps, or "he"
> That his own "he" can neither feel nor see? . . ."
>
> —Samuel Butler

There Is No Fiction

Imaginative writers communicate not their vision of the world but their attitudes which result in their vision. Just a short while before Katherine Mansfield died, she said to her friend Orage:

"There are in life as many aspects as attitudes toward it; and aspects change with attitudes . . . Could we change our attitude, we should not only see life differently, but life itself would come to be different. Life would under go a change of appearance because we ourselves had undergone a change in attitude . . . Perception of a new pattern is what I call a creative attitude towards life."

"Prophets," wrote Blake, "in the modern sense of the word, have never existed. Jonah was no prophet in the modern sense, for his prophecy of Nineveh failed. Every honest man is a prophet; he utters his opinion both of private & public matters. Thus: If you go on So, the result is So. He never says, such a thing shall happen let you do what you will. A Prophet is a Seer, not an Arbitrary Dictator." The function of the Prophet is not to tell us what is inevitable, but to tell us what can be built up out of persistent imaginal activities.

The future is determined by the imaginal activities of humanity, activities in their creative march, activities which can be seen in "Your dreams and the visions of your head as you lay in bed." "Would that all the Lord's people were prophets" in the true sense of the word like this dancer who now, from the summit of his realized ideal, sights yet higher peaks that are to be scaled. After you have read this story you will understand why he is so confident that he can predetermine any materialistic future he desires and why he is equally sure that others give reality to what were otherwise a mere figment of his imagination, that there exists and can exist nothing outside imagining on some level or other. Nothing continues in being save what imagining supports. ". . . The mind can make Substance, and people planets of its own with beings brighter than have been, and give a breath to forms which can outlive all flesh . . ."

"As my story begins at the age of nineteen, I was a mildly successful dancing teacher and continued in this static state for almost five years. At the end of this time I met a young lady who talked me into attending your lectures. My thought, upon hearing you say 'Imagining creates reality,' was that the entire idea was ridiculous. However, I decided to accept your challenge and disprove your thesis. I bought your book 'Out of This World' and read it many times. Still unconvinced I set myself a rather ambitious goal. My present position was as an instructor with the Arthur Murray Dance Studio and my goal was to own a franchise and be the boss of an Arthur Murray studio myself!

"This seemed the most unlikely thing in the world as franchises were extremely difficult to secure, but on top of this fact, I was completely without the necessary funds to begin such an operation. Nevertheless, I assumed the feeling of my wish fulfilled as night after night, in my imagination, I went to sleep managing my own studio. Three weeks later a friend called me from Reno, Nevada. He had the Murray Studio there and said it was too much for him to cope with alone. He offered me a partnership and I was delighted; so delighted, in fact, that I hastened to Reno on borrowed money and promptly forgot all about you and your story of Imagination!

"My partner and I worked hard and were very successful, but after a year I was still not satisfied, I wanted more. I began thinking of ways and means to get another studio. All my efforts failed. One night as I retired, I was restless and decided to read. As I looked through my collection of books I noticed your slender volume, 'Out of This World.' I thought of the 'silly non sense' I had gone through one year ago before getting my own studio. GETTING MY OWN STUDIO! The words in my mind electrified me! I reread the book that night and later, in my imagination, I heard my superior praise the good job we had done in Reno and suggest we acquire a second studio as he had a second location ready for us if we desired to expand. I re-enacted this imaginal scene nightly without fail. Three weeks from the first night of my imaginal drama, it materialized - almost word for word. My partner accepted the new studio in Bakersfield and I had the Reno Studio alone. Now I was convinced of the truth of your teaching and never again will I forget.

"Now I wanted to share this wonderful knowledge - of imaginal power with my staff. I tried to tell them of the marvels they could accomplish, but I was unable to reach many although one fantastic incident resulted from my efforts to tell this story. A young teacher told me he believed my story but said it would have probably happened anyway in time. He insisted the entire theory was nonsense but stated that if I could tell him something of an incredible nature that would actually happen and

There Is No Fiction

which he could witness-then he would believe. I accepted his challenge and conceived a truly fantastic test.

"The Reno Studio is the most insignificant in the entire Murray system because of the small population count in the city itself. There are over three hundred Murray Studios in the country with much larger populations, therefore providing greater possibilities to draw from. So, my test was this. I told the teacher that within the next three months, at the time of a national dance convention, the little Reno Studio would be the foremost topic of conversation at that convention. He calmly stated this was quite impossible.

"That night when I retired, I felt myself standing before a tremendous audience. I was speaking on 'Creative Imagining' and felt the nervousness of being before such a vast audience; but I also felt the wonderful sensation of audience acceptance. I heard the roar of applause and as I left the stage, I saw Mr. Murray, himself come forward and shake my hand. I re-enacted this entire drama night after night. It began to take on the 'tones of reality' and I knew I had *done it again*! My imaginal drama materialized down to the last detail.

"My little Reno Studio was the 'talk' of the convention and I did appear on that stage just as I had done in my imagination. But even after this unbelievable but actual happening, the young teacher who threw me the challenge remained unconvinced. He said it had all happened too *naturally*! And he was sure it would have happened *anyway*!

There Is No Fiction

"I did not mind his attitude because his challenge had given me another opportunity to prove, at least to myself, that Imagining does Create Reality. From that time on, I continued with my ambition to own the 'largest Arthur Murray Dance Studio in the world!' Night after night, in my imagination, I heard myself accepting a studio franchise for a great city. Within three weeks Mr. Murray called me and offered a studio in a city of one and a half million people! It is now my goal to make my studio the greatest and biggest in the entire system. And, of course, 'I know it will be done—through my Imagination'!" —E.O.L., Jr.

"Imagining," writes Douglas Fawcett, "may be hard to grasp, being 'quicksilver-like' it vanishes into each of its metamorphoses and thereby displays its transformative magic." We must look beyond the physical fact for the imagining which has caused it. For one year E.O.L., Jr. lost himself in his metamorphosis but fortunately he remembered "the silly nonsense" he had gone through before getting his own studio and re-read the book.

Imaginal acts on the human level need a certain interval of time to develop but imaginal acts, whether committed to print or locked in the bosom of a hermit, will realize themselves in time.

Test yourself, if only out of curiosity. You will discover the "Prophet" is your own imagining and you will know "there is no fiction."

There Is No Fiction

"We should never be certain that it was not some woman treading in the wine-press who began that subtle change in men's mind, or that the passion, because of which so many countries were given to the sword, did not begin in the mind of some shepherd boy, lighting up his eyes for a moment before it ran upon its way."

—William Butler Yeats

There is no fiction. Imagining fulfills itself in what our lives become. "And now I have told you before it takes place, so that when it does take place, you may believe." The Greeks were right: "The Gods have come down to us in the likeness of men!" But they have fallen asleep and do not realize the might they wield by their imaginal activities.

"Real are the dreams of Gods, and smoothly pass Their pleasure in a long immortal dream."

E.B., an author, is fully aware that "today's fiction can become tomorrow's fact." In this letter, she writes:

"One Spring, I completed a novelette, sold it and for got it. Not until many long months later did I sit down and nervously compare some 'facts' in my fiction with some 'facts' in my life! Please read a brief outline of my created story. Then compare it with my personal experience.

"The heroine of my story took a vacation trip to Vermont, to the small city of Stowe, Vermont, to be exact. When she reached her destination she was faced with such unpleasant behavior on the part of her

There Is No Fiction

companion that she either had to continue her lifetime pattern of allowing another's selfish demand dominate her or to break that pattern and leave. She broke it and returned to New York. When she returned (and the story continues) events took shape in a proposal of marriage which she happily accepted.

"For my part of this tale . . . as small events evolved . . . I began to remember the dictates of my own pen and in significant relationship. This is what happened to me! I received an invitation from a friend offering me a vacation at her summer place in Vermont. I accepted and was not startled, at first, when I learned her 'summer place' was in the city of Stowe. When I arrived, I found my hostess in such a highly nervous state I realized I was faced with either a wretched summer or the choice of 'walking out' on her. Never before in my life had I been strong enough to ignore what I thought were the claims of duty and friendship—but this time I did and without ceremony returned to New York. A few days after I returned to my home, I, too, received a proposal of marriage. But at this point fact and fiction parted. I refused the offer! I know, Neville, there is no such thing as fiction." —E.B.

"Forgetful is green earth, the gods alone remember ever lastingly . . . by their great memories the gods are known."

There Is No Fiction

Ends run true to their imaginal origins we reap the fruit of forgotten blossom—time. In life the events do not come up always where we have strewn the seed; so that we may not recognize our own harvest. Events are the emergence of a hidden imaginal activity. Man is free to imagine whatever he desires. This is why, despite all fatalists and misguided prophets of doom, all awakened men know that they are free. They know that they are creating reality. Is there a scriptural passage to support this claim? Yes: "And it came to pass, as he interpreted to us, so it was."

W. B. Yeats must have discovered that "there is no fiction" for after describing some of his experiences in the conscious use of imagination, he writes: "If all who have described events like this have not dreamed, we should rewrite our histories for all men, certainly all imaginative men, must be forever casting forth enchantments, glamour, illusions; and all men, especially tranquil men, who have no powerful egotistic life must be continually passing under their power. Our most elaborate thoughts, elaborate purposes, precise emotions, are often as I think, not really ours, but have on a sudden come up, as it were, out of hell or down out of heaven. . ."

"There is no fiction." Imagine better than the best you know.

CHAPTER 5

SUBTLE THREADS

*. . . all you behold; tho' it appears Without,
it is Within; In your Imagination, of which
this World of Mortality is but a Shadow.*
— Blake

Nothing appears or continues in being by a power of its own. Events happen because comparatively stable imaginal activities created them, and they continue in being by virtue of the support they receive from such imaginal activities. The part which imagining the wish fulfilled plays in consciously creating circumstances is obvious in this series of stories.

You will see how the telling of one story of the successful use of imagination can serve as a spur and a challenge to others to "try" it and "see."

One night a gentleman rose in my audience. He said that he had no question to ask but would like to tell me something. This was his story:

When he came out of the Armed Forces after World War II he got a job that gave him take-home pay of $25.00 a week. After ten years he was making $600.00 a month. At that time he bought my book "Awakened Imagination" and read the chapter "The Pruning Shears of Revision." Through the daily practice of "Revision," as set forth there, he was able to tell my audience two years later that his income was equal to that of the President of the United States.

Subtle Threads

In my audience sat a man who, by his confession, was broke. He had read the same book, but he suddenly realized he had done nothing with the use of his imagination to solve his financial problem.

He decided he would try to imagine himself as the winner of the 5-10 pool at Caliente Race Track. In his words: "In this pool, one attempts to pick winners in the fifth through the tenth races. So this is what I did: In my imagination I stood, sorting my tickets and feeling as I did so, that I had each of the six winners. I enacted this scene over and over in my imagination, until I actually felt 'goose pimples.' Then I 'saw' the cashier giving me a large sum of money which I placed beneath my imaginary shirt. This was my entire imaginal drama; and for three weeks, night after night, I enacted this scene and fell asleep in the action.

"After three weeks I traveled physically to the Caliente Race Track, and on that day every detail of my imaginative play was actually realized. The only change in the scene was that the cashier gave me a check for a total of $84,000.00 instead of currency."—T.K.

After my lecture the night this story was told, a man in the audience asked me if I thought it possible for him to duplicate T.K.'s experience. I told him he must decide the circumstances of his imaginal scene himself but that whatever scene he chose, he must create a drama he could make natural to himself and imagine the *end* intently with all the feeling he could muster; he must not labor for the means to the end but live imaginatively in the *feeling of the wish fulfilled*.

Subtle Threads

One month later he showed me a check for $16,000.00 which he had won in another 5-10 pool at the same Caliente Race Track the previous day.

This man had a sequel to his most interesting duplication of T.K.'s good fortune. His first win took care of his immediate financial difficulties although he wanted more money for future family security. Also, and more important to him, he wanted to prove that this had not been an "accident." He reasoned that if his good luck could happen a second time in succession, the so-called "law of percentages" would give way to proof for him that his imaginal structures were actually producing this miraculous "reality." And so he dared to put his imagination to a second test. He continues:

"I wanted a sizeable bank account and this, to me, meant 'seeing' a large balance on my bank statements. Therefore, in my imagination I enacted a scene which took me into two banks. In each bank I would 'see' an appreciative smile meant for me from the bank manager as I walked into his establishment and I would 'hear' the teller's cordial greeting. I would ask to see my statement. In one bank I 'saw' a balance of $10,000.00. In the other bank I 'saw' a balance of $15,000.00.

"My imaginal scene did not end there. Immediately after seeing my bank balances I would turn my attention to my horse racing system which, through a progression of ten steps, would bring my winnings to $11,533.00 with a starting capital of $200.00.

"I would divide the winnings into twelve piles on my desk. Counting the money in my imaginary hands I would

51

Subtle Threads

put $1,000.00 in each of eleven piles and the remaining five-hundred thirty-three dollars in the last pile. My 'imaginative accounting' would amount to $36,533.00 including my bank balances.

"I enacted this entire imaginative scene each morning, afternoon and night for less than one month, and, on March second, I went, to the Caliente track again. I made out my tickets, but strangely enough and not knowing why I did so, I duplicated six more tickets exactly like the six already made out but in the tenth selection I made a 'mistake' and copied two tickets twice. As the winners came in, I held two of them—each paying $16,423.50. I also had six consolation tickets, each paying $656.80. The combined total amounted to $36,788.00. My imaginary accounting one month before had totaled $36,533.00. Two points of interest, most profound to me, were that by seeming accident I had marked two winning tickets identically and also, that at the end of the ninth race (which was one of the major winners) the trainer attemped to 'scratch' the horse, but the Stewards denied the trainer's request."—A.J.F.

How subtle were the threads that led to his goal? Results must testify to our imagining or we really are not imagining the end at all. A.J.F. faithfully imagined the end, and all things conspired to aid his harvesting. His "mistake" in copying a winning ticket twice, and the Steward's refusal to allow the trainer's request were events created by the imaginal drama to move the plan of things forward to its goal.

Subtle Threads

"Chance," wrote Belfort Bax, "may be defined as that element in the reality change—that is, in the flowing synthesis of events—which is irreducible to law or the causal category."

To live wisely we must be aware of our imaginal activities or, at any rate, of the end which they are tending. We must see to it that it is the end we desire. Wise imagining identifies itself only with such activities that are of value or promise well. However much man seems to be dealing with a material world, he is actually living in a world of imagination. When he discovers that it is not the physical world of facts but imaginal activities which shape his life, then the physical world will no longer be the reality, and the world of imagination no longer the dream.

"Does the road wind uphill all the way?
Yes, to the very end.
Will the day's journey take the whole long day?
From morn to night, my friend."

CHAPTER 6

VISIONARY FANCY

> *"The Nature of Visionary Fancy, or Imagination, is very little known, & the External nature & permanence of its ever Existent Images is consider'd as less permanent than the things of Vegetative & Generative Nature; yet the Oak dies as well as the Lettuce, but Its Eternal image & Individuality never dies, but renews by its seed; just so the Imaginative Image returns by the seed of Contemplative Thought."*
> —Blake

The images of our imagination are the realities of which any physical manifestation is only the shadow. If we are faithful to vision, the image will create for itself the only physical manifestation of itself it has a right to make. We speak of the "reality" of a thing when we mean its material substance. That is exactly what an imaginist means by its "unreality" or shadow.

Imagining is spiritual sensation. Enter into the feeling of your wish fulfilled. Through spiritual sensation—through your use of imaginal sight, sound, scent, taste and touch — you will give to your image the sensory vividness necessary to produce that image in your outer or shadow world.

Here is the story of one who was faithful to his vision. F.B. being a true imaginist, remembered what he had heard in his imagination. Thus he writes:

Visionary Fancy

"A friend who knows my passionate fondness for opera tried to get Kirsten Flagstad's complete recording of Tristan and Isolde for me at Christmas. In over a dozen record stores he was told the same thing: 'RCA Victor is not reissuing this recording and there have been no copies available since June.' On December 27th, I deter mined to prove your principle again by getting the album I desired so intensely. Lying down in my living room, I mentally walked into a record shop I patronize and asked the one salesman whose face and voice I could recall, 'Do you have Flagstad's complete Isolde?' He replied, 'Yes, I have.' That ended the scene and I repeated it until it was 'real' to me.

"Late that afternoon I went to that record shop to physically enact the scene. Not one detail supplied by the senses had encouraged me to believe I could walk out of that shop with those records. I had been told last September by the same salesman in the same shop the same story my friend had received there before Christmas. Approaching the salesman I had seen in imag ination that morning, I said, 'Do you have Flagstad's complete Isolde?' He replied, 'No, we haven't.' Without saying anything audible to him, I said inwardly, 'That's not what I heard you say!'

"As I turned to leave the shop I noticed on a top shelf what I thought to be an advertisement of this set of records and remarked to the salesman, 'If you don't have the merchandise you shouldn't advertise it.' 'That's right,' he replied, and as he reached up to take it down discovered it to be a complete album, with all five records! The scene wasn't played exactly as I had

Visionary Fancy

constructed it, but the result confirmed what my imagined scene implied. How can I thank you?" —F.B.

After reading F.B.'s letter we must agree with Anthony Eden that "An assumption, though false, if persisted in will harden into fact." F.B's fancy, fusing with the sense-field of the record shop, enriched aspects of it and made them 'his'— what he perceived.

Our future is our imagining in its creative march. F.B. used his imagination for a conscious purpose representing life as he desired it to be and thereby affecting life instead of merely reflecting it. So sure was he that his imaginal drama was the reality—and the physical act but a shadow -that when the salesman said, "No, we haven't" F.B. mentally said, "That's not what I *heard* you say!" He not only *remembered* what he had *heard*, but he was still remembering it. Imagining the wish fulfilled is the seeking that finds, the asking that receives, the knocking to which is opened. He saw and heard what he desired to see and hear; and would not take "No, we haven't" for an answer. The imaginist dreams while awake. He is not the servant of his Vision, but the master of the direction of his attention. Imaginative constancy controls perception of events in space-time. Unfortunately, most men are . . .

> "Ever changing, like a joyless eye
> That finds no object worth
> its constancy . . ."

Mrs. G.R., too, had *imaginatively* heard what she wanted to physically hear and knew the outer world must confirm it.

Visionary Fancy

This is her story:

"Some time ago we advertised our home for sale which was necessary for us to buy a larger property on which we had placed a deposit. Several people would have bought our home immediately but we were obliged to explain that we could not close any deal until we learned whether or not our offer for the property we wanted had been accepted. At this time, a broker called and literally begged us to allow him to show our home to a client of his who was eager for this location and would be glad to pay even more than we were asking. We explained our situation to the broker and to his client; they both stated they did not mind waiting for our deal to be consummated. The broker asked us to sign a paper which he said was not binding in any way but would give him first chance at the sale if our other deal went through. We signed the paper and later learned that in California Real Estate law nothing could have been more binding. A few days later our deal for the new property fell through so we notified this broker and his verbal response was, 'Well, just forget it.' Two weeks later he filed suit against us for fifteen hundred dollars commission. Trial date was set and we asked for a jury trial.

"Our attorney assured us he would do all he could, but that the law on this particular point was so stringent that he could not see any possibility of our winning the case. When time for the trial arrived my husband was in the hospital and could not appear with me in our defense. I had no witnesses; but the broker brought three attorneys and a number of witnesses into court against

57

us. Our attorney now told me we had not the slightest chance to win.

"I turned to my imagination, and this is what I did. Completely disregarding all that had been said by attorneys, witnesses and the judge who seemed to favor the plaintiff, I thought only of the words I wanted to hear. In my imagination, I listened intently and heard the fore man of the jury say, 'We find the defendant not guilty.' I listened until I knew it was true. I closed my mind's ear to everything said in that courtroom and heard only those words, 'We find the defendant not guilty!' The jury deliberated from noon recess until four-thirty that afternoon, and all during those hours I sat in the court room and heard those words over and over in my imagination. When the jurors returned the judge asked the foreman to stand and give their verdict. The foreman stood up and said, 'We find the defendant NOT guilty'."

—Mrs. G.R.

"If there were dreams to sell, What would you buy?"

Would you not buy your wish fulfilled? Your dreams are without price and without money. By locking up the jury in her imagination hearing only what she wanted to hear, she called the jury to unanimity on her behalf. Imagining being the reality of all that exists, with it the lady achieved her wish fulfilled.

Hebbel's statement that "the poet creates from contemplation" is true of imaginists as well. They know how to utilize their video. audio hallucinations to create reality.

Nothing is so fatal as conformity. We must not allow our-

Visionary Fancy

selves to be girt about by the ringed fixity of fact. Change the image, and thereby change the fact. R.O. employed the art of seeing and feeling to create her vision in imagination.

"A year ago I took my children to Europe leaving my furnished apartment in the care of my maid. When we returned a few months later to the United States I found my maid and all my furniture gone. The apartment super intendent stated that the maid had had my furniture moved 'by my request.' There was nothing I could do at the moment, so I took my children and moved into a hotel. I, of course, reported the incident to the police and, also, brought in private detectives on the case. Both organizations investigated every moving company and every storage warehouse in New York City, but to no avail. There seemed to be absolutely no trace of my furniture, nor of my maid.

"Having exhausted all outside sources, I remembered your teaching and decided I would try using my imagination in this matter. So, while seated in my hotel room I closed by eyes and imagined myself in my own apartment sitting in my favorite chair and surrounded by all of my personal furnishings. I looked across the living room at the piano on which I kept pictures of my children. I would continue to stare at my piano until the entire room became vividly real to me. I could see my children's pictures and actually feel the upholstery of the chair in which, in my imagination, I sat.

"The next day, as I came out of my bank, I turned to walk in the direction of my vacant apartment instead of toward my hotel. When I reached the corner I discovered my 'mistake' and was just about to turn back when my attention was drawn to a very familiar pair of ankles. Yes, the ankles belonged to my maid. I walked up to her and took hold of her arm. She was quite frightened, but I assured her all I wanted from her was my furniture. I called a taxi and she took me to the place in which her friends had stored my furnishings. In one day, my imagi nation had found what an entire big city police force and private investigators could not find in weeks."—R. O.

This lady knew of the secret of imagining before she called in the police, but imagining -in spite of its importance- was forgotten owing to attention being fixed on facts. However, what reason failed to find by force, imagining found without effort. Nothing merely goes on—including the sense of loss —without its imaginal support. By imagining that she was seated in her own chair, in her own living room, sur- rounded by all of her own furnishings, she withdrew the imaginal support she had given to her sense of loss; and by this imaginal change she recovered her lost furniture and reestablished her home.

Your imagination is most creative when you imagine things as you desire them to be, building a new experience out of a dream of fancy. To build such a dream of fancy in her imagination, F.G. brought to play all of her senses—sight, sound, touch, smell—even taste. This is her story:

"Since childhood I have dreamed of visiting far-away places. The West Indies, particularly, fired my fancy, and I would revel in the feeling of actually being there. Dreams are wonderfully inexpensive and as an adult I continued to dream my dreams, for I had no money or time to make them 'come true.' Last year I was taken to the hospital in need of surgery. I had heard your teaching and, while recuperating, had decided to intensify my favorite day dream while I had time on my hands. I actually wrote to the Alcoa Steamship Line asking for free travel folders and pored over them, hour after hour, choosing the ship and the stateroom and the seven ports I desired most to see. I would close my eyes and, in my imagination, would walk up the gangplank of that ship and feel the movement of water as the great liner pushed its way into free ocean. I heard the thud of waves breaking against the sides of the ship, felt the steaming warmth of a tropical sun on my face and smelled and tasted salt in the air as we all sailed through blue waters.

"For one solid week, confined to a hospital bed, I lived the free and happy experience of actually being on that ship. Then, the day before my release from the hospital, I tucked the colored folders away and forgot them. Two months later I received a telegram from an advertising agency telling me I had won a contest. I remembered having deposited a contest coupon some months before in a neighborhood supermarket but had completely forgotten the act. I had won first prize and—wonder of wonders—it entitled me to a Caribbean cruise sponsored by the Alcoa Steamship Line. But the wonder didn't stop there. The very stateroom I had imaginatively lived in and moved about in while confined to a hospital bed had been assigned to me. And to make an unbelievable story even more unbelievable, I sailed on the one ship I had chosen—which stopped in not one, but all of the seven ports I had desired to visit!" —F.G.

"To travel is the privilege, not of
the rich but of the imaginative."

CHAPTER 7

MOODS

*"This is an age in which the mood decides
the fortunes of people rather than the
fortunes decide the mood."*
                    —Sir Winston Churchill

Men regard their moods far too much as effects and not sufficiently as causes. Moods are imaginal activities without which no creation is possible. We say that we are happy because we have achieved our goal; we do not realize that the process works equally well in the reverse direction—that we shall achieve our goal because we have assumed the happy feeling of the wish fulfilled.

Moods are not only the result of the conditions of our life; they are also the causes of those conditions. In "The Psychology of Emotions," Professor Ribot writes, "An idea which is only an idea produces nothing and does nothing; it only acts if it is felt, if it is accompanied by an effective state, if it awakens tendencies, that is to say, motor elements."

The lady in the following story so successfully felt the feeling of her wish fulfilled, she made her mood the character of the night frozen in a delightful dream.

"Most of us read and love fairy stories, but we all know that stories of improbable riches and good fortune are for the delight of the very young. But are they? I want to tell you of something unbelievably wonderful that happened to me through the power of my imagination— and I am not 'young' in years. We live in an age which believes in neither fable nor magic, and yet everything I

63

Moods

could possibly want in my wildest day-dreams was given to me by the simple use of what you teach—that 'imagining creates reality' and that 'feeling' is the secret of imagining.

"At the time this wonderful thing happened to me I was out of a job and had no family to fall back upon for support. I needed just about everything. To find a decent job I needed a car to look for it, and though I had a car it was so worn out it was ready to fall apart. I was behind in my rent; I had no proper clothes to seek a job; and today it's no fun for a woman of fifty-five to apply for a job of any kind. My bank account was almost depleted and there was no friend to whom I could turn.

"But I had been attending your lectures for almost a year and my desperation forced me to put my imagination to the test. Indeed, I had nothing to lose. It was natural for me, I suppose, to begin by imagining myself having everything I needed. But I needed so many things and in such short order that I found myself exhausted when I finally got through the list, and by that time I was so nervous I could not sleep. One lecture night I heard you tell of an artist who captured the 'feeling,' or 'word,' as you called it, of 'isn't it wonderful!' in his personal experience. I began to apply this idea to my case. Instead of thinking of and imagining every article I needed, I tried to capture the 'feeling' that something wonderful was happening to me not tomorrow, not next week—but right now. I would say over and over to myself as I fell asleep, 'Isn't it wonderful! Something marvelous is happening to me now! And as I fell asleep *I would feel the way I would expect to feel under such circumstances.*

Moods

"I repeated that imaginary action and feeling for two months, night after night, and one day in early October I met a casual friend I hadn't seen for months who informed me he was about to leave on a trip to New York. I had lived in New York many years ago and we talked of the city a few moments and then parted. I completely forgot the incident. One month later, to the day, this man called at my apartment and simply handed me a Certified Check in my name for twenty-five hundred dollars. After I got over the initial shock of seeing my name on a check for so much money, the story that unfolded seemed to me like a dream. It concerned a friend I had not seen nor heard from in more than twenty-five years. This friend of my past, I now learned, had become extremely wealthy in those twenty-five years. Our mutual acquaintance who had brought the check to me had met him quite by acci dent during the trip to New York last month. During their conversation they spoke of me, and for reasons I was not to know (for to this day I have not heard from him personally and have never attempted to contact him) this old friend decided to share a portion of his great wealth with me.

"For the next two years, from the office of his attorney, I received monthly checks so generous in amount they not only covered every necessary requirement of daily living, but left much over for all the lovely things of life: a car, clothes, a spacious apartment and best of all, no need to earn my daily bread.

"This past month I received a letter and some legal papers to be signed which provide the continuation of this monthly income for the rest of my natural life!"

—T.K.

"If the fool would persist in his folly He would become wise."

Sir Winston calls on us to act on the assumption that we already possess that which we sought, to "assume a virtue," if we have it not. Is this not the secret of "miracles"? Thus the man with palsy was told to rise, to take up his bed and walk —to mentally act as if he were healed; and when the actions of his imagination corresponded with the actions which he would physically perform were he healed-he was healed.

"This is a story about which some may say, 'it would have happened anyway,' but those who read it carefully will find room to wonder. It begins one year ago as I left Los Angeles to visit my daughter in San Francisco. Instead of the happy-natured individual she had always been, I found her in deep distress. Not knowing the cause of her anguish and not wishing to ask, I waited until she told me that she was in great financial trouble and must have three thousand dollars immediately. I am not a poor woman but I didn't have much cash I could put my hands on that quickly. Knowing my daughter, I knew she would not have accepted it anyway. I offered to borrow the money for her, but she refused and instead asked me to help her in 'my way' she meant using my imagination, for I had often told her of your teaching and some of my words must have struck home.

"I immediately agreed on this plan with the provision that she would help me help her. We decided on an imaginal scene we could both practice that involved 'seeing' money coming to her from everywhere. We felt money was flooding toward her from every corner, until she was in the middle of a 'sea' of money, but we did this always with the feeling of 'Joy' for anyone concerned and we had no thought of means, only happiness for all.

"The idea seemed to catch fire with her, and I know she was responsible for what happened a few days later. She was certainly transformed back to the happy, confident mood that was natural to her, though there was no evidence of any real money coming in at the time. I left to return home in the East.

"When I arrived home I called my mother (a lovely young lady of ninety-one) who immediately asked me to come and see her. I wanted a day's rest but she couldn't wait; it had to be now. Of course I went, and after greeting me, she handed me a check for three thousand dollars made out to my daughter! Before I could speak, she handed me three additional checks totaling fifteen hundred dollars made in favor of my daughter's children. Her reason? She explained that she had suddenly decided the day before to give what she had in cash to those she loved while she was still 'here' to know of their happiness in receiving it!

"It would have happened anyway? No-not like this. Not within days of my daughter's frantic need, and then her sudden transformation to a mood of joy. I know that her imaginal act caused this wonderful change bringing not only great joy to the receiver but to the giver as well."

"P.S. . . . I almost forgot to add that among the checks so lavishly given, was one for me too, for three thousand dollars!". —M.B.

The boundless opportunities opened by recognizing the shift of the focus of imagining is beyond measure. There are

67

no boundaries. The drama of life is an imaginal activity in which we bring to pass by our moods rather than by our physical acts. Moods so ably guide all towards that which they affirm, they may be said to create the circumstances of life and dictate the events. The mood of the wish fulfilled is the high tide which lifts us easily off the bar of the senses where we usually lie stranded. If we are aware of the mood and know this secret of imagining, we may announce that all that our mood affirms will come to pass.

The following story is by a mother who succeeded in sustaining a seemingly "playful" mood with startling results.

"Surely you've heard the 'old wives' tale' about warts: That, if a wart is bought, it will disappear? I've known this story from childhood but not until I heard your lectures did I realize the truth hidden in the old tale. My boy, a lad of ten, had many large ugly warts on his legs causing an irritation which had plagued him for years. I decided that my sudden 'insight' could be used to his advantage. A boy has a lot of faith in his mother as a rule so I asked him if he would like to be rid of his warts. He quickly said, 'Yes,' but he did not want to go to a doctor. I asked him to play a little game with me, that I would pay him a sum of money for each wart. This suited him fine; he said.—'he didn't see how he could lose!' We arrived at a fair price, he thought, and then I said, 'Now, I'm paying you good money for those warts; they no longer belong to you. You never keep property belonging to someone else so you can no longer keep those warts. They will disappear. It may take a day, two days or a month; but remember, that I've bought them and they belong to me.'

Moods

"My son was delighted with our game and the results sound like something read in old musty books on magic. But, believe me, within ten days the warts began to fade, and, at the end of one month every wart on his body had completely disappeared!

"There is a sequel to this story for I've bought warts from many people. They, too, thought it great fun and accepted my five, seven or ten cents a wart. In each case the wart disappeared—but really—only one person believes me when I tell him his Imagination, alone, took away the warts. That one person is my young son."

—J.R.

Man imagining himself into a mood takes on himself the results of the mood. If he does not imagine himself into the mood, he is ever free of the result. The great Irish mystic, A.E., wrote in "*The Candle of Vision*": "I became aware of a swift echo or response to my own moods in circumstance which had seemed hitherto immutable in its indifference . . . I could prophesy from the uprising of new moods in myself that I, without search, would soon meet people of a certain character, and so I met them. Even inanimate things were under the sway of these affinities." But man need not wait for the uprising of new moods in himself; he can create happy moods at will.

CHAPTER 8

THROUGH THE LOOKING GLASS

"A man that looks on glass,
On it may stay his eye;
Or if he pleaseth, through it pass,
And then the heav'n espie."
—George Herbert

Objects, to be perceived, must first penetrate in some manner our brain; but we are not—because of this—interlocked with our environment. Although normal consciousness is focused on the senses and is usually restricted to them, it is possible for man to pass through his sense fixation into any imaginal structure which he conceives and so fully occupy it that it is more alive and more responsive than that on which his senses "stay his eye." If this were not true, man would be an automaton reflecting life, never affecting it. Man, who is all Imagination, is not tenant to the brain but landlord; he need not rest content with the appearance of things; he can go beyond perceptual to conceptual awareness.

This ability, to pass through the mechanical reflective structure of the senses, is the most important discovery man can make. It reveals man as a center of imagining with powers of intervention which enable him to alter the course of observed events moving from success to success through a series of mental transformations in himself. Attention, the spearhead of imagining, may be either attracted from without as his senses "stay his eye" or directed from within "if he pleases" and through the senses pass into the wish fulfilled.

To move from perceptual awareness, or things as they seem, to conceptual awareness, or things as they ought to be, we imagine as vivid and as life-like a representation as possible of what we would see, hear, and do, were we physically present, and physically experiencing things as they ought to be and imaginatively participate in that scene.

The following story tells of one who went "through the glass" and broke the chains that bound her.

"Two years ago I was taken to the hospital with a serious blood clot condition which apparently had affected the entire vascular system causing hardening of arteries and arthritis. A nerve in my head was damaged and my thyroid enlarged. Doctors could not agree on the cause of this condition, and all their treatments were completely ineffective. I was forced to give up my every enjoyable activity and remain in bed most of the time. My body, from hips to toes, felt as though it was encased and bound by tight wires, and I couldn't put my feet on the floor without wearing heavy hip-length elastic stockings.

"I knew something of your teaching and tried very hard to apply what I had heard, but as my condition grew worse and I could no longer attend any of your lectures, my despondency grew deeper. One day a friend sent me a postcard picturing the scene of a lovely beach by the ocean. The picture was so beautiful I looked and looked at it and began to remember past summer days at the seashore with my parents. For a moment, the postcard picture seemed to become animated and flooding

71

memories of myself running free on the beach filled my mind. I felt the impact of my bare feet against the hard wet sand; I felt the icy water running over my toes and heard the crash of waves breaking on shore. This imaginal activity was so satisfying to me as I lay in bed that I continued to imagine this wonderful scene, day after day, for about one week.

"One morning I moved from my bed to a couch and had started to sit up when I was seized with such an excruciating pain my entire body became paralyzed. I could neither sit up nor lie down. This terrible pain lasted for more than a full minute, but when it stopped— I was free! It seemed as if all the wires binding my legs had been cut. One moment I was bound; the next moment I was free. Not by degrees, but instantly."

—V.H.

"We walk by faith, not by sight."
—2 Cor. 5:7

When we walk by sight, we know our way by objects which our eyes see. When we walk by faith we order our life by scenes and actions which only imagination sees.

Man perceives by the Eye of Imagination or by Sense. But two mental attitudes to perception are possible, the creative imaginative effort which meets with an imaginative response, or the unimaginative "staying of the eye" which merely reflects.

Man has within him the principle of life and the principle of death. One is the imagination building its imaginal structures out of the generous dreams of fancy. The other is the imagination building its imaginal structures from images reflected by the chill wind of fact. One creates. The other perpetuates. Man must adopt either the way of faith or the way of sight. To the extent that man builds from dreams of fancy, he is alive; and, therefore, the development of the faculty to pass through the reflective glass of the senses is an increase of life. It follows that restricting the imagination by "staying the eye" on the reflective glass of the senses is a reduction of life.

The specious surface of fact reflects rather than discloses, deflecting the "Eye of Imagination" from the truth that sets man free. "The Eye of Imagination," if not deflected, looks on what ought to be there, not what is. However familiar the scene on which sight rests, the "Eye of Imagination" could gaze on one never before witnessed. It is this "Eye of Imagination" and only this that can free us from the sense fixation of outer things which completely dominates our ordinary existence and keeps us looking on the reflective glass of facts.

It is possible to pass from thinking of to thinking from; but the crucial matter is thinking from, i.e., experiencing the state, for that experience means unification; whereas in thinking of there is always subject and object—the thinking individual and the thing thought of.

Self-abandonment. That is the secret. We have to abandon ourselves to the state, in our love for the state, and in so doing live the life of the state and no more our present state. Imagination seizes upon the life of the state and gives itself to the expression of the life of that state.

Faith plus Love is self-commission. We can't commit ourselves to what we do not love. "Never would you have made anything if you had not loved it." And to make the state alive, one must become it. "I live, yet not I, God lives in me: and the life I now live in the flesh, I live by the faith of God, who loved me and gave Himself for me." God loved man, His created, and became man in faith that this act of self commission would transform the created into the creative.

We must be "imitators of God as dear children" and commit ourselves to what we love, as God who loved us committed Himself to us. We must BE the state to experience the state. The center of conscious imagining can be shifted and what are now mere wishes—imaginal activities keyed low— brought into penetrative focus and entered. Entrance commits us to the state. The possibilities of such shifting of the center of imagining are startling. The activities concerned are psychical throughout. The shifting of the center of imagining is not brought about by spatial travel but by a change in what we are aware of. The boundary of the world of sense is a subjective barrier. So long as the senses take notice, the Eye of Imagination is deflected from the truth. We do not get far unless we let go. This lady "let go" with immediate and miraculous results.

"Thank you for the 'golden key.' It has released my brother from the hospital, from pain and probable death, for he was facing a fourth major operation with little hope of recovery. I was very concerned and attempting to use what I had learned about my Imagination, I first asked myself what my brother truly desired: 'Does he want to continue in this body or does he desire to be free of it?' The question revolved itself over and over in my mind and suddenly I felt that he would like to continue remodeling his kitchen which he had been contemplating before his confinement in the hospital. I knew my question had been answered, so I began to imagine from that point.

"Attempting to 'see' my brother in the busy activity of remodeling, I suddenly found myself gripping the back of a kitchen chair I had used many times when 'something' happened, then suddenly I found myself standing beside my brother's bed in the hospital. This was the last place I would have wanted to be, physically or mentally, but there I was and my brother's hand reached up and clasped my hand tightly as I heard him say, 'I knew you would come, Jo.' It was a well hand I clasped, strong and sure, and the joy that filled and spilled over in my voice as I heard myself say, 'It's all better now. You know it.' My brother didn't answer, but I distinctly heard a voice say to me, 'Remember this moment.' I seemed to awake then, back in my own home.

"This took place the night after he had entered the hospital. The following day his wife telephoned me saying, 'It is unbelievable! The doctor can't account for it, Jo, but no operation is necessary. He's so improved that they have agreed to release him tomorrow.' The following Monday my brother went back to his work and has been perfectly well since that day."

—J.S.

Not facts—but dreams of fancy shape our lives. She needed no compass to find her brother, nor tools to operate, only the "Eye of Imagination." In the world of sense we see what we have to see; in the world of Imagination we see what we want to see; And seeing it, we create it for the world of sense to see. We see the outer world automatically. Seeing what we want to see demands voluntary and conscious imaginative effort. Our future is our own imaginal activity in its creative march. Common sense assures us that we are living in a solid and sensible world but this so seemingly solid world is—in reality—imaginal through and through.

The following story proves that it is possible for an individual to transfer the center of imagining to some greater or lesser degree to a distant area, and not only do so without moving physically, but to be visible to others who are present at that point in space-time. And, if this be a dream, then,

"Is all that we see or seem But a dream within a dream?"

"Seated in my living room in San Francisco, I imagined I was in my daughter's living room in London, England. I surrounded myself so completely with that room which I knew intimately, that I suddenly found myself actually standing in it. My daughter was standing by her fireplace, her face turned away from me. A moment later she turned and our eyes met. I saw such a startled, frightened expression on her face that I, too, became emotionally upset and immediately found myself back in my own living room in San Francisco.

"Five days later I received an airmail letter from my daughter which had been written on the day of my experiment with imaginal travel. In her letter she told me she had 'seen' me in her living room that day just as real as though I were actually standing there in the flesh. She confessed she had been very frightened and that before she could speak, I had vanished. The time of this 'visitation,' as she gave it in her letter, was exactly the time I had begun the imaginative action allowing, of course, for the difference in time between the two points. She explained that she told her husband of this amazing experience and he insisted that she write to me immediately as he stated, 'Your mother must have died or is dying.' But I wasn't 'dead' or 'dying,' but very much alive and very excited by this marvelous experience."

—M.L.J.

"Nothing can act but where it is: with all my heart; only where is it?"
—Thomas Carlyle

Man is All Imagination. Therefore, a man must be where he is in imagination, for his Imagination is himself. Imagination is active at and through any state that it is aware of. If we take shifting of awareness seriously, there are possibilities beyond belief. The senses join man in forced and unholy wedlock to what, were he imaginatively awake, he would put asunder. We need not feed on sense-data. Shift the focus of awareness and see what happens. However little we move mentally we should perceive the world under a slightly changed aspect. Awareness is usually moved about in space by movement of the physical organism but it need not be so restricted. It can be moved by a change in what we are aware of.

Man is manifesting the power of Imagination whose limits he cannot define. To realize that the Real Self-Imagination—is not something enclosed within the spatial boundary of the body is most important. The foregoing story proves, that when we meet a person in the flesh, that his Real Self need not be present in space where his body is. It also shows that sense perception can be thrown into operation

77

outside of the normal physical means, and that the sense-data produced is of the same kind as those which occur in normal perception. The idea in the mother's mind which started the whole process going was the very definite idea of being in the place where her daughter lived. And if the mother really were in that place, and if the daughter were present, then she would have to be perceptible to her daughter.

We can only hope to understand this experience in imaginal, and not in mechanical or materialistic terms. The mother imagined 'elsewhere' as being 'here.' London was just as 'here' to her daughter living 'there' as San Francisco was 'here' to the mother living 'there.'

It hardly ever crosses our minds that this world might be different in essence from what common sense tells us it so obviously is. Blake writes: "I question not my Corporeal or Vegatative Eye any more than I would Question a Window concerning a Sight. I look thro' it and not with it." This looking through the eye not only shifts consciousness to other parts of "this world" but to "other worlds" as well. Astronomers must wish they knew more of this "looking through the eye"; this mental traveling that mystics practice so easily.

> "I travel'd thro' a land of men, A land of men and women too, And heard and saw such dreadful things As cold earth wanderers never knew."

Mental traveling has been practiced by awakened men and women since the earliest days. Paul states: "I know a man in Christ who fourteen years ago was caught up to the third heaven-whether in the body or out of the body I do not know, God knows." 2.Cor.12: Paul is telling us that he is that man and that he traveled by the power of imagination or Christ. In his next letter to the Corinthians he writes: "Test yourselves. Do you not realize that Jesus Christ is in you?" We need not be 'dead' in order to enjoy spiritual privileges. "Man is All Imagination and God is Man." Test yourselves as this mother did.

Sir Arthur Eddington said that all we have a right to say of the external world is that it is a "shared experience." Things are more or less 'real' according to the extent to which they are capable of being shared with others or with ourselves at another time. But there is no hard and fast line.

Accepting Eddington's definition of reality as "shared experience," the above story is as 'real' as the earth or a color for it was shared by both mother and daughter. The range of imagining is such that I must confess that I do not know what limits, if any, there are to its ability to create reality.

All these stories show us one thing—that an imaginal activity implying the wish fulfilled must start in the imagination apart from the evidence of the senses in that journey that leads to the realization of desire.

ENTER INTO

*"If the Spectator would Enter into these Images in
his Imagination, approaching them on the Fiery
Chariot of his Contemplative Thought, if he could .
.. make a Friend & Companion of one of these
Images of wonder, which always entreats him to
leave mortal things (as he must know) then would
he arise from his Grave, then would he meet the
Lord in the Air & then he would be happy."*
                                        —Blake

Imagination it seems will do nothing that we wish until
we enter into the image of the wish fulfilled. Does not this
entering into the image of the wish fulfilled resemble Blake's
"Void outside of Existence which if enter'd into Englobes
itself & becomes a Womb?" Is this not the true interpretation
of the mythical story of Adam and Eve? Man and his emanation? Are not man's dreams of fancy his Emanation, his Eve in
whom "He plants himself in all her Nerves, just as a Husband
man his mould; And she becomes his dwelling place and garden fruitful seventy fold?"

The secret of creation is the secret of imagining - first,
desiring and then assuming the feeling of the wish fulfilled until
the dream of fancy, 'the Void outside existence,' is enter'd and
'englobes itself and becomes a womb, a dwelling place and garden fruitful seventy fold.' Note well that Blake urges us to enter
into these images. This entering into the image makes it
'englobe itself and become a womb.' Man, by entering a state

Enter Into

impregnates it and causes it to create what the union implies. Blake tells us that these images are 'Shadowy to those who dwell not in them, mere possibilities; but to those who enter into them they seem the only substances . . . .'

On my way to the West Coast I stopped in Chicago to spend the day with friends. My host was recovering from a severe illness and his doctor advised him to move to a one-story house. Acting upon the doctor's advice, he had purchased a one-story house suited to his needs; but he now was confronted with the fact that there seemed to be no buyer for his large three-story home. When I arrived he was very discouraged. In trying to explain the law of constructive imagining to my host and his wife, I told them the story of a very prominent New York woman who had come to see me concerning the rental of her apartment. She maintained a lovely city apartment and a country home, but it was absolutely essential that she rent her apartment if she and her family were to spend the summer at their country home.

In previous years the apartment had been rented without any difficulty early in the Spring, but at the time she came to see me the season for summer sublets was seemingly over. Although the apartment had been in the hands of good real estate agents, no one had seemed interested in renting it. I told her what to do in her imagination. She did it and in less than twenty-four hours her apartment was rented.

I explained how she, by the constructive use of her imagination, had rented her apartment. At my suggestion, before she went to sleep that night in her apartment in the city, she imagined she was lying in her bed in her country home. In her imagination she viewed the world from the country house rather than from the city apartment. She smelled the fresh country air. She made this so real that she actually drifted off to sleep feeling that she was in the country. That was on a Thursday night. At nine o'clock the following Saturday morning, she phoned me from her country home and told me that on Friday a highly desirable tenant, who met all of her requirements, not only rented her apartment but rented it on the one condition that he could move in that very day.

I suggested to my friends that they build an imaginal structure as this woman had done, and that was to sleep, imagining they were physically present in their new home, feeling they had sold their old home. I explained to them the wide difference between thinking of the image of their new house, and thinking from the image of their new house. Thinking of it is a confession they are not in it; thinking from it is proof that they are in it. Entering into the image would give substance to the image. Their physical occupancy of the new house would follow automatically.

I explained that what the world looks like depends entirely on where man is when he makes his observation. And man, being "All Imagination," must be where he is in imagination. This concept of causation disturbed them, for it smacked of magic or superstition, but they promised they would try it. I left that night for California and the following evening the conductor on the train in which I was traveling handed me a telegram. It read: "House sold midnight last." One week later they wrote and told me that the very night I left Chicago they fell asleep physically in the old house but mentally in the new, viewing the world from the new home, imagining how things would "sound" if this were true. They were awakened that very night from their sleep to be told the house was sold.

Not until the image is entered, until Eve is known, does the event burst upon the world. The wish fulfilled must be conceived in the imagination of man before the event can evolve out of what Blake calls 'the Void.'

This next story proves that by shifting the focus of her imagining, Mrs. A. F. entered physically into where she had persisted in being imaginatively.

"Soon after our marriage, my husband and I decided that our greatest joint desire was a year in Europe. This objective may seem reasonable to a lot of people, but to us—tied to a narrow sphere of limited finances—it seemed not only unreasonable but completely ridiculous. Europe might as well have been another planet. But I had heard your teaching, so I persisted in falling asleep in England! Why England necessarily, I cannot tell, except that I had seen a current motion picture featuring the area around Buckingham Palace and had promptly fallen in love with the scene. All I did in my imagination was to stand quietly outside the great iron gates and feel the cold metal bars gripped tightly in my hands as I viewed the Palace.

"For many, many nights I felt an intense joy at 'being' there and fell asleep in this happy state. Soon after, my husband met a stranger at a party who, within one month, was instrumental in securing a teaching fellowship for him at a great university. Imagine my excitement when I heard the university was in England! Tied to a narrow sphere? Within another month we were crossing the Atlantic and our supposedly insurmountable difficulties melted as though they never existed. We had our year in Europe, one of the happiest years of my life."—M.F.

What the world looks like depends entirely on where man is when he makes his observations. And man, being 'All Imagination,' must be where he is in imagination.

"The stone which the builders rejected has become the

chief corner-stone." That stone is Imagining. I acquaint you with this secret and leave you to Act or Re-act.

"This is the famous stone
That turneth all to gold;
For that which God doth
   touch and own
Cannot for lesse be told."
—George Herbert

"My home is old but it is mine. I wanted the exterior painted and the interior redecorated, yet I had no money to accomplish either objective. You told us to 'live' as though our desire is already a reality, and this I began to do—imagining my old house with a brand—new coat of paint, new furnishings, new decoration and all the trimmings. I walked, in my imagination, through the newly decorated rooms. I walked around the outside admiring the fresh paint; and, at the end of my imaginal act, I handed the contractor a check for payment in full. I entered this imaginal scene faithfully as often as I could during the day and each night before I fell asleep.

"Within two weeks I received a registered letter from Lloyd's of London, telling me I had inherited seven thousand dollars from a woman I had never met! I had known her brother slightly almost forty years before and had performed a small service fifteen years ago for the lady when this brother had died in our country, and she had written to me asking for particulars regarding his death which I was able to provide. I had not heard from her since that time.

Enter Into

"Now, here was the check for seven thousand dollars—more than enough to cover the cost of my house restoration, plus many, many other things I desired."

—E.C.A.

"He who does not imagine in stronger and better lineaments, and in stronger and better light than his perishing and mortal eye can see, does not imagine at all." —Blake

Unless the individual imagines himself someone else, or somewhere else, the present conditions and circumstances of his life will continue in being and his problems recur, for all events renew themselves from his constant images. By him they were made; by him they continue in being; and by him they can cease to be.

The secret of causation is in the assembled imagery—but a word of warning—the assemblage must have meaning; it must imply something or it will not form the creative activity The Word.

CHAPTER 10

THINGS WHICH DO NOT APPEAR

. . . what is seen was made out of things which do not appear.
—Heb. 11:3

"Human history, with its forms of governments, its revolutions, its wars, and in fact the rise and fall of nations, could be written in terms of the rise and fall of ideas implanted in the minds of men."
—Herbert Hoover

"The secret of imagining is the greatest of all problems to the solution of which the mystic aspires. Supreme power, supreme wisdom, supreme delight lie in the far-off solution of this mystery."
—Douglas Fawcett

To refuse to recognize the creative power of man's invisible, imaginal activity, is too great to be argued with. Man, through his imaginal activity, literally "calls into existence the things that do not exist." By man's imaginal activity, all things are made, and without such activity, "was not anything made that was made."

Such causal activity could be defined as, an imaginal assemblage of images, which occurring, some physical event invariably takes place. It is for us to assemble the images of happy out come and then keep from interfering. The event must not be forced but allowed to happen.

If imagination is the only thing that acts, or is, in existing beings or men (as Blake believed) then we should never be certain that it was not some woman treading in the wine press who began that subtle change in men's minds.

This grandmother is daily treading the wine press for her little granddaughter. She writes:

"This is one of those things that make my family and friends say, 'we just don't understand it.' Kim is two-and-a-half years old now. I took care of her for a month after she was born and did not see her again until a year ago, and then, only for two weeks. However, during this past year every day I have taken her on my lap—in my imagination—and cuddled her and talked to her.

"In these imaginal acts I go over all the wonderful things about Kim: 'God is growing through me; God is loving through me,' etc. At first, I would get the response of a very young child. When I started 'God is growing through me'—she would reply, 'Me.' Now as I start she completes the whole sentence. Another thing that has happened is, as the months have passed, as I take her—in my imagination—on my lap she has grown constantly larger and heavier.

"Kim hasn't even seen a picture of me in this past year. At the most, I could only be a name to her. Now, some time each day, her family tells me, she starts talking about me—to no one in particular—just talking.

"Sometimes it goes on for an hour; or she goes to the phone and pretends to call. In her monologue are such bits as: 'My Dee Dee loves me. My Dee Dee always comes to see me every day.'

"Even though I know what I have been doing in my imagination, it has caused me, too, 'to wonder much.'"
—D.B.

All imaginative men and women are forever casting forth enchantments, and all passive men and women, who have no powerful imaginative lives, are continually passing under the spell of their power.

There is no form in nature, which is not produced by, and sustained by some imaginal activity. Therefore, any change in the imaginal activity must result in a corresponding change in form. To imagine a substitute-image for unwanted or defective content is to create it. If only we persist in our ideal imaginal activity and do not let lesser satisfactions suffice, ours shall be the victory.

"When I read in *Seedtime and Harvest* the story of the school teacher who, through her imagination, in daily revision, transformed a delinquent pupil into a lovely girl, I decided to 'do' something about a young boy in my husband's school.

"To tell all the problems involved would take pages, for my husband has never had such a difficult child nor such a trying parent situation. The lad was too young to be expelled, yet the teachers refused to have him in their classes. To make matters worse, the mother and grand mother literally 'camped' on the school grounds making trouble for everyone.

"I wanted to help the boy, but, I also, wanted to help my husband. So, nightly, I constructed two scenes in my imagination: one, I 'saw' a perfectly normal, happy child; two, I 'heard' my husband say, 'I can't believe it, dear, but do you know "R' is acting like a normal boy, now, and it is heaven not having those two women around.'

"After two months of persisting in my imaginal play, night after night, my husband came home and said, 'It's like heaven around school'—not exactly the same words but close enough for me. The grandmother had become involved in something that took her out of town and the mother had to accompany her.

"At the same time a new teacher had welcomed the challenge of 'R' and he was progressing wonderfully well into all I imagined for him."

—G.B.

It is useless to hold standards that we do not apply. Unlike Portia, who said: "I can easier teach twenty what were good to be done, than be one of the twenty to fol low mine own teaching."

G. B. followed her own teaching. It is fatally easy to make the acceptance of the imaginal faith a substitute for living by it.

". . . he has sent me to bind up the brokenhearted, to proclaim liberty to the captives, and the opening of the prison to those who are bound. . . ."

—Isaiah 61:1

CHAPTER 11

THE POTTER

*"Arise, and go down to the potter's house, and there
I will let you hear my words. So, I went down to the
potter's house, and there he was working at his
wheel. And the vessel he was making of clay was
spoiled in the potter's hand, and he reworked it into
another vessel, as it seemed good to the potter to do."*
—Jeremiah 18:2-4

The word translated Potter means imagination. Out of material others would have thrown away as useless, an awakened imagination refashions it as it ought to be. "O Lord, thou art our father, we are the clay, and thou art our potter; we are all the work of thy hand." —Isaiah 64:8

This conception of creation as a work of imagination, and the Lord our Father as our imagination, will take us further into the mystery of creation than any other guide.

The only reason people do not believe in this identity of God and human imagination is that they are unwilling to assume the responsibility for their frightful mis-use of imagination. Divine Imagination has descended to the level of human imagination, so that human imagination may ascend to Divine Imagination.

The 8th Psalm says that man was made a little lower than God-not a little lower than the angels-as the King James Version mistakenly translates it. Angels are the emotional dispositions of man and are therefore his servant and not his superior as the author of Hebrews tells us. Imagination is the Real Man and is one with God.—Heb. 1:14

The Potter

Imagination creates, conserves and transforms. Imagination is radically creative when all imaginative activity based on memory disappears.

Imagination is conservative when its imaginal activity is fed with images supplied mainly by memory. Imagination is transformative when it varies a theme already in being; when it mentally alters a fact of life; when it leaves the fact out of the remembered experience or puts something in its place if it upsets the harmony it desires.

Through the use of her imagination this talented young artist has made her dream a reality.

"Ever since I entered into the art field I have enjoyed doing sketches and paintings for children's rooms. However, I have been discouraged by advisers and friends who were far more experienced in the 'field' than I. They liked my work, admired my talent, but said I would not get recognition nor pay for this type of work.

"Somehow, I always felt I would—but how? Then last fall I heard your lectures and read your books and I decided to let my imagination create the reality I desired. This is what I did daily: I imagined I was in a gallery— there was a great deal of excitement about me—on the walls hung my 'art'—only mine (a one-woman show)— and I saw red stars on many of the pictures. This would indicate that they had been sold.

"This is what happened: Just before Christmas I did a mobile for a friend who showed it in turn to a friend of hers who owns an art import shop in Pasadena. He expressed a desire to meet me—so I took a few samples of my work along. When he looked at the very first

The Potter

painting he said he would like to give me 'a one-woman show' in the spring.

"The night of the opening, April 17, an interior decorator came and liked and commissioned me to do a collage for a little boy's room, which will appear in the September issue of *Good Housekeeping* for the 1961 House of the Year.

"Later, during the showing another decorator came and admired my work so much, he asked if he might arrange for me to meet the 'right' interior decorators and the 'right' owners of galleries who would buy and display my work properly. Incidentally, the show was a financial success for the owner of the gallery, as well as for me.

"The interesting thing about this is that seemingly these three men came to me 'out of the blue.' Certainly, I made no effort during the time of my 'imagining' to contact anyone; but, now, I am getting recognition and have a market for my work. And, now, I know without a shadow of doubt that there is no 'no' when you seriously apply this principle that 'imagining creates reality.'"

—G.L.

She tested the Potter and proved His creativity in performance. Only the indolent mind would fail to rise to this challenge. Paul states, "the spirit of God dwells in you," now, "Examine yourselves to see whether you are holding to your faith. Test yourselves. Do you not realize that Jesus Christ is in you? Unless indeed you fail to meet the test! I hope you will find out that we have not failed." —2.Cor.13:5-6

If "all things were made through him, and without him was not anything made that was made," it should not be difficult for man to test himself to find out who this creator in himself is. The test will prove to man that his imagination is

The Potter

the One, "who gives life to the dead and calls into existence the things that do not exist." —Rom.4:17

The Potter's presence in us is *inferred* from what He does there. We cannot see Him there as One not ourselves. The nature of the Potter—Jesus Christ—is to create and there is no creation without Him.

Every recorded story in this book is just such a test as Paul asked the Corinthians to make. God really and truly exists in man—in every human being. God wholly becomes us. He is not our virtue but our Real Selves—Our Imagination.

The following illustrations from the mineral world may help us to see how Supreme Imagining and Human Imagining could be one and the same power and yet be vastly different in their creativity. Diamond is the world's hardest mineral. Graphite, used in 'lead' pencils, is one of the softest. Yet both minerals are pure carbon. The vast difference in the properties of the two forms of carbon is believed to be caused by a different arrangement of the carbon atoms. But whether the difference is produced by a different arrangement of the carbon atoms or not—all agree that Diamond and Graphite are one substance, pure carbon.

The purpose of life is the creative realization of desire. Man, lacking desire, could not exist efficiently in a world of continuous problems requiring continuing solutions. A desire is an awareness of something we lack or need to make life more enjoyable. Desires always have some personal gain in view. The greater the anticipated gain, the more intense the desire. There is no really unselfish desire. Even when our desire is for another, we are still seeking to gratify desire. To attain our desire we should imagine scenes implying their fulfillment, and enact the scene in our imagination, if only

The Potter

momentarily, with a joy sufficiently felt within its limits to make it natural. It is like a child dressing up and playing "Queen." We must imagine we are what we would like to be. We must play it in imagination first—not as a spectator—as an actor.

This lady imaginatively played "Queen" by being where she wanted to be in her imagination. She was the true actor in this theatre.

"My desire was to attend a matinee performance of a famous pantomime currently playing in one of the largest theatres of our city. Because of the intimate nature of this art, I wanted to sit in the orchestra; but I didn't have even the price of a balcony ticket. The night I determined to have this pleasure for myself, in my imagination, I fell asleep watching the wondrous performer. In my imaginal act I sat in an orchestra-center seat, heard the applause as the curtain rose and the artist came on stage, and I actually felt the intense excitement of this experience.

"The next day—the day of the matinee performance —my financial condition had not changed. I had exactly one dollar and thirty-seven cents in my purse. I knew I must use the dollar to buy gas for my car which would leave me with thirty-seven cents, but I also knew I had faithfully slept in the feeling of *being* at that performance, so I dressed myself for the theatre. While changing articles from one purse to another, I found a dollar bill and forty-five cents in change hidden in the pocket of my seldom-used opera purse. I grinned to myself, realizing that gasoline money had been given to me; so would the balance of my theatre ticket be given to me. Gaily I finished dressing and left for the theatre.

The Potter

"Standing before the ticket window, my confidence dwindled as I gazed at the prices and saw three-seventy-five for orchestra seats. With a feeling of dismay I turned away quickly and walked across the street to a cafe for a cup of tea. I had spent sixteen cents on my tea before I remembered seeing the price of balcony seats on the ticket window list. Hurriedly, I counted my change and found I had one dollar and sixty-six cents left. Running back to the theatre, I bought the cheapest seat available which cost a dollar and fifty-five cents. With one dime left in my purse, I went through the entrance and the usher tore my ticket in half saying, "Upstairs, left, please." The performance was about to begin, but ignoring the usher's instructions, I walked into the main floor lady's restroom. Still determined to sit in the orchestra section, I sat down, closed my eyes and kept my inward 'sight' riveted on the stage *from* the direction of the orchestra. At that moment, a group of women walked into the rest room, all talking at once, but I heard only one conversation as a woman speaking to her companion, said, 'But I waited and waited until the last moment. Then she called and said she couldn't make it. I would have given her ticket away but it's too late now. Not realizing it, I handed the usher both tickets and he tore them in half before I could stop him.' I almost laughed aloud. Getting up, I walked over to this lady and asked if I might use the extra ticket she had, instead of the balcony seat I had bought. She was charming and kindly invited me to join her party. The ticket she handed me was for the orchestra section, center seat, six rows from the stage. I sat in that seat only moments before the curtain rose on

The Potter

a performance I had witnessed the night before from that seat—in my Imagination."

—J.R.

We must actually BE, in Imagination. It is one thing to think of the end, and another thing to think from the end. To think from the end; to enact the end, is to create reality. The inner actions must correspond to the actions we would physically perform "after these things should be."

To live wisely we must be aware of our imaginal activity, and see to it that it is faithfully shaping the end we desire. The world is clay; our Imagination is the Potter. We should always imagine ends that are of value or promise well.

"He who desires but acts not breeds pestilence."

What's done flows from what's imagined. Outward forms reveal the imaginings of Man.

"Man is the shuttle, to whose winding quest and passage through these looms God ordered motion, but ordained no rest."

"I run a small business, solely owned, and a few years ago it seemed that my venture would end in failure. For some months, sales had fallen steadily and I found myself in a financial 'jam'—along with thousands of other small businessmen, as this period spanned one of our country's minor recessions. I was badly in debt and needed at least three thousand dollars almost immediately. My auditors advised me to close my doors and try to salvage what I

The Potter

could. Instead, I turned to my Imagination. I knew your teaching but had never actually attempted to solve any problem in this manner. I was frankly skeptical of the entire idea that imagination can create reality but I was also desperate; and desperation forced me to test your teaching.

"I imagined my office receiving four thousand dollars unexpectedly in remittances due. This money would have to come from new orders as my accounts receivable were practically nonexistent, but this seemed far-fetched as I hadn't received this much in sales during the last four months or more. Nevertheless, I kept my imaginal picture of receiving this amount of money steadily before me for three days. Early the fourth morning a customer I had not heard from in months called me on the telephone asking me to come and see him personally. I was to bring a quotation previously given him for machinery needed by his factory. The quotation was months old, but I dug it out of my files and lost no time in arriving at his office that day. I wrote out the order which he signed, but I saw no immediate help for me in the transaction as the equipment he wanted would take from four to six months for factory delivery, and of course, my customer did not have to pay for it until delivered.

"I thanked him for the order and rose to leave. He stopped me at the door and handed me a check for a little over four thousand dollars, saying, 'I want to pay for the merchandise now, in advance—for tax purposes, you know. You don't mind?' No, I didn't mind. I realized what had happened the moment I took that check into my hands. Within three days my imaginal act had done for me

97

The Potter

what I hadn't been able to do in months of desperate
financial shuffling. I know, now, that imagination could
have brought forty thousand dollars into my business just
as easily as four thousands."—L.N.C.

"O Lord, thou art our Father; we
are the clay, and thou art our potter;
we are all the work of thy hand."

CHAPTER 12

ATTITUDES

Mental Things are alone Real; what is call'd
Corporeal, Nobody Knows of its Dwelling Place: it is
in Fallacy, and its Existence an Imposture. Where is
the Existence Out of Mind or Thought?
Where is it but in the Mind of a Fool?
> —Blake

Memory, though faulty, is adequate to the call for sameness. If we remember another as we have known him, we recreate him in that image, and the past will be recognized in the present. *Imagining creates reality.* If there is room for improvement, we should re-construct him with new content; visualize him as we would like him to be, rather than have him bear the burden of our memory of him. "Everything possible to be believed is an image of truth." The following story is by one who believes that imagining creates reality and acting on this belief changed his attitude toward a stranger and bore witness to this change in reality.

"More than twenty years ago, when I was a 'green' farm boy newly arrived in Boston to attend school, a 'panhandler' asked me for money for a meal. Although the money I had was pitifully insufficient for my own needs, I gave him what was in my pocket. A few hours later the same man, by this time staggering drunk, stopped me again and asked for money. I was so outraged to think the money I could so ill afford had been put to such use, I made myself a solemn pledge that I would never again listen to the plea of a street beggar. Through the years I kept my pledge, but every time I refused any one, my conscience needled me. I felt guilty even to the point of developing a sharp pain in my stomach, but I couldn't bring myself to unbend.

'The early part of this year, a man stopped me as I was walking my dog and asked for money so he could eat. True to the old pledge, I refused him. His manner was gracious as he accepted my refusal. He even admired my dog and spoke of a family in New York state he knew that raised cocker spaniels. This time my conscience was really pricking me! As he went on his way, I determined to remake that scene as I wished it had been, so I stopped right there on the street, closed my eyes for only a few moments and enacted the scene differently. In my imagi nation I had the same man approach me, only this time he opened the conversation by admiring my dog. After we had talked a moment, I had him say, 'I don't like to ask you this, but I really need something to eat. I have a job that begins tomorrow morning, but I've been out of work and tonight I'm hungry.' I then reached into my imaginary pocket, pulled out an imaginary five-dollar bill and gladly gave it to him. This imaginal act immediately dissolved the guilty feeling and the pain.

I know from your teaching that an imaginal act is fact, so I knew I could grant anyone what he asked and by faith in the imaginal act, consent to the reality of his having it.

"Four months later as I was again walking my dog, the same man approached me and opened the conversation by admiring my dog. 'Here's a beautiful dog,' he said.

THE LAW AND THE PROMISE

'Young man, I don't suppose you remember me, but awhile back I asked you for some money and you very kindly said "no." I say "kindly," because if you had given it to me I would still be asking for money. Instead, I got a job that very next morning, and now I'm on my feet and have some self-respect again.'

"I knew his job was a fact when I imagined it that night some four months before, but I won't deny there was immense satisfaction in having him appear in the flesh to confirm it!"—F.B.

"I have no silver and gold, but I give you what I have."
—Acts 3:6

None is to be discarded, all must be saved, and our Imagination reshaping memory is the process whereby this salvation is brought to pass. To condemn the man for having lost his way is to punish the already punished. "O whom should I pity if I pity not the sinner who is gone astray?" Not what the man was but what he may become should be our imaginal activity.

"Don't you remember sweet Alice, Ben Bolt Sweet Alice whose hair was so brown, Who wept with delight when you gave her a smile, And trembled with fear at your frown?"

Attitudes

If we imagine no worse of him than he of himself, he would pass as excellent. It's not the man at his best, but the imaginist exercising the spirit of forgiveness that performs the miracle. Imagining with new content transformed both the man who asked and the man who gave. Imagining has not yet had its due in the systems either of moralists or educators. When it does, there will be "the opening of the prison to those who are bound."

Nothing has existence for us save through the memory we have of it, therefore we should remember it not as it was —unless of course, it was altogether desirable—but as we desire it to be. Inasmuch as imagining is creative, our memory of another either furthers or hinders him, and makes his upward or downward way easier and swifter.

"There is no coal of character so dead that it will not glow and flame if but slightly turned."

The following story shows that imagining can make rings, and husbands, and move people "to China!"

"My husband, child of a broken home and raised by beloved grandparents, was never 'close' to his mother— nor she to him. A woman of sixty-three and a divorcee for thirty-two of those years, she was lonely and embittered; and my relationship with her was strained as I attempted to 'stay in the middle.' By her own admission her great desire was to remarry for companionship, but she believed this to be impossible at her age. My husband would often state to me that he hoped she would remarry and, as he fervently put it, 'perhaps live way out of town!'

"I had the same wish and, as I put it, 'perhaps move to China?' Being wary of my personal motive for this wish, I knew I must change my feeling toward her in my imaginal drama and at the same time 'give' her what she wanted. I began by seeing her in my imagination as a completely changed personality—a happy, joyous woman, secure and contented in a new relationship. Every time I thought of her, I would see her mentally as a 'new' woman.

"About three weeks later, she came to our house for a visit bringing a friend she had met many months previously. The man had recently become a widower; he was her age, secure financially and had grown children and grandchildren. We liked him and I was excited because it was obvious they liked each other. But my husband still thought 'it' was impossible. I didn't.

"From that day on, every time her image rose in my mind, I 'saw' her extending her left hand toward me; and I admired the 'ring' on her finger. One month later, she and her friend came to visit us and as I walked forward to greet them, she proudly extended her left hand. The ring was on her finger.

"Two weeks later she was married—and we haven't seen her since. She lives in a brand new home. . . 'way out of town' and as her new husband dislikes the long drive to our house, she might as well have 'moved to China'!"

—J.B.

There is a wide difference between the will to resist an activity and the decision to change it. He who changes an

Attitudes

activity acts; whereas he who resists an activity, re-acts. One creates; the other perpetuates.

Nothing is real beyond the imaginative patterns we make of it. Memory, no less than desire, resembles a day-dream. Why make it a day-mare? Man can forgive only if he treats memory as a day-dream, and shapes it to his heart's desire.

R. K. learned that we may rob others of their abilities by our attitudes toward them. He changed his attitude and thereby changed a fact.

"I am not a money lender nor am I in the investment business as such, but a friend and business acquaintance came to me for a substantial loan in order to expand his plant. Because of personal friendship, I granted the loan with reasonable interest rates and gave my friend the right of renewal at the end of one year. When the first year term expired, he was behind in his interest payments and requested a thirty-day extension on the note. I granted this request, but at the end of thirty days he was still unable to meet the note and asked for an additional extension.

"As I previously stated, I am not in the business of lending money. Within twenty days I needed full payment of the loan to meet debts of my own. But I consented again to extend the note although my own credit was now in serious jeopardy. The natural thing to do was to apply legal pressure to collect and a few years ago I would have done just that. Instead, I remembered your warning 'not to rob others of their ability,' and I realized that I had been robbing my friend of his ability to pay what he owed.

"For three nights I constructed a scene in my imagi

105

nation in which I heard my friend tell me that unexpected orders had flooded his desk so rapidly, he was now able to pay the loan in full. The fourth day I received a telephone call from him. He told me that by what he called 'a miracle' he had received so many orders, and big ones, too, he was now able to pay back my loan including all interest due and, in fact, had just mailed a check to me for the entire amount."—R.K.

There is nothing more fundamental to the secret of imagining than the distinction between imagining and the state imagined.

"Mental Things are alone Real . . ." "Every thing possible to be believ'd is an image of truth."

CHAPTER 13

ALL TRIVIA

General knowledge is remote knowledge; It is in par-
ticulars that wisdom consists And happiness too.
—Blake

We must use our imagination to achieve particular ends, even if the ends are all trivia. Because men do not clearly define and imagine particular ends the results are uncertain, while they might be perfectly certain. To imagine particular ends is to discriminate clearly. "How do we distinguish the oak from the beech, the horse from the ox, but by the bounding outline?" Definition asserts the reality of the particular thing against the formless generalizations which flood the mind.

Life on earth is a kindergarten for image making. The bigness or littleness of the object to be created is not in itself important. "The great and golden rule of art, as well as of life," said Blake, "is this: That the more distinct, sharp and wirey the bounding line, the more perfect the work of art, and the less keen and sharp, the greater is the evidence of weak imitation. What is it that builds a house and plants a garden but the definite and determinate? . . . leave out this line, and you leave out life itself."

The following stories are concerned with the acquiring of seemingly little things, or 'toys' as I call them, but they are important because of the clear imaginal images that created the toys. The author of the first story is one of whom it is said, 'she has everything.' This is true. She has financial, social and intellectual security.

She writes:

"As you know, through your teaching and through my practice of that teaching, I have completely changed myself and my life. Two weeks ago when you spoke of 'toys' I realized I had never used my imagination to acquire 'things' and I decided it would be fun to try it. You told of a young woman who was given a hat by merely wearing that hat in her imagination. The last thing on earth I needed was a hat, but I wanted to test my imagi nation for this 'getting of things,' so I selected a hat pictured in a fashion magazine. I cut the picture out and stuck it on the mirror of my dressing table. I studied the picture carefully. Then, I shut my eyes, and in my imagi nation, I put that hat on my head and 'wore' it as I walked out of the house. I did this just once.

"The following week I met some friends for luncheon and one of them was wearing 'the' hat. We all admired it. The very next day, I received a parcel by special delivery messenger. 'The' hat was in the parcel. The friend who had worn it the day before had sent the hat to me with a note saying she did not particularly care for the hat and didn't know why she had bought it in the first place, but for some reason she thought it would look well on me—and would I please accept it!"

—G.L.

Movement from 'dreams to things' is the power driving humanity.

"We must live wholly on the level of Imagination. And it must be consciously and deliberately undertaken."

"All my life I have loved birds. I enjoy watching them-hearing their chatter-feeding them; and I am particularly fond of the small sparrow. For many months I have fed them crumbs of morning bread, wild bird seed and any thing I believed they would eat.

"And for all those months I have been frustrated as I watched the larger birds—particularly the pigeons—command the area, gobbling up most of the good seed and leaving the husks for my sparrows.

"To use my imagination on this problem seemed facetious to me at first, but the more I thought of it, the more interesting the idea became. So, one night I set about 'seeing' the little birds come in for their full share of daily offerings, and I would 'tell' my wife that the pigeons no longer interfered with my sparrows but took their share like gentlemen and then left the area. I continued this imaginary action for almost one month. Then one morning I noticed that the pigeons had disappeared. The sparrows had breakfast all to themselves for a few days; for those few days no larger bird entered the area. They did return eventually, but to this day they have never again infringed on the area occupied by my sparrows. They stay together, eating what I put out for them, leaving a full share of the area to my tiny friends. And do you know . . . I actually believe the sparrows understand; they no longer seem to be afraid when I walk among them."—R.K.

This lady proves that unless our heart is in the task, unless we imagine ourselves right into the feeling of our wish fulfilled, we are not there-for we are all imagination, and must be where, and what we are in imagination.

"In early February my husband and I had been in our new house one month—a home lovely beyond telling, perched on a rugged cliff with the ocean for our front yard, wind and sky for neighbors and seagulls for guests—we were ecstatic. If you have experienced the joy and woe of building your own home, you know how completely filled with happiness you are and how completely empty your purse is: A hundred lovely things clamored to be bought for that house, but the one thing we wanted most of all was the most useless—a picture. Not just any picture but a wild wonderful scene of the sea dominated by a great white clipper ship. This picture had been in our thoughts all the months of building and we left one living room wall free of paneling to hold it. My

All Trivia

husband mounted decorative red and green ship lanterns on the wall to frame our picture, but the picture itself— would have to wait. Draperies, carpeting—all the practical items must come first. Perhaps so, but that didn't stop either one of us from 'seeing' that picture, in our imagination, on that wall.

"One day while shopping, I strolled into a small art gallery and as I walked through the door I stopped so suddenly a gentleman walking behind me crashed into an easel. I apologized and pointed to a painting hanging at head-height across the room.

"'That's what did it! I've never seen anything so wonderful!' He introduced himself as the owner of the gallery and said, 'Yes, an original by the greatest English painter of clipper ships the world has known.' He went on to tell me about the artist, but I wasn't listening. I could not take my eyes from that wonderful ship; and suddenly I experienced a very strange thing. It was only a moment in time, but the art gallery faded and I 'saw' that picture on my wall. I'm afraid the owner thought me a little giddy, and I was, but I finally managed to return my attention to his voice when he mentioned an astronomical price. I smiled and said, 'Perhaps some day . . . .'He continued to tell me about the painter and also about an American artist who was the only living lithographer capable of copying the great English master. He said, 'If you're very lucky, you may pick up one of his prints. I've seen his work. It's perfect down to the last detail. Many people prefer prints to paintings.'

"'Prints' or 'paintings,' I knew nothing about the values of either, and anyway, all I wanted was that scene. When my husband returned home that evening, I talked of nothing but that painting and pleaded with him to visit the gallery and see it. 'Maybe we could find a print of it somewhere. The man said . . .' 'Yes,' he interrupted, 'but you know we can't afford any picture now . . .' Our conversation ended there, but that night after dinner, I stood in our living room and 'saw' that picture on our wall.

"The next day my husband had an appointment with a client which he did not want to keep. But the appointment was kept, and my husband did not return home until after dark. When he walked through the front door, I was busy in another part of the house and called a greeting to him. A few minutes later I heard hammering and walked into the living room to see what he was doing. On our wall was hanging my picture. In my first moment of intense joy I remembered the man in the art gallery, saying . . . 'If you're very lucky, you may pick up one of his prints . . . 'Lucky? Well, here is my husband's part of this story:

"Making the call already mentioned, he entered one of the poorest, meanest little houses he had ever been in. The client introduced himself and led my husband into a tiny dark dining area where the two of them sat down at

All Trivia

a bare table. As my husband put his brief case on the table top, he looked up and saw the picture on a wall. He confessed to me he had conducted a very sloppy interview because he couldn't take his eyes from that picture. The client signed the contract and gave a check as down payment which, as my husband believed at the time, was ten dollars short. Mentioning this fact to the client, he said the check given was every cent he could afford but added . . . 'I've noticed your interest in that picture. It was here when I took this place. I don't know to whom it belonged, but I don't want it. If you'll put the ten dollars in for me, I'll give you the picture.'

"When my husband returned to his company's main office, he learned he had been in error about the amount. He was not charged ten dollars. Our picture is on our wall. And it costs us nothing."—A.A.

Of R. L. who writes the following letter it must be said:
"In faith, Lady, you have a merry heart."
"One day, during a bus strike, I needed to go into the downtown area and had to walk ten blocks from my home to the nearest bus in operation. Before starting home I recalled there was no food market on this new route and I wouldn't be able to shop for dinner. I had enough to manage a 'pot luck' meal but I would need bread. After shopping all day, the ten blocks back from the bus line was all I could manage and to go still farther to shop for bread was out of the question.

All Trivia

"I stood very still for a moment and allowed a vision of bread to 'dance in my head.' Then I started for home. When I boarded the bus I was so tired I grabbed the first available seat and almost sat on a paper bag. Now, on a crowded bus tired passengers rarely look directly at one another, so being naturally curious, I peeked into the bag. Of course it was a loaf of bread—not just any bread but the very same brand of bread I always buy!"—R.L.

Trifles: all trifles—but they produced their trivia without price. Imagining accomplished these things with out the means generally reputed necessary to do so. Man rates wealth in a way that bears no relation to real values.

"Come, buy wine and milk without money and without price."
—Isaiah 55:1

CHAPTER 14

THE CREATIVE MOMENT

"The natural man does not receive the gifts of the Spirit of God, for they are folly to him, and he is not able to understand them because they are spiritually discerned."

—I Cor. 2:14

"There is a Moment in each Day that Satan cannot find, Nor can his Watch Fiends find it; but the Industrious find This Moment & it multiply, & when it once is found It renovates every Moment of the Day if rightly placed."

—Blake

Whenever we imagine things as they ought to be, rather than as they seem to be, is "The Moment." For in that moment the spiritual man's work is done and all the great events of time start forth to mould a world in harmony with that moment's altered pattern.

Satan, Blake writes, is a 'Reactor.' He never acts; he only reacts. And if our attitude to the happenings of the day is "reactionary" are we not playing Satan's part? Man is only reacting in his natural or Satan state; he never acts or creates, he only re-acts or re-creates. One real creative moment, one real feeling of the wish fulfilled, is worth more than the whole natural life of re-action. In such a moment God's work is done. Once more we may say with Blake, "God only Acts and Is, in existing beings or Men."

115

There is an imaginal past and an imaginal future. If, by reacting, the past is re-created into the present—so—by acting out our dreams of fancy can the future be brought into the present.

"I feel now the future in the instant."

The spiritual man Acts: for him, anything that he wants to do, he can do and do at once in his imagination—and his motto is always, "The Moment is Now."

"Behold, now is the acceptable time; behold, now is the day of salvation."—2 Cor. 6:2

Nothing stands between man and the fulfillment of his dream but facts: And facts are the creations of imagining. If man changes his imagining, he will change the facts.

This story tells of a young woman who found the Moment and, by acting out her dream of fancy, brought the future into the instant, not realizing what she had done until the final scene.

"The incident related below must appear to be coincidence to those never exposed to your teaching— but I know I observed an imaginative act take solid form in, perhaps, four minutes. I believe you will be interested in reading this account, written down, exactly as it happened, a few minutes after the actual occurrence, yesterday morning.

"I was driving my car east on Sunset Boulevard, in the center lane of traffic, braking slowly to stop for a red signal at a three-way intersection, when my attention was caught by the sight of an elderly lady, dressed all in grey, running across the street in front of my car. Her arm was raised, signaling to the driver of a bus which was beginning to pull away from the curb. She was obviously attempting to cross in front of the bus to delay it. The driver slowed his vehicle and I thought would allow her to enter. Instead, as she jumped on to the curb, the bus pulled away leaving her standing just in the act of lowering her arm. She turned and walked swiftly toward a nearby phone booth.

"As my signal changed to green and I put my car in motion, I wished I had been behind the bus and had been able to offer her a ride. Her extreme agitation was obvious even from the distance I was away from her. My wish instantly fulfilled itself in a mental drama, and as I drove away, the fancy played itself out in the following scene.

". . . I opened the car door and a lady dressed in grey stepped in, smilingly relieved and thanking me profusely. She was out of breath from running and said, 'I only have a few blocks to go. I'm meeting friends and I was so afraid they would leave without me when I missed my bus.' I left my imaginary lady out a few blocks farther on and she was delighted to observe her friends still waiting for her. She thanked me again and walked away. . ."

"The entire mental scene was spanned in the time it takes to drive one block at a normal rate of speed. The fancy satisfied my feelings regarding the 'real' incident, and I immediately forgot it. Four blocks farther, I was still in the center lane and again had to stop for a red signal. My attention at this time was turned inward on some thing I have now forgotten, when suddenly someone tapped on the closed window of my car and I looked up to see a lovely-appearing elderly lady with grey hair, dressed all in grey. Smiling, she asked if she might ride a few blocks with me as she had missed her bus. She was out of breath, as though from running, and I was so stunned by her sudden appearance in the middle of a busy street at my window that for a moment I could only react physically, and without answering, leaned over and opened my car door. She got in and said, 'It's so annoying to rush so and then miss a bus. I wouldn't have imposed on you like this, but I'm supposed to meet some friends a few blocks down the street and if I had to walk now, I would miss them.' Six blocks farther on, she exclaimed, 'Oh, good! They're still waiting for me.' I let her out and she thanked me again and walked away.

"I'm afraid I drove to my own destination by automatic reflex, for I had fully recognized that I had just observed a waking dream take form in physical action. I recognized what was happening while it was happening. As soon as I could, I wrote down each part of the incident and found a startling consistency between the 'waking dream' and the subsequent 'reality.' Both women were elderly, gracious in manner, dressed all in grey, and out of breath from hurrying to catch a bus and missing it. Both wished to meet friends (who for some reason could not wait for them much longer) and both left my car within the space of a few blocks after successfully completing their contact with their friends.

The Creative Moment

"I am amazed, confounded and elated! If there is no such thing as coincidence or accident—then I witnessed imagination become 'reality' almost instantaneously."

—J.R.B.

"There is a Moment in each Day that Satan cannot find, Nor can his Watch Fiends find it; but the Industrious find This Moment & it multiply, & when it once is found It renovates every Moment of the Day if rightly placed."

"From the first time I read your 'Search' I have longed to experience a vision. Since you have told us of the 'Promise' this desire has been intensified. I want to tell you of my vision which was a glorious answer to my prayer; but I am sure I would not have had this experience were it not for something that occurred two weeks ago.

"It was necessary for me to park my car some distance from the University Building where I was scheduled to conduct my class. As I left my car I was conscious of the stillness about me. The street was completely deserted; no one was in sight.

"Suddenly I heard a most frightful cursing voice. I looked toward the sound and saw a man brandishing a cane, yelling, between vile words, 'I'll kill you. I'll kill you.' I continued on as he approached me, for at that moment I thought 'Now I can test what I have professed to believe; if I do believe we are one, The Father, this derelict and I, no harm can come to me.' At that moment I had no fear. Instead of seeing a man coming toward me, I felt a light. He stopped yelling, dropped his cane and

119

The Creative Moment

walked quietly as we passed with less than a foot between us.

"Having tested my faith at that moment, everything about me had seemed more alive than before flowers brighter and trees greener. I have had a sense of peace and the 'oneness' of life I had not known before.

"Last Friday I drove to our country home—nothing was unusual about the day or evening. I worked on a man uscript and not being tired did not try to fall off to sleep until around two the following morning. Then I turned off the light and drifted into that floating sensation, not asleep but drowsy, as I call it, half awake and half asleep. Often, while in this state—lovely, unknown faces float before me—but this morning the experience was different. A perfect face of a child came before me in pro file—then it turned and smiled at me. It was glowing with light and seemed to fill my own head with light.

"I was aglow and excited and thought 'this must be the Christos'; but something within me, without sound, said, 'No, this is you.' I feel I will never be the same again and some day I may experience the 'Promise.'"—G.B.

Our dreams will all be realized from the time that we know that Imagining Creates Reality and Act. But Imagination seeks from us something much deeper and more fundamental than creating things: nothing less indeed than the recognition of its own oneness, with God; that what it does is, in reality, God himself doing it. in and through Man who is All Imagination.

CHAPTER 15

"THE PROMISE"
Four Mystical Experiences

*The natural man does not receive the gifts of the
Spirit of God, for they are folly to him, and he is
not able to understand them because they are
spiritually discerned.*

—I Cor. 2:14

*There is a Moment in each Day that Satan cannot
find, Nor can his Watch Fiends find it; but the
Industrious find This Moment & it multiply, & when
it once is found It renovates every Moment of the
Day if rightly placed.*

—Blake

The promise that God will bring forth from our body a
son who will be "born, not of blood nor of the will of the flesh
nor of the will of man, but of God" does not concern them.
They want to know God's law, not His promise. However,
this miraculous birth has been stated clearly as a must for all
mankind from the earliest days of the Christian fellowship.
"You must be born from above," —John 3:7.

My purpose here is to state it again and to state it in such
language and with such reference to my own personal
mystical experiences that the reader will see that this birth
"from above" is far more than a part of a dispensable super-
structure, that it is the sole purpose for God's creation.

Specifically, my purpose in recording these four mystical
experiences is to show what "Jesus Christ the faithful witness,

121

the firstborn from the dead" (Rev. 1:5) was trying to say about this birth from above. "How can men preach unless they are sent?" —Rom. 10:15.

Many years ago, I was taken in spirit into a Divine Society, a Society of men in whom God is awake. Though it may seem strange, the gods do truly meet. As I entered this society, the first to greet me was the embodiment of infinite Might. His was a power unknown to mortals. I was then taken to meet infinite Love. He asked me, "What is the greatest thing in the world?" I answered him in the words of Paul, "faith, hope, and love, these three; but the greatest of these is love." At that moment, he embraced me and our bodies fused and became one body. I was knit to him and loved him as my own soul. The words, "love of God" so often a mere phrase, were now a reality with a tremendous meaning. Nothing ever imagined by man could be compared with this love which man feels through his union with Love. The most intimate relationship on earth is like living in separate cells compared with this union.

While I was in this state of supreme delight, a voice from outer space shouted, "Down with the blue bloods!" At this blast, I found myself standing before the one who had first greeted me, he who embodied infinite Might. He looked into my eyes and without the use of spoken words, I heard what he told me: "Time to act." I was suddenly whisked out of that Divine Society and returned to earth. I was tormented by my limitations of understanding but I knew that on that day the Divine Society had chosen me as a companion and sent me to preach Christ God's promise to man.

My mystical experiences have brought me to accept literally, the saying that "all the world's a stage" and to believe that God plays all the parts. The purpose of the play? To transform man, the created, into God, the creator. God loved man, his created, and became man in faith that this act of self-commission would transform man—the created, into God—the creator.

The play begins with the crucifixion of God on man - as man—and ends with the resurrection of man—as God. God becomes as we are, that we may be as He is. God becomes man that man may become, first—a living being, and secondly—a life-giving spirit.

"I have been crucified with Christ; it is no longer I who live, but Christ who lives in me; and the life I now live in the flesh I live by faith in the Son of God, who loved me and gave himself for me." —Gal.2:20

God took upon Himself the form of man and became obedient unto death—even death on the cross of man - and is crucified on Golgotha, the skull of man. God himself enters death's door—the human skull—and lies down in the grave of man to make man a living being. God's mercy turned death into sleep. Then began the prodigious and unthinkable metamorphosis of man, the transformation of man into God.

No man, unaided by the crucifixion of God, could cross the threshold that admits to conscious life, but now we have union with God in his crucified self. He lives in us as our wonderful human imagination. "Man is all imagination, and God is man, and exists in us and we in him. The eternal body of man is the imagination that is, God, himself." When he rises in us we will be like him and he will be like us. Then all impossibilities will dissolve in us at that touch of exaltation which his rising in us will impart to our nature.

Here is the secret of the world: God died to give man life and to set man free, for however clearly God is aware of his creation, it does not follow that man, imaginatively created, is aware of God. To work this miracle God had to die, then rise again as man, and none has ever expressed it so clearly as Blake. Blake says—or rather has Jesus say— "Unless I die, thou canst not live; but if I die I shall arise again and thou with me. Wouldest thou love one who never died for thee, or ever die for one who had not died for thee? And if God dieth not for man and giveth not himself eternally for man, man could not exist."

So God dies—that is to say—God has freely given himself for man. Deliberately, He has become man and has forgotten that He is God, in the hope that man, thus created, will eventually rise as God. God has so completely offered His own self for man, that He cries out on the cross of man, "My God, my God; why hast thou forsaken me?" He has completely forgotten that He is God. But after God rises in one man, that man will say to his brothers, "Why stand we here, trembling around, calling on God for help, and not ourselves, in whom God dwells?"

This first man that has been raised from the dead is known as Jesus Christ—the first fruits of those who have fallen asleep, the first-born of the dead. For man God died; now, by a man, has come also the resurrection of the dead. Jesus Christ resurrects his dead Father by becoming his father. In Adam—the universal man—God sleeps. In Jesus Christ— the individualized God—God wakes. In waking, man the created, has become God, the creator, and can truly say, "Before the world was, I am." Just as God in His love for man so completely identified Himself with man that He forgot that He was God, so man in his love for God must so completely identify himself with God that he lives the life of God, that is, Imaginatively.

"The Promise"

God's play which transforms man into God is revealed to us in the Bible. It is completely consistent in imagery and symbolism. The New Testament is hid in the Old Testament, and the old is manifested in the new. The Bible is a vision of God's Law and His Promise. It was never intended to teach history but rather to lead man in faith through the furnaces of affliction to the fulfillment of God's promise, to rouse man from this profound sleep and awaken him as God. Its characters live not in the past but in an imaginative eternity. They are personifications of the eternal spiritual states of the soul. They mark man's journey through eternal death and his awakening to eternal life.

The Old Testament tells us of God's promise. The New Testament tells us not how this promise was fulfilled but how it is fulfilled. The central theme of the Bible is the direct, individual, mystical experience of the birth of the child, that child of whom the prophet spoke ". . . to us a child is born, to us a son is given; and the government will be upon his shoulder; and his name will be called, Wonderful Counselor, Mighty God, Everlasting Father, Prince of Peace. Of the increase of his government and of peace, there will be no end . . ."

—Isaiah 9:6-7

When the child is revealed to us we see it, we experience it, and the response to this revelation can be stated in the words of job, "I have heard of thee by the hearing of the ear, but now my eye sees thee." The story of the incarnation is not fable, allegory or some carefully contrived fiction to enslave the minds of men, but mystical fact. It is a personal mystical experience of the birth of oneself out of one's own skull, symbolized in the birth of a child, wrapped in swaddling clothes and lying on the floor.

"The Promise"

There is a distinction between hearing of this birth of a child from one's own skull—a birth which no scientist or historian could ever possibly explain—and actually experiencing the birth—holding in your own hands and seeing with your own eyes this miraculous child—a child born from above out of your own skull, a birth contrary to all the laws of nature. The question as it is posed in the Old Testament, "Ask now, and see, can a male bear a child? Why then do I see every man with his hands delivering himself like a woman in labor? Why has every face turned pale?"—Jer. 30:6. The Hebrew word "chalats" mistranslated "loins" means: to draw out, to deliver, to withdraw self. The drawing of oneself out of one's own skull was exactly what the prophet foresaw as the necessary birth from above, a birth giving man entrance into the kingdom of God and reflective perception on the highest levels of Being. Throughout the ages "Deep calls to deep . . . Rouse thyself! Why sleepest thou, O Lord? Awake!"

The event, as it is recorded in the gospels, actually takes place in man. But of that day or that hour when the time will come for the individual to be delivered, no one knows but the Father. "Do not marvel that I said to you, You must be born from above. The wind blows where it wills, and you hear the sound of it, but you do not know whence it comes or whither it goes; so it is with every one who is born of the Spirit."

—John 3:7-8

This revelation in the Gospel of John is true. Here is my experience of this birth from above. Like Paul, I did not receive it from man—nor was I taught it. It came through the actual mystical experience of being born from above. None can speak truly of this mystical birth from above but one who has expe-

"*The Promise*"

rienced it. I had no idea that this birth from above was literally true. Who, before the experience, could believe that the child, the Wonderful Counselor, the Mighty God, the Everlasting Father, the Prince of Peace was woven into his own skull? Who, before the experience, would understand that his Maker is his Husband and the Lord of Hosts is His Name? Who would believe that the creator went in unto his own creation, man, and knew it to be himself and that this entrance into the skull of man—this union of God and man—resulted in the birth of a Son out of the skull of man; which birth gave to that man eternal life and union with his creator forever?

If I now tell what I experienced that night I do so not to impose my ideas on others but that I may give hope to those who, like Nicodemus, wonder how a man can be born when he is old? How can he enter a second time into his mother's womb and be born? How can this be? This is how it happened to me. Therefore, I will now "write the vision"; and "make it plain upon tablets, so he may run who reads it. For still the vision awaits its time; it hastens to the end—it will not lie. If it seem slow, wait for it; it will surely come, it will not delay. Behold, he whose soul is not upright in him shall fail, but the righteous shall live by his faith." —Hab. 2:2-4.

In the early hours of the morning on July 20, 1959, in the city of San Francisco, a heavenly dream in which the arts flourished was suddenly interrupted by the most intense vibration centered at the base of my skull. Then a drama, as real as those I experience when I am fully awake, began to unfold. I awoke from a dream to find myself completely entombed within my skull. I tried to force my way out through its base. Something gave way and I felt myself move head downward, through the base of my skull. I squeezed myself out, inch by inch. When I was almost out, I held what I took to be the foot of the bed and pulled the remaining portion of me out of my skull. There, on the floor, I lay for a few seconds.

Then I rose and looked at my body on the bed. It was pale of face lying on its back and tossing from side to side like one in recovery from a great ordeal. As I contemplated it, hoping that it would not fall off the bed, I became aware that the vibration which started the whole drama was not only in my head but now was also coming from the corner of the room. As I looked over to that corner I wondered if that vibration could be caused by a very high wind, a wind strong enough to vibrate the window. I did not realize that the vibration which I still felt within my head was related to that which seemed to be coming from the corner of the room.

Looking back to the bed, I discovered that my body was gone but in its place sat my three older brothers. My oldest brother sat where the head was. My second and third brothers sat where the feet were. None seemed to be aware of me, although I was aware of them and could discern their thoughts. I suddenly became aware of the reality of my own invisibility. I noticed that they, too, were disturbed by the vibration coming from the corner of the room. My third brother was the most disturbed and went over to investigate the cause of the disturbance. His attention was attracted by something on the floor and looking down he announced, "It's Neville's baby." My other two brothers, in most incredulous voices, asked "How can Neville have a baby?"

My brother lifted the infant wrapped in swaddling clothes and laid him on the bed. I, then, with my invisible hands lifted the babe and asked him "How is my sweetheart?" He looked into my eyes and smiled and I awoke in this world —to ponder this greatest of my many mystical experiences.

"The Promise"

Tennyson has a description of Death as a warrior—a skeleton "high on a night-black horse," issuing forth at midnight. But when Gareth's sword cut through the skull, there was in it. . .

". . . the bright face of a blooming boy Fresh as a flower new-born."
—Idylls of the King

Two other visions I will tell because they bear out the truth of my assertion that the Bible is mystical fact, that everything written about the promised child in the law of Moses and the Prophets and the Psalms must be mystically experienced in the imagination of the individual. The child's birth is a sign and a portent, signaling the resurrection of David, the Lord's anointed, of whom He said, "You are my son, today I have begotten you." Psalms 2:7

Five months after the birth of the child, on the morning of December 6, 1959, in the city of Los Angeles, a vibration similar to the one which preceded his birth started in my head. This time its intensity was centered at the top of my head. Then came a sudden explosion and I found myself in a modestly furnished room. There, leaning against the side of an open door was my son David of Biblical fame. He was a lad in his early teens. What struck me forcibly about him was the unusual beauty of his face and figure. He was—as he is described in the first book of Samuel—ruddy, with beautiful eyes and very handsome.

Not for one moment did I feel myself to be anyone other than who I am now. Yet, I knew that this lad, David, was my son, and he knew that I was his father; for "the wisdom from

129

above is without uncertainty." As I sat there contemplating the beauty of my son, the vision faded and I awoke.

"'I and the children whom the Lord has given me are signs and portents in Israel from the Lord of hosts, who dwells on Mount Zion.' Is. 8.18. God gave me David as my very own son. 'I will raise up your son after you, who shall come forth from your body. .. I will be his father, and he shall be my son.' —2 Sam. 7:12-14. God is known in no other way than through the Son.

"'No one knows who the Son is except the Father, or who the Father is except the Son and any one to whom the Son chooses to reveal Him.' Luke 10:22. The experience of being David's Father is the end of man's pilgrimage on earth. The purpose of life is to find the Father of David, the Lord's anointed, the Christ. 'Abner, whose son is this youth?' And Abner said, 'As your soul lives, O king, I cannot tell.' And the king said, 'Inquire whose son the stripling is.' And as David returned from the slaughter of the Philistine, Abner took him and brought him before Saul with the head of the Philistine in his hand. And Saul said to him, 'Whose son are you, young man?' And David answered, 'I am the son of your servant Jesse the Bethlehemite.' 1 Sam. 17:55-58. Jesse is any form of the verb 'to be.' In other words, I Am the Son of who I Am, I am self begotten, I Am the Son of God, the Father. I And my Father are one. I am the image of the invisible God. He who has seen me has seen the Father.

"'Whose son . . . ?' is not about David but about David's Father, whom the king had promised (1 Sam: 17:25) to make free in Israel. Note: in all these passages (1 Sam. 17:55,56,58) the king's inquiry is not about David but about David's Father. 'I have found David, my servant; . . . He shall cry to me, "Thou art my Father, my God, and the Rock of my salvation. And I will make him the first-born, the highest of the kings of the earth.'"

—Psalms 89

The individual who is born from above will find David and know him to be his very own son. Then he will ask the Pharisees—who are always with us—"What do you think of the Christ? Whose son is he?" And when they say to him, "The son of David." He will say to them, "How is it then that David, in the Spirit, calls him Lord . . . If David thus calls him Lord, how is he his son?" —Matt. 22:41-45. Man's misconception of the role of the Son-which is only a sign and a portent — has made the Son an idol. "Little children, keep yourselves from idols." —1 John 5:21.

God awakes; and that man in whom he awakes becomes his own father's father. He who was David's son, "Jesus Christ, the son of David" —Matt. 1:1. has become David's Father.

No longer will I cry to "our father David, thy child." Acts 4:25. "I have found David." He has cried to me, "Thou art my Father." —Psalms 89. Now I know myself to be one of the Elohim, the God who became man, that man may become God. "Great indeed, we confess, is the mystery of our religion." —1 Tim. 3.16. If the Bible were history it would not be a mystery. "Wait for the promise of the Father." —Acts 1.4. that is, for David-God's Son-who will reveal you as the Father. This promise, says Jesus, you heard from me (Luke 24:49) and to its fulfillment at that moment in time when it pleases God to give you his Son—as "your offspring, which is Christ." —Gal. 3:16.

"The Promise"

A figure of speech is used for the purpose of calling attention to, emphasizing and intensifying the reality of the literal sense. The truth is literal; the words used are figurative. "The curtain of the temple was torn in two, from top to bottom, and the earth shook and the rocks were split."—Matt. 27:51.

On the morning of April 8, 1960—four months after it was revealed to me that I am David's father—a bolt of lightning out of my skull split me in two from the top of my skull to the base of my spine. I was cleft as though I were a tree that had been struck by lightning. Then I felt and saw myself as a golden liquid light moving up my spine in a serpentine motion; as I entered my skull it vibrated like an earthquake. "Every word of God proves true; he is a shield to those who take refuge in him. Do not add to his words, lest he rebuke you, and you be found a liar." "And as Moses lifted up the serpent in the wilderness, so must the Son of man be lifted up."—John 3:14.

These mystical experiences will help to rescue the Bible from the externals of history, persons and events, and to restore it to its real significance in the life of man. Scripture must be fulfilled "in" us. God's promise will be fulfilled. You will have these experiences: "And you shall be my witnesses in Jerusalem and in all Judea and Sa-ma-ri-a and to the end of the earth." —Acts 1:8.

The widening circle—Jerusalem . . . Judea . . . Samaria the end of the earth—is God's plan.

The Promise is still maturing to its time, its appointed time, but how long, vast and severe the trials e're you find David, your son, who will reveal you as God, The Father, were long to tell; but it hastens to the end; it will not fail. So wait, for there will be no postponement.

132

"The Promise"

"Is anything too wonderful for the Lord? At the appointed time I will return to you, in the spring, and Sarah shall have a son."

—Gen. 18:14

PRAYER
THE ART OF BELIEVING

CHAPTER 16

LAW OF REVERSIBILITY

PRAYER is the master key. A key may fit one door of a house, but when it fits all doors it may well claim to be a master key. Such and no less a key is prayer to all earthly problems.

> "Pray for my soul, more things are wrought by prayer than this world dreams of"
>
> — Tennyson

PRAYER is an art and requires practice. The first requirement is a controlled imagination. Parade and vain repetitions are foreign to prayer. Its exercise requires tranquility and peace of mind. "Use not vain repetitions," for prayer is done in secret and "thy Father which seeth in secret shall reward thee openly." The ceremonies that are customarily used in prayer are mere superstitions and have been invented to give prayer an air of solemnity. Those who do practice the art of prayer are often ignorant of the laws that control it. They attribute the results obtained to the ceremonies and mistake the letter for the spirit. The essence of prayer is faith; but faith must be permeated with understanding to be given that active quality which it does not possess when standing alone. "Therefore, get wisdom; and with all thy getting get understanding."

Law of Reversibility

This book is an attempt to reduce the unknown to the known, by pointing out the conditions on which prayers are answered, and without which they cannot be answered. It defines the conditions governing prayer in laws that are simply a generalization of our observations.

The universal law of reversibility is the foundation on which its claims are based.

Mechanical motion caused by speech was known for a long time before any one dreamed of the possibility of an inverse transformation, that is, the reproduction of speech by mechanical motion (the phonograph). For a long time electricity was produced by friction without ever a thought that friction, in turn, could be produced by electricity. Whether or not man succeeds in reversing the transformation of a force, he knows, nevertheless, that all transformations of force are reversible. If heat can produce mechanical motion, so mechanical motion can produce heat. If electricity produces magnetism, magnetism too can develop electric currents. If the voice can cause undulatory currents, so can such currents reproduce the voice, and so on. Cause and effect, energy and matter, action and reaction are the same and inter-convertible. This law is of the highest importance, because it enables you to foresee the inverse transformation once the direct transformation is verified. If you knew how you would feel were you to realize your objective, then, inversely, you would know what state—you could realize were you to awaken in yourself such feeling. The injunction, to pray believing that you already possess what you pray for, is based upon a knowledge of the law of inverse transformation. If your realized prayer produces in you a definite feeling or state of consciousness, then, inversely, that particular feeling or state of consciousness must produce your realized prayer. Because all transformations of force are reversible, you should always assume the feeling of your fulfilled wish. You should awaken within you the feeling that you are and have that which heretofore you desired to be and possess. This is easily done by contemplating the joy that would be yours were your objective an accomplished fact, so that you live and move and have your being in the feeling that your wish is realized.

The feeling of the wish fulfilled, if assumed and sustained, must objectify the state that would have created it. This law explains why "Faith is the substance of things hoped for, the evidence of things not seen" and why "He calleth things that are not seen as though they were and things that were not seen become seen." Assume the feeling of your wish fulfilled and continue feeling that it is fulfilled until that which you feel objectifies itself. If a physical fact can produce a psychological state, a psychological state can produce a physical fact. If the effect (a) can be produced by the cause (b), then inversely, the effect (b) can be produced by the cause (a). Therefore I say unto you, "What things soever ye desire, when ye pray, believe that ye have received them, and ye shall have them" (Mark 11:24, E. R. V.).

CHAPTER 17

DUAL NATURE OF CONSCIOUSNESS

A clear concept of the dual nature of man's consciousness must be the basis of all true prayer. Consciousness includes a subconscious as well as a conscious part. The infinitely greater part of consciousness lies below the sphere of objective consciousness. The subconscious is the most important part of consciousness. It is the cause of voluntary action. The subconscious is what a man is. The conscious is what a man knows. "I and my Father are one but my Father is greater than I." The conscious and subconscious are one, but the subconscious is greater than the conscious.

"I of myself can do nothing, the Father within me He doeth the work." I, objective consciousness, of myself can do nothing; the Father, the subconscious, He doeth the work. The subconscious is that in which everything is known, in which everything is possible, to which everything goes, from which everything comes, which belongs to all, to which all have access.

What we are conscious of is constructed out of what we are not conscious of. Not only do our subconscious assumptions influence our behavior but they also fashion the pattern of our objective existence. They alone have the power to say, "Let us make man-objective manifestations-in our image, after our likeness." The whole of creation is asleep within the deep of man and is awakened to objective existence by his subconscious assumptions.

Within that blankness we call sleep there is a consciousness in unsleeping vigilance, and while the body sleeps this unsleeping being releases from the treasure house of eternity the subconscious assumptions of man.

Prayer is the key which unlocks the infinite storehouse. "Prove me now herewith, saith the Lord of hosts, if I will not open you the windows of heaven, and pour you out a blessing, that there shall not be room enough to receive it." Prayer modifies or completely changes our subconscious assumptions, and a change of assumption is a change of expression.

The conscious mind reasons inductively from observation, experience and education. It therefore finds it difficult to believe what the five senses and inductive reason deny. The subconscious reasons deductively and is never concerned with the truth or falsity of the premise, but proceeds on the assumption of the correctness of the premise and objectifies results which are consistent with the premise. This distinction must be clearly seen by all who would master the art of praying. No true grasp of the science of prayer can be really obtained until the laws governing the dual nature of consciousness are understood and the importance of the subconscious realized.

Prayer-the art of believing what is denied by the senses-deals almost entirely with the subconscious. Through prayer, the subconscious is suggested into acceptance of the wish fulfilled, and, reasoning deductively, logically unfolds it to its legitimate end. "Far greater is He that is in you than he that is in the world."

The subjective mind is the diffused consciousness that animates the world; it is the spirit that giveth life. In all substance is a single soul-subjective mind. Through all creation runs this one unbroken subjective mind. Thought and feeling fused into beliefs impress modifications upon it, charge it with a mission, which mission it faithfully executes.

The conscious mind originates premises. The subjective mind unfolds them to their logical ends. Were the subjective mind not so limited in its initiative power of reasoning, objective man could not be held responsible for his actions in the world. Man transmits ideas to the subconscious through his feelings. The subconscious transmits ideas from mind to mind through telepathy. Your unexpressed convictions of others are transmitted to them without their conscious knowledge or consent, and if subconsciously accepted by them will influence their behavior.

The only ideas they subconsciously reject are your ideas of them which they could not wish to be true of anyone. Whatever they could wish for others can be believed of them, and by the law of belief which governs subjective reasoning they are compelled to subjectively accept, and therefore objectively express, accordingly.

The subjective mind is completely controlled by suggestion. Ideas are best suggested when the objective mind is partly subjective, that is, when the objective senses are diminished or held in abeyance. This partly subjective state can best be described as controlled reverie, wherein the mind is passive but capable of functioning with absorption. It is a concentration of attention. There must be no conflict in your mind when you are praying. Turn from what is to what ought to be. Assume the mood of fulfilled desire, and by the universal law of reversibility you will realize your desire.

CHAPTER 18

IMAGINATION
AND FAITH

PRAYERS are not successfully made unless there is rapport between the conscious and subconscious mind of the operator. This is done through imagination and faith.

By the power of imagination all men, certainly imaginative men, are forever casting forth enchantments, and all men, especially unimaginative men, are continually passing under their power. Can we ever be certain that it was not our mother while darning our socks who began that subtle change in our minds? If I can unintentionally cast an enchantment over persons, there is no reason to doubt that I am able to cast intentionally a far stronger enchantment.

Everything, that can be seen, touched, explained, argued over, is to the imaginative man nothing more than a means, for he functions, by reason of his controlled imagination, in the deep of himself where every idea exists in itself and not in relation to something else. In him there is no need for the restraints of reason, for the only restraint he can obey is the mysterious instinct that teaches him to eliminate all moods other than the mood of fulfilled desire.

Imagination and faith are the only faculties of mind needed to create objective conditions. The faith required for the successful operation of the law of consciousness is a purely subjective faith and is attainable upon the cessation of active opposition on the part of the objective mind of the operator. It depends upon your ability to feel and accept as true what your objective senses deny. Neither the passivity of the subject

nor his conscious agreement with your suggestion is necessary, for without his consent or knowledge he can be given a
subjective order which he must objectively express. It is a fundamental law of consciousness that by telepathy we can have
immediate communion with another.

To establish rapport you call the subject mentally. Focus
your attention on him and mentally shout his name just as you
would to attract the attention of anyone. Imagine that he has
answered, and mentally hear his voice. Represent him to yourself inwardly in the state you want him to obtain. Then imagine that he is telling you in the tones of ordinary conversation
what you want to hear. Mentally answer him. Tell him of your
joy in witnessing his good fortune. Having mentally heard
with all the distinctness of reality that which you wanted to
hear, and having thrilled to the news heard, return to objective consciousness. Your subjective conversation must awaken
what it affirmed.

"Thou shalt decree a thing and it shall be established unto
thee." It is not a strong will that sends the subjective word on
its mission so much as it is clear thinking and feeling the truth
of the state affirmed. When belief and will are in conflict,
belief invariably wins. "Not by might, nor by power, but by my
spirit, saith the Lord of hosts." It is not what you want that you
attract; you attract what you believe to be true. Therefore, get
into the spirit of these mental conversations and give them the
same degree of reality that you would a telephone conversation. "If thou canst believe, all things are possible to him that
believeth. Therefore, I say unto you, what things soever ye
desire, when ye pray, believe that ye have received them, and
ye shall have them." The acceptance of the end wills the
means. And the wisest reflection could not devise more effec-

PRAYER: THE ART OF BELIEVING

tive means than those which are willed by the acceptance of the end. Mentally talk to your friends as though your desires for them were already realized.

Imagination is the beginning of the growth of all forms, and faith is the substance out of which they are formed. By imagination, that which exists in latency or is asleep within the deep of consciousness is awakened and is given a form. The cures attributed to the influence of certain medicines, relics and places are the effects of imagination and faith. The curative power is not in the spirit that is in them, it is in the spirit in which they are accepted. "The letter killeth, but the spirit giveth life."

The subjective mind is completely controlled by suggestion, so, whether the object of your faith be true or false, you will get the same results. There is nothing unsound in the theory of medicine or in the claims of the priesthood for their relics and holy places. The subjective mind of the patient accepts the suggestion of health conditioned on such states, and as soon as these conditions are met proceeds to realize health. "According to your faith be it done unto you for all things are possible to him that believeth." Confident expectation of a state is the most potent means of bringing it about. The confident expectation of a cure does that which no medical treatment can accomplish.

Failure is always due to an antagonistic auto-suggestion by the patient, arising from objective doubt of the power of the medicine or relic, or from doubt of the truth of the theory. Many of us, either from too little emotion or too much intellect, both of which are stumbling blocks in the way of prayer, cannot believe that which our senses deny. To force ourselves to believe will end in greater doubt. To avoid such counter-suggestions the patient should be unaware, objectively, of the suggestions which are made to him. The most effective method of healing or influencing the behavior of others consists in what is known as "the silent or absent treatment." When the subject is unaware, objectively, of the suggestion given him there is no possibility of him setting up an antagonistic belief. It is not necessary that the patient know, objectively, that anything is being done for him. From what is known of the subjective and objective processes of reasoning, it is better that he should not know objectively of that which is being done for him. The more completely the objective mind is kept in ignorance of the suggestion, the better will the subjective mind perform its functions. The subject subconsciously accepts the suggestion and thinks he originates it, proving the truth of Spinoza's dictum that we know not the causes that determine our actions.

The subconscious mind is the universal conductor which the operator modifies with his thoughts and feelings. Visible states are either the vibratory effects of subconscious vibrations within you or they are the vibratory causes of corresponding vibrations within you. A disciplined man never permits them to be causes unless they awaken in him desirable states of consciousness. With a knowledge of the law of reversibility, the disciplined man transforms his world by imagining and feeling only what is lovely and of good report. The beautiful idea he awakens within himself shall not fail to arouse its affinity in others. He knows the savior of the world is not a man but the manifestation that would save. The sick man's savior is health, the hungry man's savior is food, the thirsty man's savior is water. He walks in the company of the savior by assuming the feeling of his wish fulfilled. By the laws of reversibility, that all transformations of force are reversible, the energy or feeling awakened transforms itself into the state imagined. He never waits four months for the harvest. If in four months the harvest will awaken in him a state of joy, then, inversely, the joy of harvest now will awaken the harvest now. "Now is the acceptable time to give beauty for ashes, joy for mourning, praise for the spirit of heaviness; that they might be called trees of righteousness, the planting of the Lord that he might be glorified."

CHAPTER 19

CONTROLLED REVERIE

EVERYONE is amenable to the same psychological laws which govern the ordinary hypnotic subject. He is amenable to control by suggestion. In hypnosis, the objective senses are partly or totally suspended. However, no matter how profoundly the objective senses are locked in hypnosis, the subjective faculties are alert, and the subject recognizes everything that goes on around him. The activity and power of the subjective mind are proportionate to the sleep of the objective mind. Suggestions which appear powerless when presented directly to objective consciousness are highly efficacious when the subject is in the hypnotic state. The hypnotic state is simply being unaware, objectively. In hypnotism, the conscious mind is put to sleep and the subconscious powers are exposed so as to be directly reached by suggestion. It is easy to see from this, providing you accept the truth of mental suggestions, that any one not objectively aware of you is in a profound hypnotic state relative to you. Therefore, "Curse not the king, no not in thy thought; and curse not the rich in thy bedchamber; for a bird of the air shall carry the voice, and that which hath wings shall tell the matter" (Ecc. 10:20). What you sincerely believe as true of another you awaken within him.

No one need be entranced, in the ordinary manner, to be helped. If the subject is consciously unaware of the suggestion, and if the suggestion is given with conviction and confidently accepted by the operator as true, then you have the ideal setting for a successful prayer. Represent the subject to yourself mentally as though he had already done that which you desire him to do. Mentally speak to him and congratulate him on having done what you want him to do. Mentally see him in the state you want him to obtain. Within the circle of its action, every word subjectively spoken awakens, objectively, what it affirms. Incredulity on the part of the subject is no hindrance when you are in control of your reverie.

Bold assertion by you, while you are in a partly subjective state, awakens what you affirm. Self-confidence on your part and the thorough belief in the truth of your mental assertion are all that is needed to produce results. Visualize the subject and imagine that you hear his voice. This establishes contact with his subjective mind. Then imagine that he is telling you what you want to hear. If you want to send him words of health and wealth, then imagine that he is telling you, "I have never felt better and I have never had more," and mentally tell him of your joy in witnessing his good fortune. Imagine that you see and hear his joy.

A mental conversation with the subjective image of another must be in a manner which does not express the slightest doubt as to the truth of what you hear and say. If you have the least idea that you do not believe what you have imagined you have heard and seen, the subject will not comply, for your subjective mind will transmit only your fixed ideas. Only fixed ideas can awaken their vibratory correlates in those toward whom they are directed. In the controlled reverie, ideas must be suggested with the utmost care. If you do not control your imagination in the reverie, your imagination will control you. Whatever you suggest with confidence is law to the subjective mind; it is under obligation to objectify that which you mentally affirm. Not only does the subject execute the state affirmed but he does it as though the decision had come of itself, or the idea had been originated by him.

Control of the subconscious is dominion over all. Each state obeys one mind's control. Control of the subconscious is accomplished through control of your beliefs, which in turn is the all-potent factor in the production of visible states. Imagination and faith are the secrets of creation.

CHAPTER 20

LAW OF THOUGHT TRANSMISSION

"HE sent his word and healed them, and delivered them from their destructions." He transmitted the consciousness of health and it awoke its vibratory correlate in the one toward whom it was directed. He mentally represented the subject to himself in a state of health and imagined he heard the subject confirm it. "For no word of God shall be void of power; therefore hold fast the pattern of healthful words which thou hast heard."

To pray successfully you must have clearly defined objectives. You must know what you want before you can ask for it. You must know what you want before you can feel that you have it, and prayer is the feeling of fulfilled desire.

It does not matter what it is you seek in prayer, or where it is, or whom it concerns. You have nothing to do but convince yourself of the truth of that which you desire to see manifested. When you emerge from prayer you no longer seek, for you have-if you have prayed correctly-subconsciously assumed the reality of the state sought, and by the law of reversibility your subconscious assumption must objectify that which it affirms.

You must have a conductor to transmit a force. You may employ a wire, a jet of water, a current of air, a ray of light or any intermediary whatsoever. The principle of the photophone or the transmission of voice by light will help you to understand thought transmission, or the sending of a word to heal another. There is a strong analogy between a spoken voice and a mental voice. To think is to speak low, to speak is to

151

think aloud. The principle of the photophone is this: A ray of light is reflected by a mirror and projected to a receiver at a distant point. Back of the mirror is a mouthpiece. By speaking into the mouthpiece you cause the mirror to vibrate. A vibrating mirror modifies the light reflected on it. The modified light has your speech to carry, not as speech, but as represented in its mechanical correlate. It reaches the distant station and impinges on a disk within the receiver; it causes the disk to vibrate according to the modification it undergoes—and it reproduces your voice.

"I am the light of the world." I am, the knowledge that I exist, is a light by means of which what passes in my mind is rendered visible. Memory, or my ability to mentally see what is not objectively present, proves that my mind is a mirror, and so sensitive a mirror that it can reflect a thought. The perception of an image in memory in no way differs as a visual act from the perception of my image in a mirror. The same principle of seeing is involved in both.

Your consciousness is the light reflected on the mirror of your mind and projected in space to the one of whom you think. By mentally speaking to the subjective image in your mind you cause the mirror of your mind to vibrate. Your vibrating mind modifies the light of consciousness reflected on it. The modified light of consciousness reaches the one toward whom it is directed and impinges on the mirror of his mind; it causes his mind to vibrate according to the modifications it undergoes. Thus, it reproduces in him what was mentally affirmed by you.

Your beliefs, your fixed attitudes of mind, constantly modify your consciousness as it is reflected on the mirror of your mind. Your consciousness, modified by your beliefs, objectifies itself in the conditions of your world. To change the world, you must first change your conception of it. To change a man, you must change your conception of him. You must believe him to be the man you want him to be and mentally talk to him as though he were. All men are sufficiently sensitive to reproduce your beliefs of them. Therefore, if your word is not reproduced visibly in him toward whom it is sent, the cause is to be found in you, not in the subject. As soon as you believe in the truth of the state affirmed, results follow. Everyone can be transformed; every thought can be transmitted; every thought can be visibly embodied.

Subjective words-subconscious assumptions-awaken what they affirm. "They are living and active and shall not return unto me void, but shall accomplish that which I please, and shall prosper in the thing whereto I sent them." They are endowed with the intelligence pertaining to their mission and will persist until the object of their existence is realized; they persist until they awaken the vibratory correlates of themselves within the one toward whom they are directed, but the moment the object of their creation is accomplished they cease to be. The word spoken subjectively in quiet confidence will always awaken a corresponding state in the one for whom it was spoken; but the moment its task is accomplished it ceases to be, permitting the one in whom the state is realized to remain in the consciousness of the state affirmed or to return to his former state.

Whatever state has your attention holds your life. Therefore, to become attentive to a former state is to return to that condition. "Remember not the former things, neither consider the things of old."

Nothing can be added to man, for the whole of creation is

already perfected within him. "The kingdom of heaven is within you." "Man can receive nothing, except it be given him from heaven." Heaven is your subconsciousness. Not even a sunburn is given from without. The rays without only awaken corresponding rays within. Were the burning rays not contained within man, all the concentrated rays in the universe could not burn him. Were the tones of health not contained within the consciousness of the one of whom they are affirmed, they could not be vibrated by the word which is sent. You do not really give to another-you resurrect that which is asleep within him. "The damsel is not dead, but sleepeth." Death is merely a sleeping and a forgetting. Age and decay are the sleep-not death-of youth and health. Recognition of a state vibrates or awakens it.

Distance, as it is cognized by your objective senses, does not exist for the subjective mind. "If I take the wings of the morning, and dwell in the uttermost parts of the sea; even there shall thy hand lead me." Time and space are conditions of thought; the imagination can transcend them and move in a psychological time and space. Although physically separated from a place by thousands of miles, you can mentally live in the distant place as though it were here. Your imagination can easily transform winter into summer, New York into Florida, and so on. Whether the object of your desire be near or far, results will be the same. Subjectively, the object of your desire is never far off; its intense nearness makes it remote from observation of the senses. It dwells in consciousness, and consciousness is closer than breathing and nearer than hands and feet.

Consciousness is the one and only reality. All phenomena are formed of the same substance vibrating at different rates. All is consciousness modified by belief. Out of consciousness

154

I as man came, and to consciousness I as man return. In consciousness all states exist subjectively, and are awakened to their objective existence by belief. The only thing that prevents us from making a successful subjective impression on one at a great distance, or transforming there into here, is our habit of regarding space as an obstacle.

A friend a thousand miles away is rooted in your consciousness through your fixed ideas of him. To think of him and represent him to yourself inwardly in the state you desire him to be, confident that this subjective image is as true as, though it were already objectified, awakens in him a corresponding state which he must objectify. The results will be as obvious as the cause was hidden. The subject will express the awakened state within him and remain unaware of the true cause of his action. Your illusion of free will is but ignorance of the causes which make you act. Prayers depend upon your attitude of mind for their success and not upon the attitude of the subject. The subject has no power to resist your controlled subjective ideas of him unless the state affirmed by you to be true of him is a state he is incapable of wishing as true of another. In that case, it returns to you, the sender, and will realize itself in you. Provided the idea is acceptable, success depends entirely on the operator not upon the subjects who, like compass needles on their pivots, are quite indifferent as to what direction you choose to give them. If your fixed idea is not subjectively accepted by the one toward whom it is directed, it rebounds to you from whom it came. "Who is he that will harm you, if ye be followers of that which is good? I have been young, and now am old; yet have I not seen the righteous forsaken, nor his seed begging bread." "There shall no evil happen to the just." Nothing befalls us that is not of the nature of ourselves.

A person who directs a malicious thought to another will be injured by its rebound if he fails to get subconscious acceptance of the other. "As ye sow, so shall ye reap." Furthermore, what you can wish and believe of another can be wished and believed of you, and you have no power to reject it if the one who desires it for you accepts it as true of you. The only power to reject a subjective word is to be incapable of wishing a similar state of another—to give presupposes the ability to receive. The possibility to impress an idea upon another mind presupposes the ability of that mind to receive that impression. Fools exploit the world; the wise transfigure it. It is the highest wisdom to know that in the living universe there is no destiny other than that created out of the imagination of man. There is no influence outside of the mind of man.

"Whatsoever things are lovely, whatsoever things are of good report; if there be any virtue, and if there be any praise, think on these things." Never accept as true of others what you would not want to be true of you. To awaken a state within another it first must be awake within you. The state you would transmit to another can be transmitted only if it is believed by you. Therefore, to give is to receive. You cannot give what you do not have and you have only what you believe. So to believe a state as true of another not only awakens that state within the other but it makes it alive within you. You are what you believe.

"Give and ye shall receive, full measure, pressed down and running over." Giving is simply believing, for what you truly believe of others you awaken within them. The vibratory state transmitted by your belief persists until it awakens its corresponding vibration in him of whom it is believed. But before it can be transmitted it must first be awake within the consciousness of the transmitter. Whatever is awake within your consciousness, you are. Whether the belief pertains to self or another does not matter, for the believer is defined by the sum total of his beliefs or subconscious assumptions.

"As a man thinketh in his heart (in the deep subconscious of himself)so is he." Disregard appearances and subjectively affirm as true that which you wish to be true. This awakens in you the tone of the state affirmed which in turn realizes itself in you and in the one of whom it is affirmed. Give and ye shall receive. Beliefs invariably awaken what they affirm. The world is a mirror wherein everyone sees himself reflected. The objective world reflects the beliefs of the subjective mind.

Some people are self-impressed best by visual images, others by mental sounds, and still others by mental actions. The form of mental activity which allows the whole power of your attention to be focused in one chosen direction is the one to cultivate, until you can bring all to play on your objective at the same time.

Should you have some difficulty in understanding the terms, "visual images," "mental sounds" and "mental actions," here is an illustration that should make their meanings clear: A imagines he sees a piece of music, knowing nothing at all about musical notations. The impression in his mind is a purely visual image. B imagines he sees the same piece, but he can read music and can imagine how it would sound when played on the piano; that imagination is mental sound. C also reads music and is a pianist; as he reads, he imagines himself playing the piece. The imaginary action is mental action.

The visual images, mental sounds and mental actions are creations of your imagination, and though they appear to come from without, they actually come from within yourself.

They move as if moved by another but are really launched by your own spirit from the magical storehouse of imagination. They are projected into space by the same vibratory law that governs the sending of a voice or picture. Speech and images are projected not as speech or images but as vibratory correlates. Subjective mind vibrates according to the modifications it undergoes by the thought and feelings of the operator. The visible state created is the effect of the subjective vibrations. A feeling is always accompanied by a corresponding vibration, that is, a change in expression or sensation in the operator.

There is no thought or feeling without expression. No matter how motionless you appear to be if you reflect with any degree of intensity, there is always an execution of slight muscular movements. The eye, though shut, follows the movements of the imaginary objects and the pupil is dilated or contracted according to the brightness or the remoteness of those objects; respiration is accelerated or slowed, according to the course of your thoughts; the muscles contract correspondingly to your mental movements.

This change of vibration persists until it awakens a corresponding vibration in the subject, which vibration then expresses itself in a physical fact. "And the word was made flesh." Energy, as you see in the case of radio, is transmitted and received in a "field," a place where changes in space occur. The field and energy are one and inseparable. The field or subject becomes the embodiment of the word or energy received. The thinker and the thought, the operator and the subject, the energy and the field are one. Were you still enough to hear the sound of your beliefs you would know what is meant by "the music of the spheres." The mental sound you hear in prayer as coming from without are really produced by yourself. Self-observation will reveal this fact. As the music of the spheres is defined as the harmony heard by the gods alone, and is supposed to be produced by the movements of the celestial spheres, so, too, is the harmony you subjectively hear for others heard by you alone and is produced by the movements of your thoughts and feelings in the true kingdom or "heaven within you."

CHAPTER 21

GOOD TIDINGS

"How beautiful upon the mountains are the feet of him that bringeth good tidings, that bringeth peace, that bringeth good tidings of good, that bringeth salvation."

A very effective way to bring good tidings to another is to call before your mind's eye the subjective image of the person you wish to help and have him affirm that he has done that which you desired him to do. Mentally hear him tell you that he has done it. This awakens within him the vibratory correlate of the state affirmed, which vibration persists until its mission is accomplished. It does not matter what it is you desire to have done, or whom you select to do it. As soon as you subjectively affirm that it is done, results follow. Failure can result only if you fail to accept the truth of your assertion or if the state affirmed would not be desired by the subject for himself or another. In the latter event, the state would realize itself in you, the operator.

The seemingly harmless habit of "talking to yourself" is the most fruitful form of prayer. A mental argument with the subjective image of another is the surest way to pray for an argument. You are asking to be offended by the other when you objectively meet. He is compelled to act in a manner displeasing to you, unless before the meeting you countermand or modify your order by subjectively affirming a change.

Unfortunately, man forgets his subjective arguments, his daily mental conversations with others, and so is at a loss for an explanation of the conflicts and misfortunes of his life. As mental arguments produce conflicts, so happy mental conversations produce corresponding visible states of good tidings. Man creates himself out of his own imagination.

If the state desired is for yourself and you find it difficult to accept as true what your senses deny, call before your mind's eye the subjective image of a friend and have him mentally affirm that you are already that which you desire to be. This establishes in him, without his conscious consent or knowledge, the subconscious assumption that you are that which he mentally affirmed, which assumption, because it is unconsciously assumed, will persist until it fulfills its mission. Its mission is to awaken in you its vibratory correlate, which vibration when awakened in you realizes itself as an objective fact.

Another very effective way to pray for oneself is to use the formula of job who found that his own captivity was removed as he prayed for his friends. Fix your attention on a friend and have the imaginary voice of your friend tell you that he is, or has that which is comparable to that which you desire to be or have. As you mentally hear and see him, feel the thrill of his good fortune and sincerely wish him well. This awakens in him the corresponding vibration of the state affirmed, which vibration must then objectify itself as a physical fact. You will discover the truth of the statement, "Blessed are the merciful for they shall receive mercy." "The quality of mercy is twice blessed-it blesses him who taketh and him who giveth." The good you subjectively accept as true of others will not only be expressed by them, but a full share will be realized by you.

Transformations are never total. Force A is always transformed into more than a force B. A blow with a hammer produces not only a mechanical concussion, but also heat, electricity, a sound, a magnetic change and so on. The vibratory correlate in the subject is not the entire transformation of the sentiment communicated. The gift transmitted to another is like the divine measure, pressed down, shaken together and running over, so that after the five thousand are fed from the live loaves and two fish, twelve baskets full are left over.

CHAPTER 22

THE GREATEST PRAYER

IMAGINATION is the beginning of creation. You imagine what you desire, and then you believe it to be true. Every dream could be realized by those self-disciplined enough to believe it. People are what you choose to make them; a man is according to the manner in which you look at him. You must look at him with different eyes before he will objectively change. "Two men looked from the prison bars, one saw the mud and the other saw the stars." Centuries ago, Isaiah asked the question: "Who is blind, but my servant, or deaf, as my messenger that I sent?" "Who is blind as he that is perfect, and blind as the Lord's servant?" The perfect man judges not after appearances, but judges righteously. He sees others as he desires them to be; he hears only what he wants to hear. He sees only the good in others. In him is no condemnation for he transforms the world with his seeing and hearing.

"The king that sitteth on the throne scattereth the evil with his eye." Sympathy for living things-agreement with human limitations——is not in the consciousness of the king because he has learned to separate their false concepts from their true being. To him poverty is but the sleep of wealth. He does not see caterpillars, but painted butterflies to be; not winter, but summer sleeping; not man in want, but Jesus sleeping. Jesus of Nazareth, who scattereth the evil with his eye, is asleep in the imagination of every man, and out of his own imagination must man awaken him by subjectively affirming "I AM Jesus." Then and only then will he see Jesus, for man can only see what is awake within himself. The holy womb is man's imagination. The holy child is that conception of himself which fits Isaiah's definition of perfection Heed the words of St. Augustine, "Too late have I loved thee, for behold thou wert within and it was without that I did seek thee." It is to your own consciousness that you must turn as to the only reality. There, and there alone, you awaken that which is asleep. "Though Christ a thousand times in Bethlehem be born, if He is not born in thee thy soul is still forlorn."

Creation is finished. You call your creation into being by feeling the reality of the state you would call. A mood attracts its affinities but it does not create what it attracts. As sleep is called by feeling "I am sleepy," so, too, is Jesus Christ called by the feeling, "I am Jesus Christ." Man sees only himself. Nothing befalls man that is not of the nature of himself. People emerge out of the mass betraying their close affinity to your moods as they are engendered. You meet them seemingly by accident but find they are intimates of your moods. Because your moods continually externalize themselves you could prophesy from your moods, that you, without search, would soon meet certain characters and encounter certain conditions. Therefore call the perfect one into being by living in the feeling, "I am Christ," for Christ is the one concept of self through which can be seen the unveiled realities of eternity.

Our behavior is influenced by our subconscious assumption respecting our own social and intellectual rank and that of the one we are addressing. Let us seek for and evoke the greatest rank, and the noblest of all is that which disrobes man of his mortality and clothes him with uncurbed immortal glory. Let us assume the feeling, "I am Christ," and our whole behavior will subtly and unconsciously change in accordance with that assumption.

The Greatest Prayer

Our subconscious assumptions continually externalize themselves that others may consciously see us as we subconsciously see ourselves, and tell us by their actions what we have subconsciously assumed ourselves to be. Therefore let us assume the feeling, "I AM Christ," until our conscious claim becomes our subconscious assumption that "We all with open face beholding as in a glass the glory of the Lord are changed into the same image from glory to glory." Let God awake and His enemies be destroyed. There is no greater prayer for man.

FEELING IS THE SECRET

CHAPTER 23

LAW AND ITS OPERATION

"Of making many books there is no end."
—Eccl. 11:12

"He that would perfect himself in any art whatsoever, let him betake himself to the reading of some sure and certain work upon his art many times over; for to read many books upon your art produceth confusion rather than learning."
—Aron

Foreword

THIS book is concerned with the art of realizing your desire. It gives you an account of the mechanism used in the production of the visible world. It is a small book but not slight. There is a treasure in it, a clearly defined road to the realization of your dreams.

Were it possible to carry conviction to another by means of reasoned arguments and detailed instances this book would be many times its size. It is seldom possible, however, to do so by means of written statements or arguments since to the suspended judgment it always seems plausible to say that the author was dishonest or deluded, and, therefore, his evidence was tainted.

Consequently, I have purposely omitted all arguments and testimonials, and simply challenge the open-minded reader to practice the law of consciousness as revealed in this book. Personal success will prove far more convincing than all the books that could be written on the subject.

—NEVILLE

Law and Its Operation

THE world, and all within it, is man's conditioned consciousness objectified. Consciousness is the cause as well as the substance of the entire world. So it is to consciouness that we must turn if we would discover the secret of creation.

Knowledge of the law of consciousness and the method of operating this law will enable you to accomplish all you desire in life. Armed with a working knowledge of this law, you can build and maintain an ideal world.

Consciousness is the one and only reality, not figuratively but actually. This reality may for the sake of clarity be likened unto a stream which is divided into two parts, the conscious and the subconscious. In order to intelligently operate the law of consciousness it is necessary to understand the relationship between the conscious and the subconscious. The conscious is personal and selective; the subconscious is impersonal and nonselective. The conscious is the realm of effect; the subconscious is the realm of cause. These two aspects are the male and female divisions of consciousness. The conscious is male; the subconscious is female. The conscious generates ideas and impresses these ideas on the subconscious; the subconscious receives ideas and gives form and expression to them.

By this law-first conceiving an idea and then impressing the idea conceived on the subconscious-all things evolve out of consciousness; and without this sequence there is not anything made that is made. The conscious impresses the subconscious while the subconscious expresses all that is impressed upon it.

The subconscious does not originate ideas but accepts as true those which the conscious mind feels to be true and in a way known only to itself objectifies the accepted ideas. Therefore, through his power to imagine and feel and his freedom to choose the idea he will entertain, man has control over creation.

Law and Its Operation

Control of the subconscious is accomplished through control of your ideas and feelings.

The mechanism of creation is hidden in the very depth of the subconscious, the female aspect or womb of creation. The subconscious transcends reason and is independent of induction. It contemplates a feeling as a fact existing within itself and on this assumption proceeds to give expression to it. The creative process begins with an idea and its cycle runs its course as a feeling and ends in a desire to act.

Ideas are impressed on the subconscious through the medium of feeling. No idea can be impressed on the subconscious until it is felt, but once felt-be it good, bad or indifferent-it must be expressed. Feeling is the one and only medium through which ideas are conveyed to the subconscious. Therefore, the man who does not control his feeling may easily impress the subconscious with undesirable states. By control of feeling is not meant restraint or suppression of your feeling, but rather the disciplining of self to imagine and entertain only such feeling as contributes to your happiness. Control of your feeling is all important to a full and happy life. Never entertain an undesirable feeling nor think sympathetically about wrong in any shape or form. Do not dwell on the imperfection of yourself or others. To do so is to impress the subconscious with these limitations. What you do not want done unto you, do not feel that it is done unto you or another. This is the whole law of a full and happy life. Everything else is commentary.

Every feeling makes a subconscious impression and unless it is counteracted by a more powerful feeling of an opposite nature must be expressed. The dominant of two feelings is the one expressed. I am healthy is a stronger feeling than I will be

Law and Its Operation

healthy. To feel I will be is to confess I am not; I am is stronger than I am not. What you feel you are always dominates what you feel you would like to be; therefore, to be realized the wish must be felt as a state that is rather than a state that is not.

Sensation precedes manifestation and is the foundation upon which all manifestation rests. Be careful of your moods and feelings, for there is an unbroken connection between your feelings and your visible world. Your body is an emotional filter and bears the unmistakable marks of your prevalent emotions. Emotional disturbances, especially suppressed emotions, are the causes of all disease. To feel intensely about a wrong without voicing or expressing that feeling, is the beginning of disease (dis-ease) in both body and environment. Do not entertain the feeling of regret or failure for frustration or detachment from your objective results in disease.

Think feelingly only of the state you desire to realize. Feeling the reality of the state sought and living and acting on that conviction is the way of all seeming miracles. All changes of expression are brought about through a change of feeling. A change of feeling is a change of destiny. All creation occurs in the domain of the subconscious. What you must acquire, then, is a reflective control of the operation of the subconscious, that is, control of your ideas and feelings.

Chance or accident is not responsible for the things that happen to you, nor is predestined fate the author of your fortune or misfortune. Your subconscious impressions deter-mine the conditions of your world. The subconscious is not selective; it is impersonal and no respecter of persons. The subconscious is not concerned with the truth or falsity of your feeling. It always accepts as true that which you feel to be true.

Law and Its Operation

Feeling is the assent of the subconscious to the truth of that which is declared to be true. Because of this quality of the subconscious there is nothing impossible to man. Whatever the mind of man can conceive and feel as true, the subconscious can and must objectify. Your feelings create the pattern from which your world is fashioned, and a change of feeling is a change of pattern.

The subconscious never fails to express that which has been impressed upon it. The moment it receives an impression it begins to work out the ways of its expression. It accepts the feeling impressed upon it, your feeling, as a fact existing within itself and immediately sets about to produce in the outer or objective world the exact likeness of that feeling. The subconscious never alters the accepted beliefs of man. It out-pictures them to the last detail whether or not they are beneficial.

To impress the subconscious with the desirable state you must assume the feeling that would be yours had you already realized your wish. In defining your objective you must be concerned only with the objective itself. The manner of expression or the difficulties involved are not to be considered by you. To think feelingly on any state impresses it on the subconscious. Therefore, if you dwell on difficulties, barriers or delay, the subconscious, by its very non-selective nature, accepts the feeling of difficulties and obstacles as your request and proceeds to produce them in your outer world.

The subconscious is the womb of creation. It receives the idea unto itself through the feelings of man. It never changes the idea received, but always gives it form. Hence the subconscious out-pictures the idea in the image and likeness of the feeling received. To feel a state as hopeless or impossible is to impress the subconscious with the idea of failure.

Law and Its Operation

Although the subconscious faithfully serves man it must not be inferred that the relation is that of a servant to a master as was anciently conceived. The ancient prophets called it the slave and servant of man. St. Paul personified it as a "woman" and said: "The woman should be subject to man in everything." The subconscious does serve man and faithfully gives form to his feelings. However, the subconscious has a distinct distaste for compulsion and responds to persuasion rather than to command; consequently, it resembles the beloved wife more than the servant.

"The husband is head of the wife," —Eph. 5, may not be true of man and woman in their earthly relationship but it is true of the conscious and the subconscious, or the male and female aspects of consciousness. The mystery to which Paul referred when he wrote, "This is a great mystery. . . . He that loveth his wife loveth himself. . . . And they two shall be one flesh," is simply the mystery of consciousness. Consciousness is really one and undivided but for creation's sake it appears to be divided into two.

The conscious (objective) or male aspect truly is the head and dominates the subconscious (subjective) or female aspect. However, this leadership is not that of the tyrant but of the lover. So by assuming the feeling that would be yours were you already in possession of your objective, the subconscious is moved to build the exact likeness of your assumption. Your desires are not subconsciously accepted until you assume the feeling of their reality, for only through feeling is an idea subconsciously accepted and only through this subconscious acceptance is it ever expressed.

It is easier to ascribe your feeling to events in the world than to admit that the conditions of the world reflect your feeling. However, it is eternally true that the outside mirrors the inside. "As within so without." "A man can receive nothing unless it is given him from heaven," and "The kingdom of heaven is within you." Nothing comes from without; all things come from within-from the subconscious. It is impossible for you to see other than the contents of your consciousness. Your world in its every detail is your consciousness objectified. Objective states bear witness of subconscious impressions. A change of impression results in a change of expression.

The subconscious accepts as true that which you feel as true, and because creation is the result of subconscious impressions, you, by your feeling, determine creation. You are already that which you want to be, and your refusal to believe this is the only reason you do not see it. To seek on the outside for that which you do not feel you are is to seek in vain, for we never find that which we want; we find only that which we are. In short, you express and have only that which you are conscious of being or possessing. "To him that hath it is given." Denying the evidence of the senses and appropriating the feeling of the wish fulfilled is the way to the realization of your desire.

Mastery of self-control of your thoughts and feelings-is your highest achievement. However, until perfect self-control is attained so that in spite of appearances you feel all that you want to feel, use sleep and prayer to aid you in realizing your desired states. These are the two gateways into the subconscious.

CHAPTER 24

SLEEP

SLEEP, the life that occupies one-third of our stay on earth, is the natural door into the subconscious. So it is with sleep that we are now concerned. The conscious two-thirds of our life on earth is measured by the degree of attention we give sleep. Our understanding of and delight in what sleep has to bestow will cause us, night after night, to set out for it as though we were keeping an appointment with a lover.

"In a dream, in a vision of the night, when deep sleep calleth upon men, in slumbering upon the bed; then he openeth the ears of men and sealeth their instruction." Job 33. It is in sleep and in prayer, a state akin to sleep, that man enters the subconscious to make his impressions and receive his instructions. In these states the conscious and subconscious are creatively joined. The male and female become one flesh.

Sleep is the time when the male or conscious mind turns from the world of sense to seek its lover or subconscious self. The subconscious -unlike the woman of the world who marries her husband to change him - has no desire to change the conscious, waking state, but loves it as it is and faithfully reproduces its likeness in the outer world of form. The conditions and events of your life are your children formed from the molds of your subconscious impressions in sleep. They are made in the image and likeness of your innermost feeling that they may reveal you to yourself.

"As in heaven so on earth." As in the subconscious so on earth. Whatever you have in consciousness as you go to sleep is the measure of your expression in the waking two-thirds of your life on earth. Nothing stops you from realizing your

Sleep

objective save your failure to feel that you are already that which you wish to be, or that you are already in possession of the thing sought. Your subconscious gives form to your desires only when you feel your wish fulfilled.

The unconsciousness of sleep is the normal state of the subconscious. Because all things come from within yourself, and your conception of yourself determines that which comes, you should always feel the wish fulfilled before you drop off to sleep. You never draw out of the deep of yourself that which you want; you always draw that which you are, and you are that which you feel yourself to be as well as that which you feel as true of others.

To be realized, then, the wish must be resolved into the feeling of being or having or witnessing the state sought. This is accomplished by assuming the feeling of the wish fulfilled. The feeling which comes in response to the question "How would I feel were my wish realized?" is the feeling which should monopolize and immobilize your attention as you relax into sleep. You must be in the consciousness of being or having that which you want to be or to have before you drop off to sleep.

Once asleep man has no freedom of choice. His entire slumber is dominated by his last waking concept of self. It follows, therefore, that he should always assume the feeling of accomplishment and satisfaction before he retires in sleep. "Come before me with singing and thanksgiving." "Enter into his gates with thanksgiving and into his courts with praise." Your mood prior to sleep defines your state of consciousness as you enter into the presence of your everlasting lover, the subconscious. She sees you exactly as you feel yourself to be. If, as you prepare for sleep, you assume and maintain the consciousness of success by feeling "I am successful," you must be successful. Lie flat on your back with your head on a level with your body. Feel as you would were you in possession of your wish and quietly relax into unconsciousness.

"He that keepeth Israel shall neither slumber nor sleep." Nevertheless "He giveth his beloved sleep." The subconscious never sleeps. Sleep is the door through which the conscious, waking mind passes to be creatively joined to the subconscious. Sleep conceals the creative act while the objective world reveals it. In sleep man impresses the subconscious with his conception of himself.

What more beautiful description of this romance of the conscious and subconscious is there than that told in the "Song of Solomon"! "By night on my bed I sought him whom my soul loveth . . . . I found him whom my soul loveth; I held him and I would not let him go, until I had brought him into my mother's house, and into the chamber of her that conceived me."

Preparing to sleep, you feel yourself into the state of the answered wish, and then relax into unconsciousness. Your realized wish is he whom you seek. By night on your bed you seek the feeling of the wish fulfilled that you may take it with you into the chamber of her that conceived you, into sleep or the subconscious which gave you form, that this wish also may be given expression. This is the way to discover and conduct your wishes into the subconscious. Feel yourself in the state of the realized wish and quietly drop off to sleep.

Night after night you should assume the feeling of being, having and witnessing that which you seek to be, possess and see manifested. Never go to sleep feeling discouraged or dissatisfied. Never sleep in the consciousness of failure. Your subconscious, whose natural state is sleep, sees you as you

Sleep

believe yourself to be, and whether it be good, bad, or indifferent, the subconscious will faithfully embody your belief. As you feel so do you impress her; and she, the perfect lover, gives form to these impressions and out-pictures them as the children of her beloved.

"Thou art all fair, my love; there is no spot in thee," is the attitude of mind to adopt before dropping off to sleep. Disregard appearances and feel that things are as you wish them to be, for "He calleth things that are not seen as though they were, and the unseen becomes seen." To assume the feeling of satisfaction is to call conditions into being which will mirror satisfaction. "Signs follow, they do not precede." Proof that you are will follow the consciousness that you are; it will not precede it.

You are an eternal dreamer dreaming non-eternal dreams. Your dreams take form as you assume the feeling of their reality. Do not limit yourself to the past. Knowing that nothing is impossible to consciousness begin to imagine states beyond the experiences of the past. Whatever the mind of man can imagine man can realize. All objective (visible) states were first subjective (invisible) states, and you called them into visible states by assuming the feeling of their reality. The creative process is first imagining and then believing the state imagined. Always imagine and expect the best.

The world cannot change until you change your conception of it. "As within so without." Nations as well as people are only what you believe them to be. No matter what the problem is, no matter where it is, no matter whom it concerns, you have no one to change but yourself, and you have neither opponent nor helper in bringing about the change within yourself. You have nothing to do but convince yourself.

Sleep

of the truth of that which you desire to see manifested. As soon as you succeed in convincing yourself of the reality of the state sought, results follow to confirm your fixed belief. You never suggest to another the state which you desire to see him express; instead you convince yourself that he is already that which you desire him to be.

Realization of your wish is accomplished by assuming the feeling of the wish fulfilled. You cannot fail unless you fail to convince yourself of the reality of your wish. A change of belief is confirmed by a change of expression. Every night as you drop off to sleep feel satisfied and spotless, for your subjective lover always forms the objective world in the image and likeness of your conception of it, the conception defined by your feeling.

The waking two-thirds of your life on earth ever corroborates or bears witness to your subconscious impressions. The actions and events of the day are effects; they are not causes. Free will is only freedom of choice. "Choose ye this day whom ye shall serve" is your freedom to choose the kind of mood you assume; but the expression of the mood is the secret of the subconscious. The subconscious receives impressions only through the feelings of man and in a way known only to itself gives these impressions form and expression. The actions of man are determined by his subconscious impressions. His illusion of free will, his belief in freedom of action, is but ignorance of the causes which make him act. He thinks himself free because he has forgotten the link between himself and the event.

Man awake is under compulsion to express his subconscious impressions. If in the past he unwisely impressed himself, then let him begin to change his thought and feeling, for only as he does so will he change his world. Do not waste one

Sleep

moment in regret, for to think feelingly of the mistakes of the past is to reinfect yourself. "Let the dead bury the dead." Turn from appearances and assume the feeling that would be yours were you already the one you wish to be.

Feeling a state produces that state. The part you play on the world's stage is determined by your conception of yourself. By feeling your wish fulfilled and quietly relaxing into sleep, you cast yourself in a star role to be played on earth tomorrow, and while asleep you are rehearsed and instructed in your part.

The acceptance of the end automatically wills the means of realization. Make no mistake about this. If, as you prepare for sleep, you do not consciously feel yourself into the state of the answered wish, then you will take with you into the chamber of her who conceived you the sum total of the reactions and feelings of the waking day; and while asleep you will be instructed in the manner in which they will be expressed tomorrow. You will rise believing that you are a free agent, not realizing that every action and event of the day is predetermined by your concept of self as you fell asleep. Your only freedom then is your freedom of reaction. You are free to choose how you feel and react to the day's drama, but the drama the actions, events and circumstances of the day -have already been determined.

Unless you consciously and purposely define the attitude of mind with which you go to sleep, you unconsciously go to sleep in the composite attitude of mind made up of all feelings and reactions of the day. Every reaction makes a subconscious impression and, unless counteracted by an opposite and more dominant feeling, is the cause of future action.

Sleep

Ideas enveloped in feeling are creative actions. Use your divine right wisely. Through your ability to think and feel, you have dominion over all creation.

While you are awake you are a gardener selecting seed for your garden, but "Except a corn of wheat fall into the ground and die, it abideth alone; but if it die, it bringeth forth much fruit." Your conception of yourself as you fall asleep is the seed you drop into the ground of the subconscious. Dropping off to sleep feeling satisfied and happy compels conditions and events to appear in your world which confirm these attitudes of mind.

Sleep is the door into heaven. What you take in as a feeling you bring out as a condition, action, or object in space. So sleep in the feeling of the wish fulfilled. "As in consciousness so on earth."

CHAPTER 25

PRAYER

PRAYER like sleep is also an entrance into the subconscious. "When you pray, enter into your closet, and when you have shut your door, pray to your Father which is in secret and your Father which is in secret shall reward you openly."

Prayer is an illusion of sleep which diminishes the impression of the outer world and renders the mind more receptive to suggestion from within. The mind in prayer is in a state of relaxation and receptivity akin to the feeling attained just before dropping off to sleep.

Prayer is not so much what you ask for, as how you prepare for its reception. "Whatsoever things ye desire, when ye pray believe that you have received them, and ye shall have them." The only condition required is that you believe that your prayers are already realized.

Your prayer must be answered if you assume the feeling that would be yours were you already in possession of your objective. The moment you accept the wish as an accomplished fact the subconscious finds means for its realization. To pray successfully then, you must yield to the wish, that is, feel the wish fulfilled.

The perfectly disciplined man is always in tune with the wish as an accomplished fact. He knows that consciousness is the one and only reality, that ideas and feelings are facts of consciousness and are as real as objects in space; therefore he never entertains a feeling which does not contribute to his happiness for feelings are the causes of the actions and circumstances of his life. On the other hand, the undisciplined man finds it difficult to believe that which is denied by the senses

Prayer

and usually accepts or rejects solely on appearances of the senses. Because of this tendency to rely on the evidence of the senses, it is necessary to shut them out before starting to pray, before attempting to feel that which they deny. Whenever you are in the state of mind, "I should like to but I cannot," the harder you try the less you are able to yield to the wish. You never attract that which you want but always attract that which you are conscious of being.

Prayer is the art of assuming the feeling of being and having that which you want. When the senses confirm the absence of your wish, all conscious effort to counteract this suggestion is futile and tends to intensify the suggestion.

Prayer is the art of yielding to the wish and not the forcing of the wish. Whenever your feeling is in conflict with your wish, feeling will be the victor. The dominant feeling invariably expresses itself. Prayer must be without effort. In attempting to fix an attitude of mind which is denied by the senses, effort is fatal.

To yield successfully to the wish as an accomplished fact, you must create a passive state, a kind of reverie or meditative reflection similar to the feeling which precedes sleep. In such a relaxed state the mind is turned from the objective world and easily senses the reality of a subjective state. It is a state in which you are conscious and quite able to move or open your eyes but have no desire to do so.

An easy way to create this passive state is to relax in a comfortable chair or on a bed. If on a bed, lie flat on your back with your head on a level with your body, close the eyes and imagine that you are sleepy. Feel—I am sleepy, so sleepy, so very sleepy. In a little while a faraway feeling accompanied by a general lassitude and loss of all desire to move envelops you.

Prayer

You feel a pleasant, comfortable rest and not inclined to alter your position, although under other circumstances you would not be at all comfortable. When this passive state is reached, imagine that you have realized your wish - not how it was real-ized-but simply the wish fulfilled. Imagine in picture form what you desire to achieve in life; then feel yourself as having already achieved it. Thoughts produce tiny little speech move-ments which may be heard in the passive state of prayer as pronouncements from without. However, this degree of pas-sivity is not essential to the realization of your prayers. All that is necessary is to create a passive state and feel the wish ful-filled.

All you can possibly need or desire is already yours. You need no helper to give it to you; it is yours now. Call your desires into being by imagining and feeling your wish fulfilled. As the end is accepted you become totally indifferent as to possible failure, for acceptance of the end wills the means to that end. When you emerge from the moment of prayer it is as though you were shown the happy and successful end of a play although you were not shown how that end was achieved. However, having witnessed the end, regardless of any anticli-mactic sequence you remain calm and secure in the knowl-edge that the end has been perfectly defined.

CHAPTER 26

SPIRIT - FEELING

"NOT by might, nor by power, but by my spirit, saith the Lord of hosts." Get into the spirit of the state desired by assuming the feeling that would be yours were you already the one you want to be. As you capture the feeling of the state sought, you are relieved of all effort to make it so, for it is already so. There is a definite feeling associated with every idea in the mind of man. Capture the feeling associated with your realized wish by assuming the feeling that would be yours were you already in possession of the thing you desire, and your wish will objectify itself.

Faith is feeling. "According to your faith (feeling) be it unto you." You never attract that which you want but always that which you are. As a man is, so does he see. "To him that hath it shall be given and to him that hath not it shall be taken away. . . ." That which you *feel* yourself to be you are, and you are given that which you are. So assume the feeling that would be yours were you already in possession of your wish, and your wish must be realized. "So God created man in his own image, in the image of God created he him." "Let this mind be in you which was also in Christ Jesus, who being in the form of God, thought it not robbery to be equal with God." You are that which you believe yourself to be. Instead of believing in God or in Jesus—believe you are God or you are Jesus. "He that believeth on me the works that I do shall he do also" should be "He that believes as I believe the works that I do shall he do also." Jesus found it not strange to do the works of God because he believed himself to be God. "I and my Father are one." It is natural to do the works of the one you believe yourself to be. So live in the

Spirit - Feeling

feeling of being the one you want to be and that you shall be.

When a man believes in the value of the advice given him and applies it, he establishes within himself the reality of success.

FREEDOM FOR ALL

CHAPTER 27

THE ONENESS OF GOD

PUBLIC opinion will not long endure a theory which does not work in practice. Today, probably more than ever before, man demands proof of the truth of even his highest ideal. For ultimate satisfaction man must find a principle which is for him a way of life, a principle which he can experience as true.

I believe I have discovered just such a principle in the greatest of all sacred writings, the Bible. Drawn from my own mystical illumination this book reveals the truth buried within the stories of the old and new testaments alike.

Briefly, the book states that consciousness is the one and only reality, that consciousness is the cause and manifestation is the effect. It draws the reader's attention to this fact constantly, that the reader may always keep first things first.

Having laid the foundation that a change of consciousness is essential to bring about any change of expression, this book explains to the reader a dozen different ways to bring about such a change of consciousness.

This is a realistic and constructive principle that works. The revelation it contains, if applied, will set you free.

* * *

The Oneness of God

"HEAR, O Israel: the Lord our God is one Lord."
Hear, O Israel: Hear, O man made of the very substance of
God: You and God are one and undivided! Man, the world and
all within it are conditioned states of the unconditioned one,
God. You are this one; you are God conditioned as man. All
that you believe God to be, you are; but you will never know
this to be true until you stop claiming it of another, and
recognize this seeming other to be yourself. God and man,
spirit and matter, the formless and the formed, the creator
and the creation, the cause and the effect, your Father and you
are one. This one, in whom all conditioned states live and
move and have their being, is your I AM, your unconditioned
consciousness.

Unconditioned consciousness is God, the one and only
reality. By unconditioned consciousness is meant a sense of
awareness; a sense of knowing that I AM apart from knowing
who I AM; the consciousness of being, divorced from that
which I am conscious of being. I AM aware of being man, but
I need not be man to be aware of being. Before I became aware
of being someone, I, unconditioned awareness, was aware of
being, and this awareness does not depend upon being someone. I AM self-existent, unconditioned consciousness; I
became aware of being someone; and I shall become aware of
being someone other than this that I am now aware of being;
but I AM eternally aware of being whether I am unconditioned
formlessness or I am conditioned form.

As the conditioned state, I (man), might forget who I am,
or where I am, but I cannot forget that I AM. This knowing
that I AM, this awareness of being, is the only reality. This
unconditioned consciousness, the I AM, is that knowing reality in whom all conditioned states-conceptions of myself-begin

and end, but which ever remains the unknown knowing being when all the known ceases to be. All that I have ever believed myself to be, all that I now believe myself to be, and all that I shall ever believe myself to be, are but attempts to know myself,—the unknown, undefined reality. This unknown knowing one, or unconditioned consciousness, is my true being, the one and only reality. I AM the unconditioned reality conditioned as that which I believe myself to be. I AM the believer limited by my beliefs, the knower defined by the known. The world is my conditioned consciousness objectified. That which I feel and believe to be true of myself is now projected in space as my world. The world -my mirrored self- ever bears witness of the state of consciousness in which I live.

There is no chance or accident responsible for the things that happen to me or the environment in which I find myself. Nor is predestined fate the author of my fortunes or misfortunes. Innocence and guilt are mere words with no meaning to the law of consciousness, except as they reflect the state of consciousness itself.

The consciousness of guilt calls forth condemnation. The consciousness of lack produces poverty. Man everlastingly objectifies the state of consciousness in which he abides but he has somehow or other become confused in the interpretation of the law of cause and effect. He has forgotten that it is the inner state which is the cause of the outer manifestation,-"As within so without," and in his forgetfulness he believes that an outside God has his own peculiar reason for doing things, such reasons being beyond the comprehension of mere man; or he believes that people are suffering because of past mistakes which have been forgotten by the conscious mind; or, again, that blind chance alone plays the part of God.

The Oneness of God

One day man will realize that his own I Amness is the God he has been seeking throughout the ages, and that his own sense of awareness-his consciousness of being-is the one and only reality.

The most difficult thing for man to really grasp is this: That the "I amness" in himself is God. It is his true being or father state, the only state he can be sure of. The son, his conception of himself, is an illusion. He always knows that he is, but that which he is, is an illusion created by himself (the father) in an attempt at self-definition.

This discovery reveals that all that I have believed God to be I AM. "I AM the resurrection and the life," is a statement of fact concerning my consciousness, for my consciousness resurrects or makes visibly alive that which I am conscious of being. "I AM the door . . . all that ever came before me are thieves and robbers," shows me that my consciousness is the one and only entrance into the world of expression; that by assuming the consciousness of being or possessing the thing which I desire to be or possess is the only way by which I can become it or possess it; that any attempt to express this desirable state in ways other than by assuming the consciousness of being or possessing it, is to be robbed of the joy of expression and possession. "I AM the beginning and the end," reveals my consciousness as the cause of the birth and death of all expression. "I AM hath sent me," reveals my consciousness to be the Lord which sends me into the world in the image and likeness of that which I am conscious of being to live in a world composed of all that I am conscious of. "I AM the Lord, and there is no God beside me," declares my consciousness to be the one and only Lord and beside my consciousness there is no God. "Be still and know that I AM God," means that I should still the mind and know that consciousness is God. "Thou shalt not take the name of the Lord thy God in vain." "I AM the Lord: that is my name." Now that you have discovered your I AM, your consciousness to be God, do not claim anything to be true of yourself that you would not claim to be true of God, for in defining yourself you are defining God. That which you are conscious of being is that which you have named God. God and man are one. You and your Father are one. Your unconditioned consciousness, or I AM, and that which you are conscious of being, are one. The conceiver and the conception are one. If your conception of yourself is less than that which you claim as true of God, you have robbed God, the Father, because you (the son or conception) bear witness of the Father or conceiver. Do not take the magical name of God, I AM, in vain for you will not be held guiltless; you must express all that you claim yourself to be. Name God by consciously defining yourself as your highest ideal.

CHAPTER 28

THE NAME OF GOD

IT cannot be stated too often that consciousness is the one and only reality, for this is the truth that sets man free. This is the foundation upon which the whole structure of biblical literature rests. The stories of the Bible are all mystical revelations written in an Eastern symbolism which reveals to the intuitive the secret of creation and the formula of escape. The Bible is man's attempt to express in words the cause and manner of creation. Man discovered that his consciousness was the cause or creator of his world, so he proceeded to tell the story of creation in a series of symbolical stories known to us today as the Bible.

To understand this greatest of books you need a little intelligence and much intuition-intelligence enough to enable you to read the book, and intuition enough to interpret and understand what you read. You may ask why the Bible was written symbolically. Why was it not written in a clear, simple style so that all who read it might understand it? To these questions I reply that all men speak symbolically to that part of the world which differs from their own. The language of the West is clear to us of the West, but it is symbolic to the East; and vice versa. An example of this can be found in the Easterner's instruction: "If thine hand offend thee cut it off." He speaks of the hand, not as the hand of the body, but as any form of expression, and thereby he warns you to turn from that expression in your world which is offensive to you. At the same time the man of the West would unintentionally mislead the man of the East by saying: "This bank is on the rocks," for the expression "on the rocks" to the Westerner is equivalent to bankruptcy while a rock to an Easterner is a symbol of faith and security. "I will liken him unto a wise man, which built his house upon a rock; and the rain descended, and the floods came, and the winds blew and beat upon that house; and it fell not; for it was founded upon a rock."

To really understand the message of the Bible you must bear in mind that it was written by the Eastern mind and therefore cannot be taken literally by those of the West. Biologically, there is no difference between the East and the West. Love and hate are the same; hunger and thirst are the same; ambition and desire are the same; but the technique of expression is vastly different.

The first thing you must discover if you would unlock the secret of the Bible, is the meaning of the symbolic name of the creator which is known to all as Jehovah. This word "Jehovah" is composed of the four Hebrew letters—JOD HE VAU HE. The whole secret of creation is concealed within this name. The first letter JOD represents the absolute state or consciousness unconditioned; the sense of undefined awareness; that all inclusiveness out of which all creation or conditioned states of consciousness come. In the terminology of today JOD is I AM, or unconditioned consciousness.

The second letter HE represents the only begotten Son, a desire, an imaginary state. It symbolizes an idea; a defined subjective state or clarified mental picture.

The third letter VAU symbolizes the act of unifying or joining the conceiver (JOD), the consciousness desiring to the conception (HE), the state desired, so that the conceiver and the conception become one. Fixing a mental state, consciously defining yourself as the state desired, impressing upon yourself the fact that you are now that which you imagined or conceived as your objective, is the function of VAU. It nails or

197

joins the consciousness desiring to the thing desired. The cementing or joining process is accomplished subjectively by feeling the reality of that which is not yet objectified.

The fourth letter (HE) represents the objectifying of this subjective agreement. The JOD HE VAU makes man or the manifested world (HE), in the image and likeness of itself, the subjective conscious state. So the function of the final HE is to objectively bear witness to the subjective state JOD HE VAU. Conditioned consciousness continually objectifies itself on the screen of space. The world is the image and likeness of the subjective conscious state which created it. The visible world of itself can do nothing; it only bears record of its creator, the subjective state. It is the visible son (HE) bearing witness of the invisible Father, Son and Mother-JOD HE VAU-a Holy Trinity which can only be seen when made visible as man or manifestation.

Your unconditioned consciousness (JOD) is your I AM, which visualizes or images a desirable state (HE), and then becomes conscious of being the state imaged by feeling and believing itself to be the imagined state. The conscious union between you who desire and that which you desire to be, is made possible through the VAU, or your capacity to feel and believe. Believing is simply living in the feeling of actually being the state imagined-by assuming the consciousness of being the state desired. The subjective state symbolized as JOD HE VAU then objectifies itself as HE, thereby completing the mystery of the creator's name and nature, JOD HE VAU HE (Jehovah). JOD is to be aware; HE is to be aware of something; VAU is to be aware as, or to be aware of being that which you were only aware of. The second HE is your visible objectified world which is made in the image and likeness of the JOD HE VAU, or that which you are aware of being.

"And God said, Let us make man in our image, after our likeness." Let us, JOD HE VAU, make the objective manifestation (HE) in our image, the image of the subjective state. The world is the objectified likeness of the subjective conscious state in which consciousness abides. This understanding that consciousness is the one and only reality is the foundation of the Bible. The stories of the Bible are attempts to reveal in symbolic language this secret of creation as well as to show man the one formula of escape from all of his own creations. This is the true meaning of the name of Jehovah, the name by which all things are made and without which there is nothing made that is made. First, you are aware; then you become aware of something; then you become aware as that which you were aware of; then you behold objectively that which you are aware of being.

CHAPTER 29

THE LAW OF CREATION

LET us take one of the stories of the Bible and see how the prophets and writers of old revealed the story of creation by this strange Eastern symbolism. We all know the story of Noah and the Ark; that Noah was chosen to create a new world after the world was destroyed by the flood. The Bible tells us that Noah had three sons, Shem, Ham and Japheth. The first son is called Shem, which means name. Ham, the second son, means warm, alive. The third son is called Japheth, which means extension. You will observe that Noah and his three sons Shem, Ham and Japheth contain the same formula of creation as does the divine name of JOD HE VAU HE. Noah, the Father, the conceiver, the builder of a new world is equivalent to the JOD, or unconditioned consciousness, I AM. Shem is your desire; that which you are conscious of; that which you name and define as your objective, and is equivalent to the second letter in the divine name (HE). Ham is the warm, live state of feeling, which joins or binds together consciousness desiring and the thing desired, and is therefore equivalent to the third letter in the divine name, the VAU. The last son, Japheth, means extension, and is the extended or objectified state bearing witness of the subjective state and is equivalent to the last letter in the divine name, HE.

You are Noah, the knower, the creator. The first thing you beget is an idea, an urge, a desire, the word, or your first son Shem (name). Your second son Ham (warm, alive) is the secret of FEELING by which you are joined to your desire subjectively so that you, the consciousness desiring, become conscious of being or possessing the thing desired. Your third son, Japheth, is the confirmation, the visible proof that you know the secret of creation. He is the extended or objectified state bearing witness of the invisible or subjective state in which you abide.

In the story of Noah it is recorded that Ham saw the secrets of his Father, and because of his discovery he was made to serve his brothers, Shem and Japheth. Ham, or feeling, is the secret of the Father, your I AM, for it is through feeling that the consciousness desiring is joined to the thing desired. The conscious union or mystical marriage is made possible only through feeling. It is feeling which performs this heavenly union of Father and son, Noah and Shem, unconditioned consciousness and conditioned consciousness. By performing this service, feeling automatically serves Japheth, the extended or expressed state, for there can be no objectified expression unless there is first a subjective impression. To feel the presence of the thing desired, to subjectively actualize a state by impressing upon yourself, through feeling, a definite conscious state is the secret of creation. Your present objectified world is Japheth which was made visible by Ham. Therefore Ham serves his brothers Shem and Japheth, for without feeling which is symbolized as Ham, the idea or thing desired (Shem) could not be made visible as Japheth.

The ability to feel the unseen, the ability to actualize and make real a definite subjective state through the sense of feeling is the secret of creation, the secret by which the word or unseen desire is made visible,—is made flesh. "And God calleth things that be not as though they were." Consciousness calls things that are not seen as though they were, and it does this by first defining itself as that which it desires to express, and second by remaining within the defined state until the

201

invisible becomes visible. Here is the perfect working of the law according to the story of Noah. This very moment you are aware of being. This awareness of being, this knowing that you are, is Noah, the creator.

Now with Noah's identity established as your own consciousness of being, name something that you would like to possess or express; define some objective (Shem), and with your desire clearly defined, close your eyes and feel that you have it or are expressing it. Don't question how it can be done; simply feel that you have it. Assume the attitude of mind that would be yours if you were already in possession of it so that you feel that it is done. Feeling is the secret of creation. Be as wise as Ham and make this discovery that you too may have the joy of serving your brothers Shem and Japheth; the joy of making the word or name flesh.

CHAPTER 30

THE SECRET OF FEELING

THE secret of feeling or the calling of the invisible into visible states is beautifully told in the story of Isaac blessing his second son Jacob in the belief, based solely upon feeling, that he was blessing his first son Esau. It is recorded that Isaac, who was old and blind, felt that be was about to leave this world and wishing to bless his first son Esau before he died, sent Esau hunting for savory venison with the promise that upon his return from the hunt he would receive his father's blessing.

Now Jacob, who desired the birthright or right to be born through the blessing of his father, overheard his blind father's request for venison and his promise to Esau. So, as Esau went hunting for the venison, Jacob killed and dressed a kid of his father's flock.

Placing the skins upon his smooth body to give him the feel of his hairy and rough brother Esau, he brought the tastily prepared kid to his blind father Isaac. And Isaac who depended solely upon his sense of feel mistook his second son Jacob for his first son Esau, and pronounced his blessing on Jacob! Esau on his return from the hunt learned that his smooth-skinned brother Jacob had supplanted him so he appealed to his father for justice; but Isaac answered and said, "Thy brother came with subtlety and hath taken away thy blessing. I have made him thy Lord, and all his brethren have I given to him for servants."

Simple human decency should tell man that this story cannot be taken literally. There must be a message for man hidden somewhere in this treacherous and despicable act of Jacob! The hidden message, the formula of success buried in this story was intuitively revealed to the writer in this manner. Isaac, the blind father, is your consciousness; your awareness of being.

Esau, the hairy son, is your present objectified world-the rough or sensibly felt; the present moment; the present environment; your present conception of yourself; in short, the world you know by reason of your objective senses. Jacob, the smooth-skinned lad, the second son, is your desire or subjective state; an idea not yet embodied; a subjective state which is perceived and sensed but not objectively known or seen; a point in time and space removed from the present. In short, Jacob is your defined objective. The smooth-skinned Jacob-or subjective state seeking embodiment or the right of birth - when properly felt or blessed by his father (when consciously felt and fixed as real), becomes objectified; and in so doing he supplants the rough, hairy Esau, or the former objectified state. Two things cannot occupy a given place at one and the same time, and so as the invisible is made visible, the former visible state vanishes. Your consciousness is the cause of your world. The conscious state in which you abide determines the kind of world in which you live. Your present concept of yourself is now objectified as your environment, and this state is symbolized as Esau, the hairy, or sensibly felt; the first son. That which you would like to be or possess is symbolized as your second son, Jacob, the smooth-skinned lad who is not yet seen but is subjectively sensed and felt, and will, if properly touched, supplant his brother Esau, or your present world.

Always bear in mind the fact that Isaac, the father of these two sons, or states, is blind. He does not see his smooth-skinned son Jacob; he only feels him. And through the sense of feeling he actually believes Jacob, the subjective, to be Esau,

the real, the objectified. You do not see your desire objectively; you simply sense it (feel it) subjectively. You do not grope
in space after a desirable state. Like Isaac, you sit still and send
your first son hunting by removing your attention from your
objective world. Then in the absence of your first son, Esau,
you invite the desirable state, your second son, Jacob, to come
close so that you may feel it. "Come close, my son, that I may
feel you." First, you are aware of it in your immediate environment; then you draw it closer and closer and closer until you
sense it and feel it in your immediate presence so that it is real
and natural to you.

"If two of you shall agree on earth as touching on any
point that they shall ask, it shall be done for them of my Father
which is in heaven." The two agree through the sense of feel;
and the agreement is established on earth-is objectified; is
made real. The two agreeing are Isaac and Jacob-you and that
which you desire; and the agreement is made solely on the
sense of feeling. Esau symbolizes your present objectified
world whether it be pleasant or otherwise. Jacob symbolizes
any and every desire of your heart. Isaac symbolizes your true
self—with your eyes closed to the present world-in the act of
sensing and feeling yourself to be or to possess that which you
desire to be or to possess. The secret of Isaac-this sensing, feeling state is simply the act of mentally separating the sensibly felt
(your present physical state) from the insensibly felt (that which
you would like to be). With the objective senses tightly shut
Isaac made, and you can make the insensibly felt (the subjective
state) seem real or sensibly known; for faith is knowledge.

Knowing the law of self-expression, the law by which the
invisible is made visible, is not enough. It must be applied; and
this is the method of application.

The Secret of Feeling

First: Send your first son Esau—your present objectified world or problem-hunting. This is accomplished simply by closing your eyes and taking your attention away from the objectified limitations. As your senses are removed from your objective world, it vanishes from your consciousness or goes hunting.

Second: With your eyes still closed and your attention removed from the world round about you, consciously fix the natural time and place for the realization of your desire.

With your objective senses closed to your present environment you can sense and feel the reality of any point in time or space, for both are psychological and can be created at will. It is vitally important that the natural time-space condition of Jacob, that is, the natural time and place for the realization of your desire be first fixed in your consciousness. If Sunday is the day on which the thing desired is to be realized, then Sunday must be fixed in consciousness now. Simply begin to feel that it is Sunday until the quietness and naturalness of Sunday is consciously established. You have definite associations with the days, weeks, months and seasons of the year. You have said time and again "Today feels like Sunday, or Monday, or Saturday; or this feels like Spring, or Summer, or Fall, or Winter." This should convince you that you have definite, conscious impressions that you associate with the days, weeks, and seasons of the year. Then because of these associations you can select any desirable time, and by recalling the conscious impression associated with such time, you can make a subjective reality of that time now.

Do the same with space. If the room in which you are seated is not the room in which the thing desired would be naturally placed or realized, feel yourself seated in the room or place where it would be natural. Consciously fix this time-

The Secret of Feeling

space impression before you start the act of sensing and feeling the nearness, the reality, and the possession of the thing desired. It matters not whether the place desired be ten thousand miles away or only next door, you must fix in consciousness the fact that right where you are seated is the desired place. You do not make a mental journey; you collapse space. Sit quietly where you are and turn "thereness" into "hereness." Close your eyes and feel that the very place where you are is the place desired; feel and sense the reality of it until you are consciously impressed with this fact, for your knowledge of this fact is based solely on your subjective sensing.

Third: In the absence of Esau (the problem) and with the natural time-space established, you invite Jacob (the solution) to come and fill this space-to come and supplant his brother. In your imagination see the thing desired. If you cannot visualize it, sense the general outline of it; contemplate it. Then mentally draw it close to you. "Come close, my son, that I may feel you." Feel the nearness of it; feel it to be in your immediate presence; feel the reality and solidity of it; feel it and see it naturally placed in the room in which you are seated; feel the thrill of actual accomplishment, and the joy of possession.

Now open your eyes. This brings you back to the objective world-the rough or sensibly felt world. Your hairy son Esau has returned from the hunt and by his very presence tells you that you have been betrayed by your smooth skinned son Jacob,—the subjective, psychologically felt. But, like Isaac, whose confidence was based upon the knowledge of this changeless law, you too will say- "I have made him thy Lord and all his brethren have I given to him for servants." That is, even though your problem appears fixed and real, you have felt the subjective, psychological state to be real to the point

207

The Secret of Feeling

of receiving the thrill of that reality; you have experienced the secret of creation for you have felt the reality of the subjective.

You have fixed a definite psychological state which in spite of all opposition or precedent will objectify itself, thereby fulfilling the name of Jacob-the supplanter.

Here are a few practical examples of this drama.

First: The blessing or making a thing real. Sit in your living room and name a piece of furniture, rug or lamp that you would like to have in this particular room. Look at that area of the room where you would place it if you had it.

Close your eyes and let all that now occupies that area of the room vanish. In your imagination see this area as empty space-there is absolutely nothing there. Now begin to fill this space with the desired piece of furniture; sense and feel that you have it in this very area. Imagine you are seeing that which you desired to see. Continue in this consciousness until you feel the thrill of possession.

Second: The blessing or the making of a place real. You are now seated in your apartment in New York City, contemplating the joy that would be yours if you were on an ocean liner sailing across the great Atlantic. "I go to prepare a place for you. And if I go and prepare a place for you, I will come again, and receive you unto myself: that where I am there ye may be also." Your eyes are closed; you have consciously released the New York apartment and in its place you sense and feel that you are on an ocean liner. You are seated in a deck chair; there is nothing round you but the vast Atlantic. Fix the reality of this ship and ocean so that in this state you can mentally recall the day when you were seated in your New York apartment dreaming of this day at sea. Recall the mental picture of yourself seated there in New York dreaming of this day. In your imagination see the memory picture of yourself back there in your New York apartment. If you succeed in looking back on your New York apartment without consciously returning there, then you have successfully prepared the reality of this voyage. Remain in this conscious state feeling the reality of the ship and the ocean; feel the joy of this accomplishment-then open your eyes. You have gone and prepared the place; you have fixed a definite psychological state and where you are in consciousness there you shall be in body also.

Third: The blessing or making real of a point in time. You consciously let go of this day, month or year, as the case may be, and you imagine that it is now that day, month or year which you desire to experience. You sense and feel the reality of the desired time by impressing upon yourself the fact that it is now accomplished. As you sense the naturalness of this time, you begin to feel the thrill of having fully realized that which before you started this psychological journey in time you desired to experience at this time.

With the knowledge of your power to bless you can open the doors of any prison—he prison of illness or poverty or of a humdrum existence. "The Spirit of the Lord God is upon me; because the Lord hath anointed me to preach good tidings unto the meek; he hath sent me to bind up the brokenhearted, to proclaim liberty to the captives, and the opening of the prison to them that are bound."

THE SABBATH

*"SIX days shall work be done, but on the seventh
day there shall be to you a holy day, a Sabbath of rest
to the Lord."*

These six days are not twenty-four-hour periods of time.
They symbolize the psychological moment a definite subjective state is fixed. These six days of work are subjective experiences, and consequently cannot be measured by sidereal
time, for the real work of fixing a definite psychological state
is done in consciousness. The time spent in consciously defining yourself as that which you desire to be is the measure of
these six days. A change of consciousness is the work done in
these six creative days; a psychological adjustment, which is
measured not by sidereal time but by actual (subjective)
accomplishment. Just as a life in retrospect is measured not by
years but by the content of those years, so too is this psychological interval measured, not by the time spent in making the
adjustment but by the accomplishment of that interval.

The true meaning of six days of work (creation) is
revealed in the mystery of the VAU, which is the sixth letter in
the Hebrew alphabet, and the third letter in the divine name-
JOD HE VAU HE. As previously explained in the mystery of
the name of Jehovah, VAU means to nail or join. The creator is
joined to his creation through feeling; and the time that it
takes you to fix a definite feeling is the true measure of these
six days of creation. Mentally separating yourself from the
objective world and attaching yourself through the secret of

210

The Sabbath

feeling to the subjective state is the function of the sixth letter of the Hebrew alphabet, VAU, or the six days of work.

There is always an interval between the fixed impression, or subjective state, and the outward expression of that state. This interval is called the Sabbath. The Sabbath is the mental rest which follows the fixed psychological state; it is the result of your six days of work. "The Sabbath was made for man." This mental rest which follows a successful conscious impregnation is the period of mental pregnancy; a period which is made for the purpose of incubating the manifestation. It was made for the manifestation; the manifestation was not made for it. Automatically you keep the Sabbath a day of rest-a period of mental rest-if you succeed in accomplishing your six days of work. There can be no Sabbath, no seventh day, no period of mental rest, until the six days are over,-until the psychological adjustment is accomplished and the mental impression is fully made.

Man is warned that if he fails to keep the Sabbath, if he fails to enter into the rest of God he will also fail to receive the promise-he will fail to realize his desires. The reason for this is simple and obvious. There can be no mental rest until a conscious impression is made. If a man fails to fully impress upon himself the fact that he now has that which heretofore he desired to possess, he will continue to desire it, and therefore he will not be mentally at rest or satisfied. If, on the other hand, he succeeds in making this conscious adjustment so that upon emerging from the period of silence or his subjective six days of work, he knows by his feeling that he has the thing desired, then he automatically enters the Sabbath or the period of mental rest. Pregnancy follows impregnation. Man does not continue desiring that which he has already acquired. The Sabbath can be kept as a day of rest only after man succeeds in

211

becoming conscious of being that which before entering the silence he desired to be.

The Sabbath is the result of the six days of work. The man who knows the true meaning of these six work days realizes that the observance of one day of the week as a day of physical quietness is not keeping the Sabbath. The peace and the quiet of the Sabbath can be experienced only when man has succeeded in becoming conscious of being that which he desires to be. If he fails to make this conscious impression he has missed the mark; he has sinned, for to sin is to miss the mark-to fail to achieve one's objective; a state in which there is no peace of mind. "If I had not come and spoken unto them, they had not had sin." If man had not been presented with an ideal state toward which to aim, a state to be desired and acquired, he would have been satisfied with his lot in life and would never have known sin. Now that man knows that his capacities are infinite, knows that by working six days or by making a psychological adjustment he can realize his desires, he will not be satisfied until he achieves his every objective. He will, with the true knowledge of these six work days, define his objective and set about becoming conscious of being it. When this conscious impression is made it is automatically followed by a period of mental rest, a period the mystic calls the Sabbath, an interval in which the conscious impression will be gestated and physically expressed. The word will be made flesh. But that is not the end! This Sabbath or rest which will be broken by the embodiment of the idea will sooner or later give way to another six days of work as man defines another objective and begins anew the act of defining himself as that which he desires to be.

Man has been stirred out of his sleep through the medium of desire, and can find no rest until he realizes his desire. But

The Sabbath

before he can enter into the rest of God, or keep the Sabbath, before he can walk unafraid and at peace, he must become a good spiritual marksman and learn the secret of hitting the mark or working six days-the secret by which he lets go the objective state and adjusts himself to the subjective. This secret was revealed in the divine name Jehovah, and again in the story of Isaac blessing his son Jacob. If man will apply the formula as it is revealed in these Bible dramas he will hit a spiritual bull's-eye every time, for he will know that the mental rest or Sabbath is entered only as he succeeds in making a psychological adjustment.

The story of the crucifixion beautifully dramatizes these six days (psychological period) and the seventh day of rest. It is recorded that it was the custom of the Jews to have someone released from prison at the feast of the Passover; and that they were given the choice of having released unto them either Barabbas the robber, or Jesus the Savior. And they cried, "Release Barabbas." Whereupon Barabbas was released and Jesus was crucified.

It is further recorded that Jesus the Savior was crucified on the sixth day, entombed or buried on the seventh day, and resurrected on the first day. The savior in your case is that which would save you from that which you are now conscious of being, while Barabbas the thief is your present conception of yourself which robs you of that which you would like to be. In defining your savior you define that which would save you and not how you would be saved. Your savior or desire has ways ye know not of; his ways are past finding out. Every problem reveals its own solution. If you were imprisoned you would automatically desire to be free. Freedom, then, is the thing that would save you. It is your savior.

Having discovered your savior the next step in this great

The Sabbath

drama of the resurrection is to release Barabbas, the robber-your present concept of yourself—and to crucify your savior, or fix the consciousness of being or having that which would save you. Barabbas represents your present problem. Your savior is that which would free you from this problem. You release Barabbas by taking your attention away from your problem-away from your sense of limitation-for it robs you of the freedom that you seek. And you crucify your savior by fixing a definite psychological state by feeling that you are free from the limitations of the past.

You deny the evidence of the senses and begin to feel subjectively the joy of being free. You feel this state of freedom to be so real that you too cry out- "I am free!" "It is finished." The fixing of this subjective state-the crucifixion—takes place on the sixth day. Before the sun sets on this day you must have completed the fixation by feeling-" It is so"— "It is finished."

This subjective knowing is followed by the Sabbath or mental rest. You will be as one buried or entombed for you will know that no matter how mountainous the barriers, how impassable the walls appear to be, your crucified and buried savior (your present subjective fixation) will resurrect himself. By keeping the Sabbath a period of mental rest, by assuming the attitude of mind that would be yours if you were already visibly expressing this freedom, you will receive the promise of the Lord, for the word will be made flesh,-the subjective fixation will embody itself. "And God did rest the seventh day from all his works." Your consciousness is God resting in the knowledge that — "It is well" — "It is finished." And your objective senses shall confirm that it is so for the day shall reveal it.

CHAPTER 32

HEALING

THE formula for the cure of leprosy as revealed in the fourteenth chapter of Leviticus is most illuminating when viewed through the eyes of a mystic. This formula can be prescribed as the positive cure of any disease in man's world, be it physical, mental, financial, social, moral,-anything. It matters not about the nature of the disease or its duration, for this formula can be successfully applied to any and all of them.

Here is the formula as it is recorded in the book of Leviticus. "Then shall the priest command to take for him that is to be cleansed two birds alive and clean . . . and the priest shall command that one of the birds be killed . . . As for the living bird, he shall take it and shall dip it in the blood of the bird that was killed; and he shall sprinkle upon him that is to be cleansed from the leprosy seven times and shall pronounce him clean and shall let the living bird loose into the open field. . . . And he shall be clean." A literal application of this story would be stupid and fruitless, while on the other hand a psychological application of this formula is wise and fruitful.

A bird is a symbol of an idea. Every man who has a problem or who desires to express something other than that which he is now expressing can be said to have two birds. These two birds or conceptions can be defined as follows: The first bird is your present out-pictured conception of yourself; it is the description which you would give if you were asked to define yourself,—your physical condition, your income, your obligations, your nationality, family, race and so on. Your sincere answer to these questions would necessarily be based solely upon the evidence of your senses and not upon any

Healing

wishful thinking. This true conception of yourself (based entirely upon the evidences of your senses) defines the first bird. The second bird is defined by the answer you wish you might give to these questions of self-definition. In short, these two birds can be defined as that which you are conscious of being and that which you desire to be.

Another definition of the two birds would be, the first-your present problem regardless of its nature; and the second-the solution to that problem. For example: If you were sick, good health would be the solution. If you were in debt, freedom from debt would be the solution. If you were hungry, food would be the solution. As you have noticed, the how, the manner of realizing the solution, is not considered. Only the problem and the solution are considered. Every problem reveals its own solution. For sickness it is health; for poverty it is riches; for weakness it is strength; for confinement it is freedom.

These two states then, your problem and its solution, are the two birds you bring to the priest. You are the priest who now performs the drama of the curing of the man of leprosy-you and your problem. You are the priest; and with this formula for the cure of leprosy you now free yourself from your problem.

First: Take one of the birds (your problem) and kill it by extracting the blood from it. Blood is man's consciousness. "He hath made of one blood all nations of men to dwell on all the face of the earth." Your consciousness is the one and only reality which animates and makes real that which you are conscious of being. So turning your attention away from the problem is equivalent to extracting the blood from the bird. Your consciousness is the one blood which makes all states living

216

Healing

realities. By removing your attention from any given state you have drained the lifeblood from that state. You kill or eliminate the first bird (your problem) by removing your attention from it. Into this blood (your consciousness) you dip the live bird (the solution), or that which heretofore you desired to be or possess. This you do by feeling yourself to be the desirable state now.

This dipping of the live bird into the blood of the bird that was killed is similar to the blessing of Jacob by his blind father Isaac. As you recall, blind Isaac could not see his objective world, his son Esau. You, too, are blind to your problem—the first bird-for you have removed your attention from it and therefore you do not see it. Your attention (blood) is now placed upon the second bird (subjective state), and you feel and sense the reality of it.

Seven times you are told to sprinkle the one to be cleansed. This means you must dwell within this new conception of yourself until you mentally enter the seventh day (the Sabbath); until the mind is stilled or fixed in the belief that you are actually expressing or possessing that which you desire to be or to possess. At the seventh sprinkle you are instructed to loose the living bird and pronounce the man clean. As you fully impress upon yourself the fact that you are that which you desire to be, you have symbolically sprinkled yourself seven times; then you are as free as the bird that is loosed. And like the bird in flight which must in a little while return to the earth, so must your subjective impression or claim in a little while embody itself in your world.

This story and all the other stories of the Bible are psychological plays dramatized within the consciousness of man. You are the high priest; you are the leper; you are the birds. Your

217

Healing

consciousness or I AM is the high priest; you, the man with the problem, are the leper. The problem, your present concept of yourself, is the bird that is killed; the solution of the problem, what you desire to be, is the living bird that is freed. You re-enact this great drama within yourself by turning your attention away from your problem and placing it upon that which you desire to express. You impress upon yourself the fact that you are that which you desire to be until your mind is stilled in the belief that it is so. Living in this fixed attitude of mind, living in the consciousness that you are now that which you formerly desired to be, is the bird in flight, unfettered by the limitations of the past and moving toward the embodiment of your desire.

CHAPTER 33

DESIRE—
THE WORD OF GOD

"SO shall my word be that goeth forth out of my mouth; it shall not return unto me void, but it shall accomplish that which I please, and it shall prosper in the thing whereunto I sent it."

God speaks to you through the medium of your basic desires. Your basic desires are words of promise or prophecies that contain within themselves the plan and power of expression.

By basic desire is meant your real objective. Secondary desires deal with the manner of realization. God, your I AM, speaks to you, the conditioned conscious state, through your basic desires. Secondary desires or ways of expression are the secrets of your I AM, the all wise Father. Your Father, I AM, reveals the first and last—"I am the beginning and the end," but never does He reveal the middle or secret of His ways; that is, the first is revealed as the word, your basic desire. The last is its fulfillment-the word made flesh. The second or middle (the plan of unfoldment) is never revealed to man but remains forever the Father's secret.

"For I testify unto every man that heareth the words of the prophecy of this book, if any man shall add unto these things, God shall add unto him the plagues that are written in this book; and if any man shall take away from the words of the book of this prophecy, God shall take away his part out of the book of life."

The words of prophecy spoken of in the book of Revelation are your basic desires which must not be further

Desire-The Word of God

conditioned. Man is constantly adding to and taking from these words. Not knowing that the basic desire contains the plan and power of expression man is always compromising and complicating his desires. Here is an illustration of what man does to the word of prophecy—his desires.

Man desires freedom from his limitation or problem. The first thing he does after he defines his objective is to condition it upon something else. He begins to speculate on the manner of acquiring it. Not knowing that the thing desired has a way of expression all of its own he starts planning how he is going to get it, thereby adding to the word of God. If, on the other hand, he has no plan or conception as to the fulfillment of his desire, then he compromises his desire by modifying it. He feels that if he will be satisfied with less than his basic desire, then he might have a better chance of realizing it. In doing so he takes from the word of God. Individuals and nations alike are constantly violating this law of their basic desire by plotting and planning the realization of their ambitions; they thereby add to the word of prophecy, or they compromise with their ideals, thus taking from the word of God. The inevitable result is death and plagues or failure and frustration as promised for such violations.

God speaks to man only through the medium of his basic desires. Your desires are determined by your conception of yourself. Of themselves they are neither good nor evil. "I know and am persuaded by the Lord Christ Jesus that there is nothing unclean of itself but to him that seeth anything to be unclean to him it is unclean." Your desires are the natural and automatic result of your present conception of yourself. God, your unconditioned consciousness, is impersonal and no respecter of persons. Your unconditioned consciousness, God,

Desire-The Word of God

gives to your conditioned consciousness, man, through the medium of your basic desires that which your conditioned state (your present conception of yourself) believes it needs.

As long as you remain in your present conscious state so long will you continue desiring that which you now desire. Change your conception of yourself and you will automatically change the nature of your desires.

Desires are states of consciousness seeking embodiment. They are formed by man's consciousness and can easily be expressed by the man who has conceived them. Desires are expressed when the man who has conceived them assumes the attitude of mind that would be his if the states desired were already expressed. Now because desires regardless of their nature can be so easily expressed by fixed attitudes of mind, a word of warning must be given to those who have not yet realized the oneness of life, and who do not know the fundamental truth that consciousness is God, the one and only reality. This warning was given to man in the famous Golden Rule—"Do unto others that which you would have them do unto you."

You may desire something for yourself or you may desire for another. If your desire concerns another, make sure that the thing desired is acceptable to that other. The reason for this warning is that your consciousness is God, the giver of all gifts. Therefore, that which you feel and believe to be true of another is a gift you have given to him. The gift that is not accepted returns to the giver. Be very sure then that you would love to possess the gift yourself for if you fix a belief within yourself as true of another and he does not accept this state as true of himself, this unaccepted gift will embody itself within your world. Always hear and accept as true of others that which you would desire for yourself. In so doing you are building heaven on earth. "Do unto others as you would have them do unto you" is based upon this law. Only accept such states as true of others that you would willingly accept as true of yourself that you may constantly create heaven on earth. Your heaven is defined by the state of consciousness in which you live, which state is made up of all that you accept as true of yourself and true of others. Your immediate environment is defined by your own conception of yourself plus your convictions regarding others which have not been accepted by them.

Your conception of another which is not his conception of himself is a gift returned to you.

Suggestions, like propaganda, are boomerangs unless they are accepted by those to whom they are sent. So your world is a gift you have given to yourself. The nature of the gift is determined by your conception of yourself plus the unaccepted gifts you offered others. Make no mistake about this; law is no respecter of persons. Discover the law of self-expression and live by it; then you will be free. With this understanding of the law, define your desire; know exactly what you want; make certain that it is desirable and acceptable.

The wise and disciplined man sees no barrier to the realization of his desire; he sees nothing to destroy. With a fixed attitude of mind he recognizes that the thing desired is already fully expressed, for he knows that a fixed subjective state has ways and means of expressing itself of which no man knows. "Before they ask I have answered." "I have ways ye know not of." "My ways are past finding out." The undisciplined man, on the other hand, constantly sees opposition to the fulfillment of his desire, and because of this frustration he forms desires of destruction which he firmly believes must be expressed before his basic desire can be realized. When man discovers this law of one consciousness he will understand the great wis-

Desire-The Word of God

dom of the Golden Rule and so he will live by it and prove to himself that the kingdom of heaven is on earth.

You will realize why you should "Do unto others that which you would have them do unto you." You will know why you should live by this Golden Rule because you will discover that it is just good common sense to do so since the rule is based upon life's changeless law and is no respecter of persons. Consciousness is the one and only reality. The world and all within it are states of consciousness objectified. Your world is defined by your conception of yourself plus your conception of others which are not their conceptions of themselves.

The story of the Passover is to help you turn your back on the limitations of the present and pass over into a better and freer state. The suggestion to "Follow the man with the pitcher of water" was given to the disciples to guide them to the last supper or the feast of the Passover. The man with the pitcher of water is the eleventh disciple, Simon of Canaan, the disciplined quality of mind which hears only dignified, noble and kindly states. The mind that is disciplined to hear only the good feasts upon good states and so embodies the good on earth. If you, too, would attend the last supper-the great feast of the Passover-then follow this man. Assume this attitude of mind symbolized as the "man with the pitcher of water," and you will live in a world that is really heaven on earth. The feast of the Passover is the secret of changing your consciousness. You turn your attention from your present conception of yourself and assume the consciousness of being that which you want to be, thereby passing from one state to another.

CHAPTER 34

FAITH

"AND Jesus said unto them, Because of your unbelief; for verily I say unto you, if ye have faith as a grain of mustard seed, ye shall say unto this mountain, remove hence to yonder place; and it shall remove; and nothing shall be impossible unto you."

This faith of a grain of mustard seed has proved a stumbling block to man. He has been taught to believe that a grain of mustard seed signifies a small degree of faith. So he naturally wonders why he, a mature man, should lack this insignificant measure of faith when so small an amount assures success.

"Faith," he is told, "is the substance of things hoped for, the evidence of things not seen." And again, "Through faith . . . the worlds were framed by the word of God, so that things which are seen were not made of things which do appear." Invisible things were made visible. The grain of mustard seed is not the measure of a small amount of faith. On the contrary, it is the absolute in faith. A mustard seed is conscious of being a mustard seed and a mustard seed alone. It is not aware of any other seed in the world. It is sealed in the conviction that it is a mustard seed in the same manner that the spermatozoa sealed in the womb is conscious of being man and only man. A grain of mustard seed is truly the measure of faith necessary to accomplish your every objective; but like the mustard seed you too must lose yourself in the consciousness of being only the thing desired. You abide within this sealed state until it bursts itself and reveals your conscious claim. Faith is feeling or living in the consciousness of being the thing desired; faith is the secret

224

Faith

of creation, the VAU in the divine name JOD HE VAU HE; faith is the Ham in the family of Noah; faith is the sense of feeling by which Isaac blessed and made real his son Jacob. By faith God (your consciousness) calleth things that are not seen as though they were and makes them seen.

It is faith which enables you to become conscious of being the thing desired; again, it is faith which seals you in this conscious state until your invisible claim ripens to maturity and expresses itself, is made visible. Faith or feeling is the secret of this appropriation. Through feeling, the consciousness desiring is joined to the thing desired.

How would you feel if you were that which you desire to be? Wear this mood, this feeling that would be yours if you were already that which you desire to be; and in a little while you will be sealed in the belief that you are. Then without effort this invisible state will objectify itself; the invisible will be made visible. If you had the faith of a grain of mustard seed you would this day through the magical substance of feeling seal yourself in the consciousness of being that which you desire to be. In this mental stillness or tomblike state you would remain, confident that you need no one to roll away the stone, for all the mountains, stones and inhabitants of earth are as nothing in your sight. That which you now recognize to be true of yourself (this present conscious state) will do according to its nature among all the inhabitants of earth, and none can stay its hand or say unto it, What doest thou? None can stop this conscious state in which you are sealed from embodying itself, nor question its right to be.

This conscious state when properly sealed by faith is a word of God, I AM, for the man so sealed is saying, "I AM so and so;" and the word of God (my fixed conscious state) is

Faith

spirit and cannot return unto me void but must accomplish whereunto it is sent. God's word (your conscious state) must embody itself that you may know: "I AM the Lord . . . there is no God beside me;" "The word was made flesh and dwelt among us;" and "He sent his word and healed him."

You too can send your word, God's word, and heal a friend. Is there something that you would like to hear of a friend? Define this something that you know he would love to be or to possess. Now with your desire properly defined you have a word of God. To send this word on its way, to speak this word into being, you simply do this: Sit quietly where you are and assume the mental attitude of listening; recall your friend's voice; with this familiar voice established in your consciousness, imagine that you are actually hearing his voice and that he is telling you that he is or has that which you wanted him to be or to have. Impress upon your consciousness the fact that you actually heard him and that he told you what you wanted to hear; feel the thrill of having heard. Then drop it completely. This is the mystic's secret of sending words into expression-of making the word flesh. You form within yourself the word, the thing you want to hear; then you listen, and tell it to yourself. "Speak, Lord, for thy servant heareth." Your consciousness is the Lord speaking through the familiar voice of a friend and impressing on yourself that which you desire to hear. This self-impregnation, the state impressed upon yourself, the word, has ways and means of expressing itself of which no man knows. As you succeed in making the impression you will be unmoved by appearances.

CHAPTER 35

THE ANNUNCIATION

THE use of a friend's voice to impregnate one's self with a desirable state is beautifully told in the story of the Immaculate Conception.

It is recorded that God sent an angel to Mary to announce the birth of His son. "And the angel said unto her, thou shalt conceive in thy womb, and bring forth a son. Then said Mary unto the angel, 'How shall this be, seeing I know not a man?' And the angel answered and said unto her, 'The Holy Ghost shall come upon thee, and the power of the highest shall overshadow thee: therefore also that holy thing which shall be born of thee shall be called the son of God.' For with God nothing shall be impossible."

This is the story that has been told for centuries the world over, but man was not told that it was written about himself so he has failed to receive the benefit it was intended to give him. This story reveals the method by which the idea or word was made flesh. God, we are told, germinated or begat an idea, a son, without the aid of another. Then He placed His germinal idea in the womb of Mary with the help of an angel who made the announcement to her and impregnated her with the idea. No simpler method was ever recorded of consciousness impregnating itself than is found in the story of the Immaculate Conception. The four characters in this drama of creation are the Father, the Son, Mary and the Angel. The Father symbolizes your consciousness; the Son symbolizes your desire; Mary symbolizes your receptive attitude of mind; and the Angel symbolizes the method used to make the impregnation. The drama unfolds in this manner. The Father begets a son without the aid of another. You define your

227

objective—you clarify your desire without the help or suggestion of another.

Then the Father selects that angel who is best qualified to bear this message or germinal possibility to Mary. You select the person in your world who would be sincerely thrilled in witnessing the fulfillment of your desire. Then Mary learns through the angel that she has already conceived a son without the aid of man. You assume a receptive attitude of mind, a listening attitude, and imagine you are hearing the voice of the one you have chosen to tell you what you desire to know. Imagine that you hear him tell you that you are and have that which you desire to be and to have. You remain in this receptive state until you feel the thrill of having heard the good and wonderful news. Then like Mary of the story, you go about your business in secret telling no one of this wonderful and immaculate self-impregnation, confident that in due season you will express this impression.

The Father generates the seed or germinal possibility of a son but in a eugenic impregnation; he does not convey the spermatozoa from himself to the womb. He has it borne through another medium. Consciousness desiring is the Father generating the seed or idea. A clarified desire is the perfectly formed seed or the only begotten son. This seed is then carried from the Father (consciousness desiring) to the Mother (consciousness of being and having the state desired). This change in consciousness is accomplished by the angel or imaginary voice of a friend telling you that you have already achieved your objective.

The use of an angel or friend's voice to make a conscious impression is the shortest, safest and surest way to be self-impregnated. With your desire properly defined, you assume an attitude of listening. Imagine you are hearing the voice of a friend; then make him tell you (imagine he is telling you) how lucky and fortunate you are to have fully realized your desire. In this receptive attitude of mind you are receiving the message of an angel; you are receiving the impression that you are and have that which you desire to be and to have. The emotional thrill of having heard that which you desire to hear is the moment of conception. It is the moment you become self-impregnated, the moment you actually feel you are now that or have that which heretofore you but desired to be or to possess.

As you emerge from this subjective experience, you, like Mary of the story, will know by your changed attitude of mind that you have conceived a son; that you have fixed a definite subjective state and will in a little while express or objectify this state.

OUT OF THIS WORLD

CHAPTER 36

THINKING FOURTH-
DIMENSIONALLY

*"And now I have told you before it come to pass, that,
when it is come to pass, ye might believe."*
                                        —John 14:29

MANY persons, myself included, have observed events
before they occurred; that is, before they occurred in this
world of three dimensions. Since man can observe an event
before it occurs in the three dimensions of space, life on earth
must proceed according to plan, and this plan must exist elsewhere in another dimension and be slowly moving through
our space.

If the occurring events were not in this world when they
were observed, then, to be perfectly logical, they must have
been out of this world. And whatever is *there* to be seen before
it occurs *here* must be "Predetermined" from the point of
view of man awake in a three-dimensional world.

Thus the question arises: "Are we
able to alter our future?"

My object in writing these pages is to indicate possibilities inherent in man, to show that man can alter his future;
but, thus altered, it forms again a deterministic sequence
starting from the point of interference—a future that will be
consistent with the alteration. The most remarkable feature of
man's future is its flexibility. It is determined by his attitudes

rather than by his acts. The cornerstone on which all things are based is man's concept of himself. He acts as he does and has the experiences that he does, because his concept of himself is what it is, and for no other reason. Had he a different concept of self, he would act differently. A change of concept of self automatically alters his future; and a change in any term of his future series of experiences reciprocally alters his concept of self. Man's assumptions which he regards as insignificant produce effects that are considerable; therefore man should revise his estimate of an assumption, and recognize its creative power.

All changes take place in consciousness. The future, although prepared in every detail in advance, has several outcomes. At every moment of our lives we have before us the choice of which of several futures we will choose.

There are two actual outlooks on the world possessed by everyone—a natural focus and a spiritual focus. The ancient teachers called the one "the carnal mind," the other "the mind of Christ." We may differentiate them as ordinary waking consciousness-governed by our senses, and a controlled imagination-governed by desire. We recognize these two distinct centers of thought in the statement: "The natural man receiveth not the things of the spirit of God for they are foolishness unto him; neither can he know them for they are spiritually discerned." The natural view confines reality to the moment called now. To the natural view, the past and future are purely imaginary. The spiritual view, on the other hand, sees the contents of time. It sees events as distinct and separated as objects in space. The past and future are a present whole to the spiritual view. What is mental and subjective to the natural man is concrete and objective to the spiritual man.

Thinking Fourth-Dimensionally

The habit of seeing only that which our senses permit, renders us totally blind to what we otherwise could see. To cultivate the faculty of seeing the invisible, we should often deliberately disentangle our minds from the evidence of the senses and focus our attention on an invisible state, mentally feeling it and sensing it until it has all the distinctness of reality.

Earnest, concentrated thought focused in a particular direction shuts out other sensations and causes them to disappear. We have but to concentrate on the state desired in order to see it. The habit of withdrawing attention from the region of sensation and concentrating it on the invisible develops our spiritual outlook and enables us to penetrate beyond the world of sense and to see that which is invisible. "For the invisible things of him from the creation of the world are clearly seen."—Romans 1:20. This vision is completely independent of the natural faculties. Open it and quicken it! Without it, these instructions are useless, for "the things of the spirit are spiritually discerned."

A little practice will convince us that we can, by controlling our imagination, reshape our future in harmony with our desire. Desire is the mainspring of action. We could not move a single finger unless we had a desire to move it. No matter what we do, we follow the desire which at the moment dominates our minds. When we break a habit, our desire to break it is greater than our desire to continue in the habit.

The desires which impel us to action are those that hold our attention. A desire is but an awareness of something we lack or need to make our life more enjoyable. Desires always have some personal gain in view, the greater the anticipated gain, the more intense is the desire. There is no absolutely unselfish desire. Where there is nothing to gain there is no desire, and consequently no action.

The spiritual man speaks to the natural man through the language of desire. The key to progress in life and to the fulfillment of dreams lies in ready obedience to its voice. Unhesitating obedience to its voice is an immediate assumption of the wish fulfilled. To desire a state is to have it. As Pascal has said, "You would not have sought me had you not already found me." Man, by assuming the feeling of his wish fulfilled, and then living and acting on this conviction, alters the future in harmony with his assumption.

Assumptions awaken what they affirm. As soon as man assumes the feeling of his wish fulfilled, his four-dimensional self finds ways for the attainment of this end, discovers methods for its realization. I know of no clearer definition of the means by which we realize our desires than to *experience in imagination what we would experience in the flesh were we to achieve our goal.* This experience of the end wills the means. With its larger outlook the four-dimensional self then constructs the means necessary to realize the accepted end.

The undisciplined mind finds it difficult to assume a state which is denied by the senses. Here is a technique that makes it easy to encounter events before they occur, to "call things which are not seen as though they were." People have a habit of slighting the importance of simple things; but this simple formula for changing the future was discovered after years of searching and experimenting. The first step in changing the future is *desire*; that is: define your objective-know definitely what you want. Secondly: construct an event which you believe you would encounter *following* the fulfillment of your desire-an event which implies fulfillment of your desire-something that will have the action of *self* predominant. Thirdly: immobilize the physical body and induce a condition akin to sleep-lie on a bed or relax in a chair and imagine that you are sleepy; then, with eyelids closed and your attention focused on the action you intend to experience in imagination-mentally feel yourself right into the proposed action - imagining all the while that you are actually performing the action here and now. You must always participate in the imaginary action, not merely stand back and look on, but you must feel that you are actually performing the action so that the imaginary sensation is real to you.

It is important always to remember that the proposed action must be one which *follows* the fulfillment of your desire; and, also, you must feel yourself into the action until it has all the vividness and distinctness of reality. For example: suppose you desired promotion in office. Being congratulated would be an event you would encounter following the fulfillment of your desire. Having selected this action as the one you will experience in imagination, immobilize the physical body, and induce a state akin to sleep-a drowsy state-but one in which you are still able to control the direction of your thoughts-a state in which you are attentive without effort. Now, imagine that a friend is standing before you. Put your imaginary hand into his. First feel it to be solid and real, then carry on an imaginary conversation with him in harmony with the action. Do not visualize yourself at a distance in point of space and at a distance in point of time being congratulated on your good fortune. Instead, make elsewhere here, and the future now. The future event is a reality now in a dimensionally larger world; and, oddly enough, now in a dimensionally larger world, is equivalent to here in the ordinary three-dimensional space of everyday life. The difference between feeling yourself in action, *here* and *now*, and visualizing yourself in action, as though you were on a motion-picture screen, is the difference between success and failure. The difference will be appreciated if you will now visualize yourself climbing a ladder. Then with eyelids closed imagine that a ladder is right in front of you and feel you are actually climbing it.

Desire, physical immobility bordering on sleep, and imaginary action in which self feelingly predominates, *here* and *now*, are not only important factors in altering the future, but they are essential conditions in consciously projecting the spiritual self. If, when the physical body is immobilized we become possessed of the idea to do something-and imagine that we are doing it *here* and *now* and keep the imaginary action feelingly going right up until sleep ensues—we are likely to awaken out of the physical body to find ourselves in a dimensionally larger world with a dimensionally larger focus and actually doing what we desired and imagined we were doing in the flesh. But whether we awaken there or not, we are actually performing the action in the fourth-dimensional world, and we will re-enact it in the future, here in the third-dimensional world.

Experience has taught me to restrict the imaginary action, to condense the idea which is to be the object of our meditation into a single act, and to re-enact it over and over again until it has the feeling of reality. Otherwise, the attention will wander off along an associational track, and hosts of associated images will be presented to our attention. In a few seconds they will lead us hundreds of miles away from our objective in point of space, and years away in point of time. If we decide to climb a particular flight of stairs, because that is the likely event to follow the realization of our desire, then we must restrict the action to climbing that particular flight of stairs. Should our attention wander off, we must bring it back to its task of climbing that flight of stairs and keep on doing so until the imaginary action has all the solidity and distinctness of reality. The idea must be maintained in the field of presentation without any sensible effort on our part. We must, with the minimum of effort, permeate the mind with the feeling of the wish fulfilled.

Drowsiness facilitates change because it favors attention without effort, but it must not be pushed to the stage of sleep, in which we shall no longer be able to control the movements of our attention, but rather a moderate degree of drowsiness in which we are still able to direct our thoughts. A most effective way to embody a desire is to assume the feeling of the wish fulfilled and then, in a relaxed and sleepy state, repeat over and over again, like a lullaby, any short phrase which implies fulfillment of our desire, such as "Thank you" as though we addressed a higher power for having done it for us. If, however, we seek a conscious projection into a dimensionally larger world, then we must keep the action going right up until sleep ensues.

Experience in imagination, with all the distinctness of reality, what would be experienced in the flesh were you to achieve your goal; and you shall, in time, meet it in the flesh as you met it in your imagination. Feed the mind with *premises*—that is, assertions *presumed* to be true, because assumptions, though unreal to the senses, if persisted in, until they have the *feeling of reality*, will harden into facts. To an assumption all means which promote its realization are good. It influences the behavior of all by inspiring in all the movements, the actions, and the words which tend towards its fulfillment.

To understand how man molds his future in harmony with his assumption we must know what we mean by a dimensionally larger world, for it is to a dimensionally larger world that we go to alter our future. The observation of an event before it occurs implies that the event is predetermined from the point of view of man in the three-dimensional world. Therefore, to change the conditions here in the three dimensions of space we must first change them in the four dimensions of space.

Man does not know exactly what is meant by a dimensionally larger world, and would no doubt deny the existence of a dimensionally larger self. He is quite familiar with the three dimensions of length, width and height, and he feels that if there were a fourth dimension, it should be just as obvious to him as the dimensions of length, width and height. A dimension is not a line; it is any way in which a thing can be measured that is entirely different from all other ways. That is, to measure a solid fourth-dimensionally, we simply measure it in any direction except that of its length, width and height.

Is there another way of measuring an object other than those of its length, width and height? Time measures my life without employing the three dimensions of length, width and height. There is no such thing as an instantaneous object. Its appearance and disappearance are measurable. It endures for a definite length of time. We can measure its life span without using the dimensions of length, width and height. Time is definitely a fourth way of measuring an object.

The more dimensions an object has, the more substantial and real it becomes. A straight line, which lies entirely in one dimension, acquires shape, mass and substance by the addition of dimensions. What new quality would time, the fourth dimension, give which would make it just as vastly superior to solids as solids are to surfaces and surfaces are to lines? Time is a medium for changes in experience because all changes take time. The new quality is *changeability*.

Observe that if we bisect a solid, its cross section will be a surface; by bisecting a surface, we obtain a line; and by bisecting a line, we get a point. This means that a point is but a cross section of a line, which is, in turn, but a cross section of a surface, which is, in turn, but a cross section of a solid, which is, in turn, if carried to its logical conclusion, but a cross section of a four-dimensional object.

We cannot avoid the inference that all three-dimensional objects are but cross sections of four-dimensional bodies. Which means: when I meet you, I meet a cross section of the four-dimensional you-the four-dimensional *self* that is not seen. To see the four-dimensional *self* I must see every cross section or moment of your life from birth to death and see them all as coexisting. My focus should take in the entire array of sensory impressions which you have experienced on earth plus those you might encounter. I should see them, not in the order in which they were experienced by you, but as a present whole. Because change is the characteristic of the fourth dimension, I should see them in a state of flux as a living, animated whole.

If we have all this clearly fixed in our minds, what does it mean to us in this three-dimensional world? It means that, if we can move along time's length, we can see the future and alter it as we so desire. This world, which we think so solidly real, is a shadow out of which and beyond which we may at any time pass. It is an abstraction from a more fundamental and dimensionally larger world—a more fundamental world abstracted from a still more fundamental and dimensionally larger world and so on to infinity. The absolute is unattainable by any means or analysis, no matter how many dimensions we add to the world.

Man can prove the existence of a dimensionally larger world simply by focusing his attention on an invisible state and imagining that he sees and feels it. If he remains concentrated in this state, his present environment will pass away, and he will awaken in a dimensionally larger world where the object of his contemplation will be seen as a concrete objective reality. Intuitively I feel that, were he to abstract his thoughts from this dimensionally larger world and retreat still farther within his mind, he would again bring about an externalization of time. He would discover that every time he retreats into his inner mind and brings about an externalization of time, space becomes dimensionally larger. And he would, therefore, conclude that both time and space are serial, and that the drama of life is but the climbing of a multitudinous dimensional time block.

Scientists will one day explain *why* there is a Serial Universe. But in practice *how* we use this Serial Universe to change the future is more important. To change the future, we need only concern ourselves with two worlds in the infinite series, the world we know by reason of our bodily organs, and the world we perceive independently of our bodily organs.

CHAPTER 37

ASSUMPTIONS
BECOME FACTS

MEN believe in the reality of the external world because they do not know how to focus and condense their powers to penetrate its thin crust. This book has only one purpose-the removing of the veil of the senses—the traveling into another world. To remove the veil of the senses we do not employ great effort; the objective world vanishes by turning our attention away from it.

We have only to concentrate on the state desired in order to mentally see it, but to give it reality so that it will become an objective fact, we must focus attention upon the invisible state until it has the feeling of reality. When, through concentrated attention, our desire appears to possess the distinctness and feeling of reality, we have given it the right to become a visible concrete fact.

If it is difficult to control the direction of your attention while in a state akin to sleep, you may find gazing fixedly into an object very helpful. Do not look at its surface but into and beyond any plain object such as a wall, a carpet, or any other object which possesses depth. Arrange it to return as little reflection as possible. Imagine then that in this depth you are seeing and hearing what you want to see and hear until your attention is exclusively occupied by the imagined state.

At the end of your meditation, when you awake from your "controlled waking dream," you feel as though you had returned from a great distance. The visible world which you had shut out returns to consciousness and by its very presence informs you that you have been self-deceived into believing that the object of your contemplation was real. But, if you know that consciousness is the one and only reality, you will - remain faithful to your vision, and by this sustained mental attitude confirm your gift of reality, and prove that you have the power to give reality to your desires that they may become visible concrete facts.

Define your ideal and concentrate your attention upon the idea of identifying yourself with your ideal. Assume the feeling of being it, the feeling that would be yours were you already the embodiment of your ideal. Then live and act upon this conviction. This assumption, though denied by the senses, if *persisted* in, will become fact. You will know when you have succeeded in fixing the desired state in consciousness by simply looking *mentally* at the people you know. In dialogues with yourself you are less inhibited and more sincere than in actual conversations with others, therefore the opportunity for self-analysis arises when you are surprised by your mental conversations with others. If you see them as you formerly saw them, you have not changed your concept of self, for all changes of concepts of self result in a changed relationship to your world.

In your meditation allow others to see you as they would see you were this new concept of self a concrete fact. You always seem to others an embodiment of the ideal you inspire. Therefore, in meditation, when you contemplate others, you must be seen by them mentally as you would be seen by them physically were your concept of self an objective fact; that is, in meditation you imagine that they see you expressing that which you desire to be.

If you assume that you are what you want to be your desire is fulfilled, and in fulfillment all longing is neutralized.

Assumptions Become Facts

You cannot continue desiring what you have already realized. Your desire is not something you labor to fulfill, it is recognizing something you already possess. It is assuming the feeling of *being* that which you desire to be. Believing and being are one. The conceiver and his conception are one, therefore that which you conceive yourself to be can never be so far off as even to be near, for nearness implies separation. "If thou canst believe, all things are possible to him that believeth." Being is the substance of things hoped for, the evidence of things not yet seen. If you assume that you are what you want to be, then you will see others as they are related to your assumption.

If, however, it is the good of others that you desire, then, in meditation, you must represent them to yourself as already being that which you desire them to be. It is through desire that you rise above your present sphere and the road from longing to fulfillment is shortened as you experience in imagination what you would experience in the flesh were you already the embodiment of the ideal you desire to be.

I have stated that man has at every moment of time the choice before him which of several futures he will encounter; but the question arises: "How is this possible when the experiences of man, awake in the three-dimensional world, are predetermined?" as his observation of an event before it occurs implies. This ability to change the future will be seen if we liken the experiences of life on earth to this printed page. Man experiences events on earth singly and successively in the same way that you are now experiencing the words of this page.

Imagine that every word on this page represents a single sensory impression. To get the context, to understand my meaning, you focus your vision on the first word in the upper left-hand corner and then move your focus across the page from left to right, letting it fall on the words singly and successively. By the time your eyes reach the last word on this page you have extracted my meaning. Suppose, however, on looking at the page, with all the printed words thereon equally present, you decided to rearrange them. You could, by rearranging them, tell an entirely different story; in fact, you could tell many different stories.

A dream is nothing more than uncontrolled four-dimensional thinking, or the rearrangement of both past and future sensory impressions. Man seldom dreams of events in the order in which he experiences them when awake. He usually dreams of two or more events which are separated in time, fused into a single sensory impression; or, in his dream, he so completely rearranges his single waking sensory impressions that he does not recognize them when he encounters them in his waking state.

For example: I dreamed that I delivered a package to the restaurant in my apartment building. The hostess said to me, "You can't leave that there"; whereupon, the elevator operator gave me a few letters and as I thanked him for them, he, in turn, thanked me. At this point, the night elevator operator appeared and waved a greeting to me.

The following day, as I left my apartment, I picked up a few letters which had been placed at my door. On my way down I gave the day elevator operator a tip and thanked him for taking care of my mail; whereupon, he thanked me for the tip. On my return home that day I overheard a doorman say to a delivery man, "You can't leave that there." As I was about to take the elevator up to my apartment, I was attracted by a familiar face in the restaurant, and, as I looked in, the hostess greeted me with a smile. Late that night I escorted my dinner

Assumptions Become Facts

guests to the elevator and as I said good-by to them, the night operator waved good-night to me.

By simply rearranging a few of the single sensory impressions I was destined to encounter, and by fusing two or more of them into single sensory impressions, I constructed a dream which differed quite a bit from my waking experience.

When we have learned to control the movements of our attention in the four-dimensional world, we shall be able to consciously create circumstances in the three-dimensional world. We learn this control through the waking dream, where our attention can be maintained without effort, for attention minus effort is indispensable to changing the future. We can, in a controlled waking dream, consciously construct an event which we desire to experience in the three-dimensional world.

The sensory impressions we use to construct our waking dream are present realities displaced in time or the four-dimensional world. All that we do in constructing the waking dream is to select from the vast array of sensory impressions those, which, when they are properly arranged, imply that we have realized our desire. With the dream clearly defined we relax in a chair and induce a state of consciousness akin to sleep-a state, which, although bordering on sleep, leaves us in conscious control of the movements of our attention. When we have achieved that state, we experience in imagination what we would experience in reality were this waking dream an objective fact. In applying this technique to change the future it is important always to remember that the only thing which occupies the mind during the waking dream is the waking dream, the predetermined action which implies the fulfillment of our desire. How the waking dream becomes physical fact is not our concern. Our acceptance of the waking dream as physical reality wills the means for its fulfillment.

Let me again lay the foundation of changing the future, which is nothing more than a controlled waking dream.

1. Define your objective-know definitely what you want.

2. Construct an event which you believe you will encounter *following* the fulfillment of your desire-something which will have the action of *self* predominant-an event which implies the fulfillment of your desire.

3. Immobilize the physical body and induce a state of consciousness akin to sleep; then, mentally feel yourself right into the proposed action-imagining all the while that you are actually performing the action here and now so that you experience in imagination what you would experience in the flesh were you now to realize your goal.

Experience has convinced me that this is the perfect way to achieve my goal. However, my own many failures would convict me were I to imply that I have completely mastered the movements of my attention. I can, however, with the ancient teacher say: "This one thing I do, forgetting those things which are behind, and reaching forth unto those things which are before, I press toward the mark for the prize."

CHAPTER 38

POWER OF IMAGINATION

"Ye shall know the truth, and the truth shall make you free."

— John 8:32

MEN claim that a true judgment must conform to the external reality to which it relates. This means that if I, while imprisoned, suggest to myself that I am free and succeed in believing that I am free, it is true that I believe in my freedom; but it does not follow that I am free for I may be the victim of illusion. But, because of my own experiences, I have come to believe in so many strange things that I see little reason to doubt the truth of things that are beyond my experience.

The ancient teachers warned us not to judge from appearances because, said they, the truth need not conform to the external reality to which it relates. They claimed that we bore false witness if we imagined evil against another -that no matter how real our belief appears to be-how truly it conforms to the external reality to which it relates-if it does not make free the one of whom we hold the belief, it is untrue and therefore a false judgment.

We are called upon to deny the evidence of our senses and to imagine as true of our neighbor that which makes him free. "Ye shall know the truth, and the truth shall make you free." To know the truth of our neighbor we must assume that he is already that which he desires to be. Any concept we hold of

Power of Imagination

another that is short of his fulfilled desire will not make him free and therefore cannot be the truth.

Instead of learning my craft in schools where attending courses and seminars is considered a substitute for self-acquired knowledge, my schooling was devoted almost exclusively to the power of imagination. I sat for hours imagining myself to be other than that which my reason and my senses dictated until the imagined states were vivid as reality-so vivid that passersby became but a part of my imagination and acted as I would have them. By the power of imagination my fantasy led theirs and dictated to them their behavior and the discourse they held together while I was identified with my imagined state. Man's imagination is the man himself, and the world as imagination sees it is the real world, but it is our duty to imagine all that is lovely and of good report. "The Lord seeth not as man seeth, for man looketh upon the outward appearance, but the Lord looketh upon the heart." "As a man thinketh in his heart so is he."

In meditation, when the brain grows luminous, I find my imagination endowed with the magnetic power to attract to me whatsoever I desire. Desire is the power imagination uses to fashion life about me as I fashion it within myself. I first desire to see a certain person or scene, and then I look *as though I were seeing* that which I want to see, and the imagined state becomes objectively real. I desire to hear, and then I listen as *though I were hearing*, and the imagined voice speaks that which I dictate as though it had initiated the message. I could give you many examples to prove my arguments, to prove that these imagined states do become physical realities; but I know that my examples will awaken in all who have not met the like or who are not inclined towards my arguments, a most natu-

250

ral incredulity. Nevertheless, experience has convinced me of the truth of the statement, "He calleth those things which be not as though they were."—Romans 4:17. For I have, in intense meditation, called things that were not seen as though they were, and the unseen not only became seen, but eventually became physical realities.

By this method-first desiring and then imagining that we are experiencing that which we desire to experience-we can mold the future in harmony with our desire. But let us follow the advice of the prophet and think only the lovely and the good, for the imagination waits on us as indifferently and as swiftly when our nature is evil as when it is good. From us spring forth good and evil. "I have set before thee this day life and good, and death and evil." —Deuteronomy 30:15.

Desire and imagination are the enchanter's wand of fable and they draw to themselves their own affinities. They break forth best when the mind is in a state akin to sleep. I have written with some care and detail the method I use to enter the dimensionally larger world, but I shall give one more formula for opening the door of the larger world. "In a dream, in a vision of the night, when deep sleep calleth upon men, in slumberings upon the bed; Then he openeth the ears of men, and sealeth their instruction."—Job 33:15, 16

In dream we are usually the servant of our vision rather than its master, but the *internal fantasy* of dream can be turned into an *external reality*. In dream, as in meditation, we slip from this world into a dimensionally larger world, and I know that the forms in dream are not flat two-dimensional images which modern psychologists believe them to be. They are substantial realities of the dimensionally larger world, and I can lay hold of them. I have discovered that, if I surprise myself dreaming,

Power of Imagination

I can lay hold of any inanimate or stationary form of the dream (a chair, a table, a stairway, a tree) and command myself to awake. At the command to awake, while firmly holding on to the object of the dream, I am pulled through myself with the distinct feeling of awakening from dream. I awaken in another sphere holding the object of my dream, to find that I am no longer the servant of my vision but its master, for I am fully conscious and in control of the movements of my attention. It is in this fully conscious state, when we are in control of the direction of thought, that we call things that are not seen as though they were. In this state we call things by wishing and assuming the feeling of our wish fulfilled. Unlike the world of three dimensions where there is an interval between our assumption and its fulfillment, in the dimensionally larger world there is an immediate realization of our assumption. The external reality instantly mirrors our assumption. Here there is no need to wait four months till harvest. We look again as though we saw, and lo and behold, the fields are already white to harvest.

In this dimensionally larger world "Ye shall not need to fight: set yourselves, stand ye still, and see the salvation of the Lord with you." —Chronicles 20:17. And because that greater world is slowly passing through our three-dimensional world, we can by the power of imagination mold our world in harmony with our desire. Look *as though you saw*; listen *as though you heard*; stretch forth your imaginary hand *as though you touched* . . . and your assumptions will harden into facts.

To those who believe that a true judgment must conform to the external reality to which it relates, this will be foolishness and a stumbling-block. But I preach and practice the fixing in consciousness of that which man desires to realize.

Power of Imagination

Experience convinces me that fixed attitudes of mind which do not conform to the external reality to which they relate and are therefore called imaginary—"things which are not"—will, nevertheless, "bring to nought things that are."

I do not wish to write a book of wonders, but rather to turn man's mind back to the one and only reality that the ancient teachers worshiped as God. All that was said of God was in reality said of man's consciousness so we may say, "That, according as it is written, He that glorify, let him glory in his own consciousness."

No man needs help to direct him in the application of this law of consciousness. "I am" is the self-definition of the absolute. The root out of which everything grows. "I am the vine."

What is your answer to the eternal question, "Who am I?" Your answer determines the part you play in the world's drama. Your answer-that is, your concept of self-need not conform to the external reality to which it relates. This great truth is revealed in the statement, "Let the weak say, I am strong." —Joel 3:10

Look back over the good resolutions with which many past new years are encumbered. They lived a little while and then they died. Why? Because they were severed from their root. Assume that you are that which you want to be. Experience in imagination what you would experience in the flesh were you already that which you want to be. Remain faithful to your assumption, so that you define yourself as that which you have assumed. Things have no life if they are severed from their roots, and our consciousness, our "I amness," is the root of all that springs in our world.

"If ye believe not that I am he, ye shall die in your sins." — John 8:24. That is, if I do not believe that I am already that

Power of Imagination

which I desire to be, then I remain as I am and die in my present concept of self. There is no power, outside of the consciousness of man, to resurrect and make alive that which man desires to experience. That man who is accustomed to call up at will whatever images he pleases, will be, by virtue of the power of his imagination, master of his fate. "I am the resurrection, and the life: he that believeth in me, though he were dead, yet shall he live." —John 11:25. "Ye shall know the truth, and the truth shall make you free."

CHAPTER 39

NO ONE TO CHANGE BUT SELF

"And for their sakes I sanctify myself, that they also might be sanctified through the truth."
—John 17:19

THE ideal we serve and strive to attain could never be evolved from us were it not potentially involved in our nature.

It is now my purpose to retell and to emphasize an experience of mine printed by me two years ago. I believe these quotations from "THE SEARCH" will help us to understand the operation of the law of consciousness, and show us that we have no one to change but self.

Once in an idle interval at sea I meditated on "the perfect state," and wondered what I would be, were I of too pure eyes to behold iniquity, if to me all things were pure and were I without condemnation. As I became lost in this fiery brooding, I found myself lifted above the dark environment of the senses. So intense was feeling I felt myself a being of fire dwelling in a body of air. Voices as from a heavenly chorus, with the exaltation of those who had been conquerors in a conflict with death, were singing, "He is risen—He is risen," and intuitively I knew they meant me.

Then I seemed to be walking in the night. I soon came upon a scene that might have been the ancient Pool of Bethesda for in this place lay a great multitude of impotent folk-blind, halt, withered, waiting not for the moving of the water as of tradition, but waiting for me. As I came near, with-

255

out thought or effort on my part they were, one after the other, molded as by the Magician of the Beautiful. Eyes, hands, feet-all missing members-were drawn from some invisible reservoir and molded in harmony with that perfection which I felt springing within me. When all were made perfect, the chorus exulted, "It is finished." Then the scene dissolved and I awoke.

I know this vision was the result of my intense meditation upon the idea of perfection, for my meditations invariably bring about union with the state contemplated. I had been so completely absorbed within the idea that for a while I had become what I contemplated, and the high purpose with which I had for that moment identified myself drew the companionship of high things and fashioned the vision in harmony with my inner nature. The ideal with which we are united works by association of ideas to awaken a thousand moods to create a drama in keeping with the central idea.

My mystical experiences have convinced me that there is no way to bring about the outer perfection we seek other than by the transformation of ourselves. As soon as we succeed in transforming ourselves, the world will melt magically before our eyes and reshape itself in harmony with that which our transformation affirms.

In the divine economy nothing is lost. We cannot lose anything save by descent from the sphere where the thing has its natural life. There is no transforming power in death and, whether we are here or there, we fashion the world that surrounds us by the intensity of our imagination and feeling, and we illuminate or darken our lives by the concepts we hold of ourselves. Nothing is more important to us than our conception of ourselves, and especially is this true of our concept of the dimensionally greater One within us.

No One to Change but Self

Those who help or hinder us, whether they know it or not, are the servants of that law which shapes outward circumstances in harmony with our inner nature. It is our conception of ourselves which frees or constrains us, though it may use material agencies to achieve its purpose.

Because life molds the outer world to reflect the inner arrangement of our minds, there is no way of bringing about the outer perfection we seek other than by the transformation of ourselves. No help cometh from without; the hills to which we lift our eyes are those of an inner range. It is thus to our own consciousness that we must turn as to the only reality, the only foundation on which all phenomena can be explained. We can rely absolutely on the justice of this law to give us only that which is of the nature of ourselves.

To attempt to change the world before we change our concept of ourselves is to struggle against the nature of things. There can be no outer change until there is first an inner change. As within, so without. I am not advocating philosophical indifference when I suggest that we should imagine ourselves as already that which we want to be, living in a mental atmosphere of greatness, rather than using physical means and arguments to bring about the desired change. Everything we do, unaccompanied by a change of consciousness, is but futile readjustment of surfaces. However we toil or struggle, we can receive no more than our assumptions affirm. To protest against anything which happens to us is to protest against the law of our being and our rulership over our own destiny.

The circumstances of my life are too closely related to my conception of myself not to have been formed by my own spirit from some dimensionally larger storehouse of my being. If there is pain to me in these happenings, I should look within myself for the cause, for I am moved here and there and made to live in a

No One to Change but Self

world in harmony with my concept of myself.

Intense meditation brings about a union with the state contemplated, and during this union we see visions, have experiences and behave in keeping with our change of consciousness. This shows us that a transformation of consciousness will result in a change of environment and behavior.

All wars prove that violent emotions are extremely potent in precipitating mental rearrangements. Every great conflict has been followed by an era of materialism and greed in which the ideals for which the conflict ostensibly was waged are submerged. This is inevitable because war evokes hate which impels a descent in consciousness from the plane of the ideal to the level where the conflict is waged. If we would become as emotionally aroused over our ideals as we become over our dislikes, we would ascend to the plane of our ideal as easily as we now descend to the level of our hates.

Love and hate have a magical transforming power, and we grow through their exercise into the likeness of what we contemplate. By intensity of hatred we create in ourselves the character we imagine in our enemies. Qualities die for want of attention, so the unlovely states might best be rubbed out by imagining "beauty for ashes and joy for mourning" rather than by direct attacks on the state from which we would be free. "Whatsoever things are lovely and of good report, think on these things," for we become that with which we are en rapport.

There is nothing to change but our concept of self. As soon as we succeed in transforming self, our world will dissolve and reshape itself in harmony with that which our change affirms.

RESSURECTION

CHAPTER 40

A CONFESSION
OF FAITH

"Now after John was arrested, Jesus came into Galilee, preaching the gospel of God, and saying, The time is fulfilled, and the kingdom of God is at hand; repent, and believe in the gospel."

—Mark 1:14-15

Jesus' ministry began after that of John ended in Judea. "Jesus, when he began his ministry, was about thirty years of age."

—Luke 3:23

The soil of the centuries had been ploughed and harrowed for the gospel of God. And men began to experience God's plan of salvation.

The authors of the gospel of God are anonymous, and all that we can really know about them must be derived from our own experience of scripture. Their authority was not in scripture as a dead written code but in their own experience of scripture. Their gospel was not a new religion but the fulfillment of one as old as the faith of Abraham. "And the scripture, foreseeing that God would justify the heathen by faith, preached the gospel beforehand to Abraham" (Gal. 3:8). And Abraham believed God and lived in accordance with the preview of the story of salvation that God granted to him.

The unknown authors of the gospel emphasize the fulfillment of scripture in the life of Jesus Christ. Christ in us fulfills the scripture. "Do you not realize that Jesus Christ is in you?" (2 Cor. 13:5). "I have been crucified with Christ; it is no longer I who live, but Christ who lives in me" (Gal. 2:20). "For if we have been united with him in a death like his, we shall certainly be united with him in a resurrection like his" (Rom. 6:4).

The repetition in us, through his indwelling, has been expressed by Johann Scheffler, a seventeenth-century mystic.

> "Though Christ a thousand times
> In Bethlehem be born, If he's not
> born in thee, Thy soul is still forlorn."
> —Edward Thomas

"And he said to them, "O foolish men, and slow of heart to believe all that the prophets have spoken! Was it not necessary that the Christ should suffer these things and enter into his glory? And beginning with Moses and all the prophets, he interpreted to them in all the scriptures the things concerning himself . . . everything written about me in the law of Moses and the prophets and the psalms must be fulfilled. Then he opened their minds to understand the scriptures." (Luke 24:25, 27, 44-45).

"And they read from the book, from the law of God, with interpretation, and they gave the sense, so that the people understood the reading" (Nehemiah 8:8).

The Old Testament is a prophetic blueprint of the life of Jesus Christ. The gospel of God is the revelation of the future granted to Abraham. "Abraham rejoiced that he was to see my day" (John 8:56). It is about the risen Christ. Participation in the life of the age to come depends on God's act of raising the dead. The resurrection of Jesus Christ is God's victory. That we shall be "united with him in a resurrection like his" is the promise of God's victory for all.

But before the day of victory, man must be refined in the furnace of affliction. "I have tried you in the furnace of affliction. For my own sake, for my own sake, I do it, for how should my name be profaned? My glory I will not give to another" (Isaiah 48:10-11). It takes the furnace of affliction to conform us to the image of his Son, and therefore to the image of the Father, for the Father and the Son are one.

"Then came to him all his brothers and sisters and all who had known him before... and comforted him for all the evil that the Lord had brought upon him... And the Lord blessed the latter days of job more than his beginning" (Job 42:11-12). The story of job is the story of man, the innocent victim of a cruel experiment on the part of God, "And God said, 'Let us make man in our image'" (Gen. 1:26). Yet "I consider that the sufferings of this present time are not worth comparing with the glory that is to be revealed in us" (Rom. 8:18) and that glory is nothing less than the unveiling of God the Father in us, as us.

Nothing can take the place of personal witness to God's plan of salvation. The plan of the mystery is inherent in the creation. What is so prophetically spoken to the world in the Old Testament is realized in one's own personality. All was foretold me but naught could I foresee, but I learned who Jesus Christ really is after the story was re-enacted in me.

The man who has experienced Scripture cannot escape the responsibility of telling its meaning to his fellow men. The unknown writers of the gospel of God were not describing situations and events of the past as historians. Their story of

Jesus Christ is their own experience of God's plan of redemption as men who themselves had experienced redemption. They related their own experiences. They are witnesses of the first order testifying to the truth of God's Word, not hesitating to interpret the Old Testament according to their own supernatural experiences.

Having experienced the story of salvation I can add my testimony to theirs and say that all is done as they have told it. Their experiences, thus attested, confront men with the responsibility of accepting or rejecting their interpretation of the Old Testament. Their testimony should be heard and responded to. One must experience Scripture for himself before he can begin to understand how wonderful it is. They give no account of the personal appearance of Jesus, because when the story of salvation is recreated in man, man will know that "I am He." "He who is united to the Lord becomes one spirit with him" (1 Cor. 6:17).

* * *

"Being in the form of God, . . . he emptied himself, taking the form of a slave, being born in the likeness of men. And being found in human form he humbled himself and became obedient unto death, even death on the cross" (Phil. 2:6-8) of man. He abdicated his divine form and assumed the form of a slave. He did not merely disguise himself as a slave but became one, subject to all human weaknesses and limitations. God who entered death's door, the human skull, Golgotha, is now the world's Savior. "God is our salvation.

Our God is a God of salvation; and to God, the Lord, belongs escape from death" (Ps. 68:19-20). "Unless I die

264

thou canst not live; But if I die I shall arise again and thou with me. "The grain of wheat sets out the mystery of life through death. "Unless a grain of wheat falls into the earth and dies, it remains alone; but if it dies, it bears much fruit" (John 12:24). This is the secret of God's plan of salvation. God achieves his purpose by self-limitation, by contraction in order to expand. God himself enters Death's Door, my skull, and lays down in the Grave with me. And with apologies to William Blake

> "What'er is done to me I cannot know, And if you'll ask me I will swear it so. Whether 'tis good or evil none's to blame: Only God can take the pride, only God the shame."

"And I am sure that he who began a good work in me will bring it to completion at the day of Jesus Christ" (Phil. 1:6). When the image of the unbegotten is formed in me, then He who was so long tightly furled within me, unwinds Himself, and I am He. "No one has ascended into Heaven but he who descended from heaven, the Son of Man" (John 3:13). God himself voluntarily descended into his grave Golgotha, my skull. "I lay down my life, that I may take it again. No one takes it from me, but I lay it down of my own accord" (John 10:17-18). "For your maker is your husband, the Lord of hosts is his name" (Isa. 54:5). And, "He cleaves to his wife and they become one flesh" (Gen. 2:24). For, "He who is united to the Lord becomes one Spirit with him" (I Cor. 6:17). "What therefore God has joined together, let not man put asunder" (Mark 10:9). Man is God's emanation, yet his wife till the sleep of death is past. "Rouse thyself! Why sleepest thou O Lord? Awake!" (Ps. 44:23). When he awakes, "I am He." God laid Himself down within me to sleep, and as He slept He dreamed a dream; he dreamed that He is I and when He awakes He is I. But how do I know that I am He? Through the revelation of His Son David who in the Spirit calls me Father.

* * *

"I am the way, and the truth, and the life; no one comes to the Father, but by me . . . He who has seen me has seen the Father" (John 14:6, 9). Union with the risen Christ is the only way to the Father. Because, "Christ and the Father are one" (John 10:30). The way leads through death to life eternal.

Man's search for Christ as the authority which he can trust, which he can respect, to which he can submit is his longing for the Father that lives in him, for that same Father whom the Christ of the Gospel claims to be. The Christ of the Gospel is the Eternal Father in man. This longing for the Father is the cry of man that ends the New Testament. "Come, Lord Jesus!" (Rev. 22:20). "Do you not realize that Jesus Christ is in you?" (2 Cor. 13:5). "And in him the whole fullness of deity dwells bodily?" (Col. 2:9), not figuratively, but genuinely in a body. This is "the mystery hidden for ages and generations which is Christ in you, the hope of glory" (Col. 1:26, 27).

Imperfect knowledge of Jesus has blinded man to the true nature of the Father. The Lord Jesus is God the Father who became man that man might become the Lord Jesus, the Father. Historian's researches cannot yield knowledge of who the Father is. "No one can say 'Jesus is Lord' except by the

Holy Spirit" (I Cor. 12:3). Man's goal is to find the Father, but God the Father is made known only through his Son. "No one knows the Son except the Father, and no one knows the Father except the Son and any one to whom the Son chooses to reveal him." (Matt. 11:27). Only the Father and the Son know each other. "Call no man your Father on earth, for you have one Father, who is in Heaven" (Matt. 23:9) and Heaven is "within you" (Luke 17:21).

And David said: "I will tell of the decree of the Lord; He said to me, 'You are my son, today I have begotten you'" (Ps. 2:7). David's divine sonship is unique, the only one of its kind and wholly supernatural. He was "born, not of blood nor of the will of the flesh nor of the will of man, but of God" (John 1:13).

The Father will be found by man only in a first person singular, present tense experience when David in the Spirit calls him Father, that is, my Lord. Jesus asked them a question, saying, "What do you think of the Christ? Whose son is he?" They said to him, "The son of David." He said to them, "How is it then that David, in the Spirit, calls him Lord . . . If David thus calls him Lord, how is he his son?" (Matt. 22:41-45).

In Hebrew thought, history consists of all the generations of men and their experiences fused into one great whole and this concentrated time, into which all the generations are fused, and from which they spring, is called "Eternity." Scripture states that: "God has put eternity into man's mind, yet so that man cannot find out what God has done from the beginning to the end" (Ecc. 3:11). The Hebrew word for "eternity" means also "youth, stripling, young man."

Saul saw David and said to Abner "Whose son is this *youth* . . . Inquire whose son the *stripling* is?" Then turning to David he said: "Whose son are you, young *man*?" And David answered "I am the son of your servant Jesse the Bethemite" (I Sam.

267

17:55-58). Whose son....? Note in all the passages (I Sam. 17:55, 56, 58: Matt. 22:42), the inquiry is not about the Son, but about his Father. The Father made known by David is the eternally true Father.

It is in us as persons that God the Father is revealed. David said "I am the son of Jesse." Jesse is any form of the verb to be. David's answer was "I am the son of Him" whose name is "I AM." "I am the son of the Lord."

One of the names for God is the name He gave to Moses. "Say to the people of Israel 'I AM has sent me to you'" (Exod. 3:14). He is the Eternal "I AM." God's first revelation of Himself is as "God Almighty" (Exod. 6:3). His second self-revelation is as "The Eternal I AM" (Exod. 3:14). His final revelation of Himself is as "the Father" (John 17). Only the Son can reveal God as Father. "No one (i.e. no human eye) has ever seen God; the only begotten Son, who is in the bosom of the Father, he has made him known" (John 1:18).

It is God Himself, the Eternal I AM, and His only begotten Son, the eternal youth David, who entered man's mind. At the end of his journey through the fires of affliction in this Age of Eternal death, man will find David and exclaim "I have found David... He shall cry to me, Thou art my Father, my God, and the Rock of my salvation" (Ps. 89: 20, 26).

I do not reveal myself to myself directly as God or as Jesus Christ, but by implication parallel with Scripture, when David in the Spirit calls me Father. And this wisdom from within is without uncertainty.

"When it pleased God to reveal his Son in me, I did not confer with flesh and blood" (Gal. 1:15-16). The man in whom the Son of God appears finds it difficult to convince others of the reality of the revelation, because these supernatural experiences of Scripture take place in a realm of action too remote from our common experience. The whole drama belongs to a world far more real and vital than that which the intellect inhabits for the historic imagination to understand it.

> "Oh could I tell ye surely would believe it! Oh could I only say what I have seen! How should 1 tell or how can ye receive it, How, till he bringeth you where I have been?"
>
> —F. W. H. Myers

This entrance into the Father-Son relationship is truly by the Grace of God. "For God so loved the world that he gave his only Son" (John 3:16). It was the eternal plan of God to give Himself to man. And it is the Son, calling him Father, who makes him sure that he really is the Father.

When David in the Spirit calls Him Father, he does not lose his distinctive individuality or cease to be the self he was before, but that self now includes a far greater self, which is none other than Jesus Christ whom David in the Spirit called "Lord" Man is heir to a Promise and to a Presence! "Abraham having patiently endured, obtained the promise." (Heb. 6:15). Grace is the final expression of God's love in action which man will experience when the Son is revealed in him, and who in turn reveals man as the Father.

The authority which underlies the story of Jesus Christ is a two-fold witness; the inward testimony of the Father, and the external testimony of Scripture. God Himself came, and comes, into human history in the person of the incarnate Jesus within us. This will be confirmed by the "signs," which will be experienced by man as foretold in Scripture.

"The Father who dwells in me does his works. Believe me that I am in the Father and the Father in me; or else believe me for the sake of the works themselves. Truly, truly, I say to you, he who believes in me will also do the works that I do: and greater works than these will he do, because I go to the Father" (John 14:10-12). "I came from the Father and have come into the world; again, I am leaving the world and going to the Father" (John 16:28). "I and the Father are one" (John 10:30).

The Vision of God is granted to those who have had the revelation of the Father in the life of the incarnate Jesus in them, when the only begotten Son David calls them Father.

Only as the "signs" become our experience is God's purpose-and therefore the Scripture's purpose-fulfilled in us. "Scripture must be fulfilled in me . . . for what is written about me has its fulfillment" (Luke 22:37).

God gave Himself to all of us, to each of us. And it is His only begotten Son David, in the Spirit, calling us Father, who makes us sure that it is really so. "So if the Son makes you free, you will be free indeed" (John 8:36). "And as David returned from the slaughter of the Philistine . . . with the head of the Philistine in his hand. Saul said to him "Whose son are you young man?" (I Sam. 17:57, 58) for he did not know David's father, whom he had promised (I Sam. 17:25) to make free in Israel. The king had promised to make free the father of the man who destroyed the enemy of Israel.

We must not ignore the very personal and supernatural character of God's plan of salvation. The fulfillment of the plan takes place in man; it is inaugurated by the event called "his resurrection from the dead." "We have been born anew . . . through the resurrection of Jesus Christ from the dead" (I Peter 1:3). It is Christ in you—your I AM—who is resurrected. The resurrection marks the beginning of the freeing of Jesus Christ the Father from the body of sin and death, and His return to His divine body of Love, the human form divine. This was the Lord's purpose from the beginning "which he set forth in Christ as a plan for the fullness of time" (Eph. 1:9, 10). "The Lord of hosts has sworn: As I have planned, so shall it be, and as I have purposed, so shall it stand" (Isa. 14.24).

Live and act on the assurance that God has brought his plan to fulfillment and continues to do so. God Himself came, and comes, into human history in the person of Jesus Christ in you, in me, in all. God awoke in the anonymous authors of the gospels, and continues to awake in individual man. Believe their testimony, do not seek new ways of access to a goal already attained.

Perhaps the best description of the unknown writers of the gospel of God is given in the words: "That which... we have heard, which we have seen with our eyes, which we have looked upon, and our hands have handled, of the Word of life . . . That which we have seen and heard declare we unto you" (I John 1:1, 3). Faith is not complete till it has become experience. It is essential that those whose eyes have seen and whose hands have handled the Word of life, be sent and be conscious of themselves as sent, to declare it to the world.

It is the resurrected Christ, the twice-born man, who says: "Take my yoke upon you, and learn from me... and you will find rest for your souls" (Matt. 11:29). He offers his knowledge of Scripture based on his own experience, for that of others based on speculation. Accept his offer. And it will keep you from losing your way among the tangled speculations that pass for religious truth. And show you the only way to the Father.

The man who is sent to preach the gospel of God is first called, and taken in Spirit into the divine assembly where the gods hold judgment. "God has taken his place in the divine council; in the midst of the gods he holds judgment" (Ps. 82:1).

The Hebrew word Elokim is plural, a compound unity, one made up of others. In this sentence it is translated as God and gods. The man who is called is brought before the Elokim, the risen Christ. He is asked to name the greatest thing in the world; he answers in the words of Paul, "faith, hope, arid love, these three; but the greatest of these is love" (I Cor. 13:13). At that moment God embraces him, and they fuse and become One. For "he who is united to the Lord becomes one spirit with him" (I Cor. 6:17). "So they are no longer two but one. What therefore God has joined together, let no man put asunder" (Matt. 19:6). Men are called one by one to unite into a single Man, who is God. "The Lord will thresh out the grain, and you will be gathered one by one, O people of Israel" (Isa. 27:12). This union with the risen Christ is baptism with the Holy Spirit. From his baptism with the Holy Spirit to his resurrection, fall the "days of the Messiah," a period of thirty years. During this period, he is so overwhelmingly in love with his mission, as messenger and preacher of the Gospel of God, a gospel which has laid such constraint upon him that he can do no other, feels that "if I preach the gospel, that gives me no ground for boasting. For necessity is laid upon me. Woe to me if I do not preach the gospel!" (I Cor. 9:16). A divine compulsion drives him as it had Jeremiah, who said; "If I say, 'I will not mention him, or speak any more in his name,' there is in my heart as it were a burning fire shut up in my bones, and I am weary with holding it in, and I cannot'" (Jer. 20:9).

The end of this thirty year period arrives with such dramatic suddenness that he has no time to observe its coming. "Jesus, when he began his ministry, was about thirty years of age" (Luke 3:23). Now the story of Jesus Christ unfolds in him in a series of the most personal, first person singular, present tense experiences. The entire series of events takes three and a half years. It begins with his resurrection and birth from above.

> "The dead heard the voice of the child And began to awake from sleep: All things heard the voice of the child And began to awake to life."
> —William Blake

While sleeping on his bed and dreaming of the redeemed society of a city "full of boys and girls playing in the streets thereof" (Zech. 8:5), an intense vibration centered at the base of his skull awakens him, "Awake, O sleeper, and arise from the dead, and Christ shall give you light" (Eph. 5:14). As he wakes, he finds that he is not in the room where he fell asleep, but in his own skull (Golgotha). His skull is a completely sealed tomb. He does not know how he got there, but his one consuming desire is to get out. He pushes the base of his skull, and something rolls away leaving a small opening. He pushes his head through the opening and squeezes himself out inch by inch in the same manner that a child is born from his mother's womb. He looks at his body out of which he has just emerged. It is pale of face lying on its back and tossing its head from side to side like one in recovery from a great ordeal. "You will be sorrowful, but your sorrow will turn into joy. When a woman is in travail she has sorrow, because her hour has come; but when she is delivered of the child, she no longer remembers the anguish, for joy that a child is born into the world" (John 16:20, 21).

"For there the Babe is born in joy
That was begotten in dire woe;
Just as we Reap in joy the fruit
Which we in bitter tears did sow."
—William Blake

"You must be born from above" (John 3:7). "The Jerusalem above is free, and she is our mother" (Gal. 4:26). The skull that was his tomb became the womb from which he is born anew. The vibration within his skull which roused him from sleep, appears now to be coming from without, it sounds like a great wind. He turns his head in the direction where the wind appears to be. Looking back to where his body was, he is surprised to find that it is gone but in its place sit three men.

This experience that faces him will be the fulfillment of the promise made to Abraham. "And the Lord appeared to him . . . He lifted up his eyes and looked, and behold, three men stood in front of him . . . They said to him, "Where is Sarah your wife?" And he said, "She is in the tent." He said, "I will surely return to you according to the time of life; and Sarah your wife shall have a son . . . Abraham called the name of his son who was born to him . . . Isaac" (he laughs), (Gen. 18:1, 2, 9, 10, 21:3). The three men suddenly appeared, they had not been seen approaching. Abraham does not at once realize the significance of this. They are ordinary men who have chanced to come his way. They too are disturbed by the wind. The youngest of the three is the most disturbed and goes over to investigate the source of the disturbance. His attention is attracted by a babe wrapped in swaddling cloths lying on the floor. He takes the babe in his arms and proclaiming it to be the resurrected man's babe, lays it on the bed. The man then lifts the babe in his arms and says: "How is my sweetheart?" The child smiles and the first act comes to an end.

"And in that region there were shepherds out in the field . . . And an angel of the Lord appeared to them . . . And the angel said to them, "Be not afraid; for behold, I bring you good news of a great joy which will come to all the people; for to you is born this day in the city of David a Savior, who is Christ the Lord. And this will be a sign for you: you will find a babe wrapped in swaddling cloths and lying in a manger" (Luke 2:8-12). God is born, for God is called Savior (Isa. 43:3, 45:15, Luke 1:47).

After the revelation, man searches the ancient scriptures for intimations and foreshadowings of his supernatural experience, and finding them there, knows that:

> "All was foretold me: naught
> Could I foresee: But I learned
> how the wind would sound
> After these things should be."
> —Edward Thomas

The unpredictable nature of the wind's course illustrates the spontaneity of the divine birth all the more easily since both in Greek and in Hebrew the word is used both for wind and spirit.

The plan of the Lord is described in the ancient scripture, but it cannot really be known until after it has been experienced by the individual. God has spoken, and what He has foretold is written there for all to understand. But His prophecy appears in a quite different light in prospect from what it is seen to be in retrospect.

Everyone will know that Jesus Christ is the Father in the light of his own experience of the Christian Mystery.

"In these last days he has spoken to us by His Son" (Heb. 1:2). Five months after man is resurrected and born from above, a vibration similar to that which began the first act starts in his head. This time it is centered at the top of his head. It increases in intensity until it explodes. After the explosion he finds himself seated in a modestly furnished room. Leaning against the side of an open door, and looking out on a pastoral scene, is his son David of Biblical fame. He is a youth in his early teens. David addresses him as "My Father." The resurrected man knows that he is David's Father, and David knows that he is his Son. Two men look at David lustfully and the Father reminds them of his Son's victory over the giant Philistine. And while he is sitting there and contemplating the unearthly beauty of his Son, the second act comes to its end. God the Father gave Himself to man that man might become God the Father. "I will tell of the decree of the Lord: He said to me, "You are my son, today I have begotten you" (Ps. 2:7).

The third act unfolds four months after the Father-Son relationship has been revealed. It is dramatic from beginning to end. A bolt of lightning splits the body of the resurrected man from the top of his skull to the base of his spine. Now the new and living way is opened for him through the curtain, that is, through his body. Revelation is always in personal terms, and the human agents of God's revelation are never suppressed to the level of the impersonal. "Consequently, when he came into the world, he said, "Sacrifices and offerings thou has not desired, but a body hast thou prepared for me; in burnt offerings and sin offerings thou hast taken no pleasure. Then I said 'Lo, I have come to do thy will, O God, as it is

276

written of me in the roll of the book'" (Heb. 10:5-7. Ps. 40:6-8 is quoted). God's will is done. God must save and God alone. At the base of his spine, he sees a pool of golden liquid light and knows that it is himself. He now has "confidence to enter the sanctuary by the blood of Jesus, by the new and living way which he opened for us through the curtain, that is, through his flesh" (Heb. 10:19, 20). As he contemplates the pool of golden liquid light, the blood of God, the living water, he fuses with it, and knows that it is himself, his divine Creator and Redeemer. Now like a bolt of spiral lightning, he ascends his spine entering the heavenly sanctuary of his skull violently. His head reverberates like thunder. "And as Moses lifted up the serpent in the wilderness, so must the Son of man be lifted up" (John 3:14). "From the days of John the Baptist until now the kingdom of heaven has been coming violently, and men of violence take it by force" (Matt. 11:12). To such men the new age has come.

Two years and nine months later, fulfilling the three and a half years of the ministry of Jesus, the fourth and final act of the drama of salvation comes to its climax. "And the Holy Spirit descended upon him in bodily form, as a dove, and a voice came from heaven, "Thou art my beloved Son; with thee I am well pleased" (Luke 3:22).

The head of the resurrected one suddenly becomes translucent. Hovering above him, as though floating, a dove with its eyes focused lovingly upon him, descends upon his outstretched hand, he draws her to his face, and the dove smothers him with love, kissing his face, his head and his neck. A woman, daughter of the voice of God says to him: "He loves you" and the drama of salvation comes to its end in him. He is now a son of God, a son of the resurrection. He "cannot die any more, because he is a son of God, being a son of the resurrection" (Luke 20:36). "I and the Father are one" (John 10:30). "I am the root and the offspring of David" (Rev. 22:16). He is the Father of humanity and its offspring. By becoming man, the limit of contraction and opacity, he breaks the shell, and expanding into translucence achieves his purpose. He has "found him of whom Moses in the law and also the prophets wrote" (John 1:45).

The anonymous authors of the gospel of God are twice-born men, sons of God, sons of the resurrection, who can die no more, having escaped from the body of sin and death. The gospel is the story of God's plan of salvation.

It will be helpful to all readers of the Word of God, to end this confession of faith with a quote from William Blake.

"It ought to be understood that the Persons, Moses and Abraham, are not here meant, but the States Signified by those Names, the Individuals being representatives or Visions of those States as they were reveal'd to Mortal Man in the Series of Divine Revelations as they are written in the Bible: these various States I have seen in my Imagination; when distant they appear as One Man, but as you approach they appear Multitudes of Nations."

There is no secular history in the Bible. The Bible is the history of salvation and is wholly supernatural.

SEEDTIME AND HARVEST

CHAPTER 41

THE END OF A GOLDEN STRING

"I Give you the end of a golden string; Only wind it into a ball, It will lead you in at Heaven's gate, Built in Jerusalem's wall."

—Blake

IN THE following essays I have tried to indicate certain ways of approach to the understanding of the Bible and the realization of your dreams.

"That ye be not slothful, but followers of them who through faith and patience inherit the promises."

—Hebrews 6:12

Many who enjoy the old familiar verses of Scripture are discouraged when they themselves try to read the Bible as they would any other book because, quite excusably, they do not understand that the Bible is written in the language of symbolism. Not knowing that all of its characters are personifications of the laws and functions of Mind; that the Bible is psychology rather than history, they puzzle their brains over it for awhile and then give up. It is all too mystifying. To understand the significance of its imagery, the reader of the Bible must be imaginatively awake.

According to the Scriptures, we sleep with Adam and wake with Christ. That is, we sleep collectively and wake individually.

"And the Lord God caused a deep sleep to fall upon Adam, and he slept."
—Genesis 2:21

If Adam, or generic man, is in a deep sleep, then his experiences as recorded in the Scriptures must be a dream. Only he who is awake can tell his dream, and only he who understands the symbolism of dreams can interpret the dream.

"And they said one to and all, Did not our heart burn within us, while He talked with us by the way, and while He opened to us the Scriptures?"
—Luke 24:32

The Bible is a revelation of the laws and functions of Mind expressed in the language of that twilight realm into which we go when we sleep. Because the symbolical language of this twilight realm is much the same for all men, the recent explorers of this realm—human imagination—call it the "collective unconscious."

The purpose of this book, however, is not to give you a complete definition of Biblical symbols or exhaustive interpretations of its stories. All I hope to have done is to have indicated the way in which you are most likely to succeed in realizing your desires. "What things soever ye desire" can be obtained only through the conscious, voluntary exercise of imagination in direct obedience to the laws of Mind. Somewhere within this realm of imagination there is a mood, a feeling of the wish fulfilled which, if appropriated, means success to you. This realm, this Eden—your imagination —is vaster than you know and repays exploration. "I Give you the end of a golden string;" You must wind it into a ball.

CHAPTER 42

THE FOUR
MIGHTY ONES

*"And a river went out of Eden to water the garden;
and from thence it was parted, and became into
four heads."*

—Genesis 2:10

"And every one had four faces: . . ."

—Ezekiel 10:14

*"I see four men loose, walking in the midst of the
fire, and they have no hurt; and the form of the
fourth is like the Son of God."*

—Daniel 3:25

"Four Mighty Ones are in every Man."

—Blake

The "Four Mighty Ones" constitute the selfhood of man, or God in man. There are "Four Mighty Ones" in every man, but these "Four Mighty Ones" are not four separate beings, separated one from the other as are the fingers of his hand. The "Four Mighty Ones" are four different aspects of his mind, and differ from one another in function and character without being four separate selves inhabiting one man's body.

The "Four Mighty Ones" may be equated with the four Hebrew characters: יהוה, which form the four-lettered mystery-name of the Creative Power, derived from and combining within itself the past, present and future forms of the verb "to be." The Tetragrammaton is revered as the symbol of the Creative Power in man - I AM - the creative four functions in man reaching forth to realize in actual material phenomena qualities latent in Itself.

We can best understand the "Four Mighty Ones" by comparing them to the four most important characters in the production of a play.

> "All the world's a stage,
> And all the men and women
> merely players;
> They have their exits and
> their entrances;
> And one man in his time plays
> many parts . . ."
> —As You Like It: Act II, Scene VII.

The producer, the author, the director and the actor are the four most important characters in the production of a play. In the drama of life, the producer's function is to suggest the theme of a play. This he does in the form of a wish, such as, "I wish I were successful"; "I wish I could take a trip"; "I wish I were married", and so on. But to appear on the world's stage, these general themes must somehow be specified and worked out in detail. It is not enough to say, "I wish I were successful" that is too vague. Successful at what? However, the first "Mighty One" only suggests a theme.

The dramatization of the theme is left to the originality of the second "Mighty One", the author. In dramatizing the theme, the author writes only the last scene of the play-but this scene he writes in detail. The scene must dramatize the wish fulfilled. He mentally constructs as life-like a scene as possible of what he would experience had he realized his wish. When the scene is clearly visualized, the author's work is done.

The third "Mighty One" in the production of life's play is the director. The director's tasks are to see that the actor remains faithful to the script and to rehearse him over and over again until he is natural in the part. This function may be likened to a controlled and consciously directed attention -an attention focused exclusively on the action which implies that the wish is already realized.

"The form of the Fourth is like the Son of God"— human imagination, the actor. This fourth "Mighty One" performs within himself, in imagination, the predetermined action which implies the fulfillment of the wish. This function does not visualize or observe the action. This function actually enacts the drama, and does it over and over again until it takes on the tones of reality. Without the dramatized vision of fulfilled desire, the theme remains a mere theme and sleeps forever in the vast chambers of unborn themes. Nor without the co-operant attention, obedient to the dramatized vision of fulfilled desire, will the vision perceived attain objective reality.

These "Four Mighty Ones" are the four quarters of the human soul. The first is Jehovah's King, who suggests the theme; the second is Jehovah's servant, who faithfully works out the theme in a dramatic vision; the third is Jehovah's man, who was attentive and obedient to the vision of fulfilled desire, who brings the wandering imagination back to the script "seventy times seven". The "Form of the Fourth" is

Jehovah himself, who enacts the dramatized theme on the stage of the mind.

> "Let this mind be in you, which was also in Christ Jesus: Who, being in the form of God, thought it not robbery to be equal with God:. . ."
>
> —Philippians 2:5, 6

The drama of life is a joint effort of the four quarters of the human soul.

> "All that you behold, tho' it appears without, it is within, in your imagination, of which this world of mortality is but a shadow."
>
> —Blake

All that we behold is a visual construction contrived to express a theme - a theme which has been dramatized, rehearsed and performed elsewhere. What we are witnessing on the stage of the world is an optical construction devised to express the themes which have been dramatized, rehearsed and performed in the imaginations of men.

These "Four Mighty Ones" constitute the Selfhood of man, or God in man; and all that man beholds, tho' it appears without, are but shadows cast upon the screen of space - optical constructions contrived by Selfhood to inform him in regard to the themes which he has conceived, dramatized, rehearsed and performed within himself.

"The creature was made subject unto vanity" that he may become conscious of Selfhood and its functions, for with consciousness of Selfhood and its functions, he can act to a purpose; he can have a consciously self-determined history. Without such consciousness, he acts unconsciously, and cries to an objective God to save him from his own creation.

> "O Lord, how long shall I cry, and Thou wilt not hear! even cry out unto Thee of violence, and Thou wilt not save!"
>
> —Habakkuk 1:2

When man discovers that life is a play which he, himself, is consciously or unconsciously writing, he will cease from the blind, self-torture of executing judgment upon others. Instead, he will rewrite the play to conform to his ideal, for he will realize that all changes in the play must come from the cooperation of the "Four Mighty Ones" within himself. They alone can alter the script and produce the change.

All the men and women in his world are merely players and are as helpless to change his play as are the players on the screen of the theatre to change the picture. The desired change must be conceived, dramatized, rehearsed and performed in the theatre of his mind. When the fourth function, the imagination, has completed its task of rehearsing the revised version of the play until it is natural, then the curtain will rise upon this so seemingly solid world and the "Mighty Four" will cast a shadow of the real play upon the screen of space. Men and women will automatically play their parts to bring about the fulfillment of the dramatized theme. The players, by reason of their various parts in the world's drama, become relevant to the individual's dramatized theme and, because relevant, are drawn into his drama. They will play their parts, faithfully believing all the while that it was they themselves who initiated the parts they play. This they do because:

> "Thou, Father, art in me, and I in thee, . . . I in them, and thou in me."
>
> —John 17:21, 23

I am involved in mankind. We are one. We are all playing the four parts of producer, author, director and actor in the drama of life. Some of us are doing it consciously, others unconsciously. It is necessary that we do it consciously. Only in this way can we be certain of a perfect ending to our play. Then we shall understand why we must become conscious of the four functions of the one God within ourselves that we may have the companionship of God as His Sons.

> "Man should not stay a man: His aim should higher be. For God will only gods Accept as company."
>
> —Angelus Silesius

In January of 1946, I took my wife and little daughter to Barbados in the British West Indies for a holiday. Not knowing there were any difficulties in getting a return passage, I had not booked ours before leaving New York. Upon our arrival in Barbados, I discovered that there were only two ships serving the islands, one from Boston and one from New York. I was told there was no available space on either ship before

September. As I had commitments in New York for the first week in May, I put my name on the long waiting list for the April sailing.

A few days later, the ship from New York was anchored in the harbor. I observed it very carefully, and decided that this was the ship we should take. I returned to my hotel and determined on an inner action that would be mine were we actually sailing on that ship. I settled down in an easy chair in my bedroom, to lose myself in this imaginative action.

In Barbados, we take a motor launch or rowboat out into the deep harbor when we embark on a large steamer. I knew I must catch the feeling that we were sailing on that ship. I chose the inner action of stepping from the tender and climbing up the gangplank of the steamer. The first time I tried it, my attention wandered after I had reached the top of the gangplank. I brought myself back down, and tried again and again. I do not recall how many times I carried out this action in my imagination until I reached the deck and looked back at the port with the feeling of sweet sadness at departing. I was happy to be returning to my home in New York, but nostalgic in saying goodbye to the lovely island and our family and friends. I do recall that in one of my many attempts at walking up the gangplank in the feeling that I was sailing, I fell asleep. After I awoke, I went about the usual social activities of the day and evening.

The following morning, I received a call from the steamship company requesting me to come down to their office and pick up our tickets for the April sailing. I was curious to know why Barbados had been chosen to receive the cancellation and why I, at the end of the long waiting list, was to have the reservation, but all that the agent could tell me was that a cable had been received that morning from New York, offering passage for three. I was not the first the agent had called, but for reasons she could not explain, those she had called said that now they found it inconvenient to sail in April. We sailed on April 20th and arrived in New York on the morning of May the first.

In the production of my play—sailing on a boat that would bring me to New York by the first of May—I played the four most important characters in my drama. As the producer, I decided to sail on a specific ship at a certain time. Playing the part of the author, I wrote the script—I visualized the inner action which conformed to the outer action I would take if my desire were realized. As the director, I rehearsed myself, the actor, in that imagined action of climbing the gangplank until that action felt completely natural.

This being done, events and people moved swiftly to conform, in the outer world, to the play I had constructed and enacted in my imagination.

> "I saw the mystic vision flow
> And live in men and woods and
> streams, Until I could no longer
> know The stream of life from my
> own dreams."
> —George William Russell (AE)

I told this story to an audience of mine in San Francisco, and a lady in the audience told me how she had unconsciously used the same technique, when she was a young girl.

The incident occurred on Christmas Eve. She was feeling very sad and tired and sorry for herself. Her father, whom she adored, had died suddenly. Not only did she feel this loss at the Christmas season, but necessity had forced her to give up her planned college years and go to work. This rainy Christmas Eve she was riding home on a San Diego street car. The car was filled with gay chatter of happy young people home for the holidays. To hide her tears from those around about her, she stood on the open part at the front of the car and turned her face into the skies to mingle her tears with the rain. With her eyes closed, and holding the rail of the car firmly, this is what she said to herself: "This is not the salt of tears that I taste, but the salt of the sea in the wind. This is not San Diego, this is the South Pacific and I am sailing into the Bay of Samoa". And looking up, in her imagination, she constructed what she imagined to be the Southern Cross. She lost herself in this contemplation so that all faded round about her. Suddenly she was at the end of the line, and home.

Two weeks later, she received word from a lawyer in Chicago that he was holding three thousand dollars in American bonds for her. Several years before, an aunt of hers had gone to Europe, with instructions that these bonds be turned over to her niece if she did not return to the United States. The lawyer had just received word of the aunt's death, and was now carrying out her instructions.

A month later, this girl sailed for the islands in the South Pacific. It was night when she entered the Bay of Samoa. Looking down, she could see the white foam like a "bone in the lady's mouth" as the ship ploughed through the waves, and brought the salt of the sea in the wind. An officer on duty said to her: "There is the Southern Cross", and looking up, she saw the Southern Cross as she had imagined it.

In the intervening years, she had many opportunities to use her imagination constructively, but as she had done this unconsciously, she did not realize there was a Law behind it all. Now that she understands, she, too, is consciously playing her four major roles in the daily drama of her life, producing plays for the good of others as well as herself.

"Then the soldiers, when they had crucified Jesus, took his garments, and made four parts, to every soldier a part; and also his coat: now the coat was without seam, woven from the top throughout."

—John 19:23

CHAPTER 43

THE GIFT OF FAITH

"I Give you the end of a golden string; Only wind it into a ball, It will lead you in at Heaven's gate, Built in Jerusalem's wall."

—Blake

"And the Lord had respect unto Abel and to his offerings: But unto Cain and to his offering he had not respect."

—Genesis 4:4, 5

If we search the Scriptures, we will become aware of a far deeper meaning in the above quotation than that which a literal reading would give us. The Lord is none other than your own consciousness. ". . . say unto the children of Israel, I AM hath sent me unto you. . ." Exodus 3:14. "I AM" is the self-definition of the Lord.

Cain and Abel, as the grandchildren of the Lord, can be only personifications of two distinct functions of your own consciousness. The author is really concerned to show the "Two Contrary States of the Human Soul," and he has used two brothers to show these states. The two brothers represent two distinct outlooks on the world, possessed by everyone. One is the limited perception of the senses, and the other is an imaginative view of the world. Cain—the first view—is a passive surrender to appearances and an acceptance of life on the basis of the world without: a view which inevitably leads to unsatisfied longing or to contentment with disillusion.

Abel —the second view—is a vision of fulfilled desire, lifting man above the evidence of the senses to that state of relief where he no longer pines with desire. Ignorance of the second view is a soul on fire. Knowledge of the second view is the wing whereby it flies to the Heaven of fulfilled desire.

> ## "Come, eat my bread and drink of the wine that I have mingled, forsake the foolish and live."
>
> —Proverbs 9:56

In the epistle to the Hebrews, the writer tells us that Abel's offering was faith and, states the author, "Without faith it is impossible to please Him"—Hebrews 11:6.

> ## "Now faith is the substance of things hoped for, the evidence of things not seen. . . Through faith we understand that the worlds were framed by the word of God, so that things which are seen were not made of things which do appear."
>
> —Hebrews 11:1,3

Cain offers the evidence of the senses which consciousness, the Lord, rejects, because acceptance of this gift as a mold of the future would mean the fixation and perpetuation of the present state forever. The sick would be sick, the poor would be poor, the thief would be a thief, the murderer a murderer, and so on, without hope of redemption.

The Lord, or consciousness, has no respect for such passive use of imagination—which is the gift of Cain. He delights in the gift of Abel, the active, voluntary, loving exercise of the imagination on behalf of man for himself and others.

"Let the weak man say, I am strong."
—Joel 3:10

Let man disregard appearances and declare himself to be the man he wants to be. Let him imagine beauty where his senses reveal ashes, joy where they testify to mourning, riches where they bear witness to poverty. Only by such active, voluntary use of imagination can man be lifted up and Eden restored.

The ideal is always waiting to be incarnated, but unless we ourselves offer the ideal to the Lord, our consciousness, by assuming that we are already that which we seek to embody, it is incapable of birth. The Lord needs his daily lamb of faith to mold the world in harmony with our dreams.

"By faith Abel offered unto God a more excellent sacrifice than Cain . . ."
—Hebrews 11:4

Faith sacrifices the apparent fact for the unapparent truth. Faith holds fast to the fundamental truth that through the medium of an assumption, invisible states become visible facts.

"For what is faith unless it is to believe what you do not see?"
—St. Augustine

The Gift of Faith

Just recently, I had the opportunity to observe the wonderful results of one who had the faith to believe what she did not see.

A young woman asked me to meet her sister and her three-year-old nephew. He was a fine, healthy lad with clear blue eyes and an exceptionally fine unblemished skin. Then, she told me her story.

At birth, the boy was perfect in every way save for a large, ugly birthmark covering one side of his face. Their doctor advised them that nothing could be done about this type of scar. Visits to many specialists only confirmed his statement. Hearing the verdict, the aunt set herself the task of proving her faith-that an assumption, though denied by the evidence of the senses, if persisted in, will harden into fact.

Every time she thought of the baby, which was often, she saw, in her imagination, an eight-month-old baby with a perfect face-without any trace of a scar. This was not easy, but she knew that in this case, that was the gift of Abel which pleased God. She persisted in her faith-she believed what was not there to be seen. The result was that she visited her sister on the child's eight-month birthday and found him to have a perfect, unblemished skin with no trace of a birthmark ever having been present. "Luck! Coincidence!" shouts Cain. No. Abel knows that these are names given by those who have no faith, to the works of faith.

"We walk by faith, not by sight."
—II. Corinthians 5:7

The Gift of Faith

When reason and the facts of life oppose the idea you desire to realize and you accept the evidence of your senses and the dictates of reason as the truth, you have brought the Lord-your consciousness—the gift of Cain. It is obvious that such offerings do not please Him.

Life on earth is a training ground for image making. If you use only the molds which your senses dictate, there will be no change in your life. You are here to live the more abundant life, so you must use the invisible molds of imagination and make results and accomplishments the crucial test of your power to create. Only as you assume the feeling of the wish fulfilled and continue therein are you offering the gift that pleases.

"When Abel's gift is my attire Then I'll realize my great desire."

The Prophet Malachi complains that man has robbed God:

"But ye say, Wherein have we robbed thee? In tithes and offerings?"
—Malachi 3:8

Facts based upon reason and the evidence of the senses which oppose the idea seeking expression, rob you of the belief in the reality of the invisible state. But "faith is the evidence of things not seen", and through it "God calleth those things which be not as though they were . . ." Romans 4:17. Call the thing not seen; assume the feeling of your wish fulfilled.

The Gift of Faith

". . . that there may be meat in mine house, and prove me now herewith, sayeth the Lord of hosts, if I will not open you the windows of heaven, and pour you out a blessing, that there shall not be room enough to receive it."

—Malachi 3:10

This is the story of a couple living in Sacramento, California, who refused to accept the evidence of their senses, who refused to be robbed, in spite of a seeming loss. The wife had given her husband a very valuable wristwatch. The gift doubled its value because of the sentiment he attached to it. They had a little ritual with the watch. Every night as he removed the watch he gave it to her and she put it away in a special box in the bureau. Every morning she took the watch and gave it to him to put on.

One morning the watch was missing. They both remembered playing their usual parts the night before, therefore the watch was not lost or misplaced, but stolen. Then and there, they determined not to accept the fact that it was really gone. They said to each other, "This is an opportunity to practice what we believe." They decided that, in their imagination, they would enact their customary ritual as though the watch were actually there. In his imagination, every night the husband took off the watch and gave it to his wife, while in her imagination she accepted the watch and carefully put it away. Every morning she removed the watch from its box and gave it to her husband and he, in turn, put it on. This they did faithfully for two weeks.

After their fourteen-day vigil, a man went into the one

and only jewelry store in Sacramento where the watch would be recognized. As he offered a gem for appraisal, the owner of the store noticed the wristwatch he was wearing. Under the pretext of needing a closer examination of the stone, he went into an inner office and called the police. After the police arrested the man, they found in his apartment over ten thousand dollars worth of stolen jewelry. In walking "by faith, not by sight", this couple attained their desire-the watch-and also aided many others in regaining what had seemed to be lost forever.

> "If one advances confidently in the direction of his dream, and endeavors to live the life which he has imagined, he will meet with a success unexpected in common hours."
>
> —Thoreau

CHAPTER 44

THE SCALE OF BEING

"Now after John was arrested, Jesus came into Galilee, preaching the gospel of God, and saying, The time is fulfilled, and the kingdom of God is at hand; repent, and believe in the gospel."

—Mark 1:14-15

Jesus' ministry began after that of John ended in Judea. "Jesus, when he began his ministry, was about thirty years of age"

—Luke 3:23

"And he dreamed, and behold a ladder set up on the earth, and the top of it reached to heaven: and behold the angels of God ascending and descending on it. And, behold, the Lord stood above it . . ."

—Genesis 28:12, 13

In a dream, in a vision of the night, when deep sleep fell upon Jacob, his inner eye was opened and he beheld the world as a series of ascending and descending levels of awareness. It was a revelation of the deepest insight into the mysteries of the world. Jacob saw a vertical scale of ascending and descending values, or states of consciousness. This gave meaning to everything in the outer world, for without such a scale of values there would be no meaning to life.

At every moment of time, man stands upon the eternal scale of meaning. There is no object or event that has ever taken place or is taking place now that is without significance.

The Scale of Being

The significance of an object or event for the individual is a direct index to the level of his consciousness.

You are holding this book, for example. On one level of consciousness, it is an object in space. On a higher level, it is a series of letters on paper, arranged according to certain rules. On a still higher level, it is an expression of meaning.

Looking outwardly, you see the book first, but actually, the meaning comes first. It occupies a higher grade of significance than the letter arrangement on paper or the book as an object in space. Meaning determined the arrangement of letters; the arrangement of letters only expresses the meaning. The meaning is invisible and above the level of the visible arrangement of letters. If there had been no meaning to be expressed, no book would have been written and published.

"And, behold, the Lord stood above it."

The Lord and meaning are one-the Creator, the cause of the phenomena of life.

> "In the beginning was the Word, and the Word was with God, and the Word was God."
>
> —John 1:1

In the beginning was the intention the meaning - and the intention was with the intender, and the intention was the intender. The objects and events in time and space occupy a lower level of significance than the level of meaning which produced them. All things were made by meaning, and without meaning was not anything made that was made. The fact that everything seen can be regarded as the effect, on a lower level of significance, of an unseen higher order of significance is a very important one to grasp.

Our usual mode of procedure is to attempt to explain the higher levels of significance—why things happen-in terms of the lower levels-what and how things happen. For example, let us take an actual accident and try to explain it.

Most of us live on the level of what happened—the accident was an event in space—one automobile struck another and practically demolished it. Some of us live on the higher level of "how" the accident happened-it was a rainy night, the roads were slippery and the second car skidded into the first. On rare occasions, a few of us reach the highest or causal level of "why" such an accident occurs. Then we become aware of the invisible, the state of consciousness which produced the visible event.

In this case, the ruined car was driven by a widow, who, though she felt she could not afford to, greatly desired to change her environment. Having heard that, by the proper use of her imagination, she could do and be all she wished to be, this widow had been imagining herself actually living in the city of her desire. At the same time, she was living in a consciousness of loss, both personal and financial. Therefore, she brought upon herself an event which was seemingly another loss, but the sum of money the insurance company paid her allowed her to make the desired change in her life.

When we see the "why" behind the seeming accident, the state of consciousness that produced the accident, we are led to the conclusion that there is no accident. Everything in life has its invisible meaning.

The man who learns of an accident, the man who knows "how" it happened, and the man who knows "why" it happened, are on three different levels of awareness in regard to that accident. On the ascending scale, each higher level carries us a step in advance towards the truth of the accident.

We should strive constantly to lift ourselves to the higher level of meaning, the meaning that is always invisible and above the physical event. But, remember, the meaning or cause of the phenomena of life can be found only within the consciousness of man.

Man is so engrossed in the visible side of the drama of life —the side of "what" has happened, and "how" it happened that he rarely rises to the invisible side of "why" it happened. He refuses to accept the Prophet's warning that:

"Things which are seen were not made of things that do appear."
—Hebrews 11:3

His descriptions of "what" has happened and "how" it happened are true in terms of his corresponding level of thought, but when he asks "why" it happened, all physical explanations break down and he is forced to seek the "why", or meaning of it, on the invisible and higher level. The mechanical analysis of events deals only with external relationships of things. Such a course will never reach the level which holds the secret of why the events happen. Man must recognize that the lower and visible sides flow from the invisible and higher level of meaning.

Intuition is needed to lift us up to the level of meaning-to the level of why things happen. Let us follow the advice of the Hebrew prophet of old and "lift up our eyes unto the hills" within ourselves, and observe what is taking place there. See what ideas we have accepted as true, what states we have consented to, what dreams, what desires -and, above all, what intentions. It is from these hills that all things come to reveal our stature—our height—on the vertical scale of meaning. If we lift our eyes to "the Thee in Me who works behind the Veil", we will see the meaning of the phenomena of life.

Events appear on the screen of space to express the different levels of consciousness of man. A change in the level of his consciousness automatically results in a change of the phenomena of his life. To attempt to change conditions before he changes the level of consciousness from whence they came, is to struggle in vain. Man redeems the world as he ascends the vertical scale of meaning.

We saw, in the analogy of the book, that as consciousness was lifted up to the level where man could see meaning expressed in the arrangement of its letters, it also included the knowledge that the letters were arranged according to certain rules, and that such arrangements, when printed on paper and bound together, formed a book. What is true of the book is true of every event in the world.

> "They shall not hurt nor destroy in all my holy mountain: for the earth shall be full of the knowledge of the Lord, as the waters cover the sea."
>
> —Isaiah 11:9

Nothing is to be discarded; all is to be redeemed. Our lives, ascending the vertical scale of meaning towards an ever increasing awareness—an awareness of things of higher significance—are the process whereby this redemption is brought to pass. As man arranges letters into words, and words into sentences to express meaning, in like manner, life arranges circumstances, conditions and events to express the unseen meanings or attitudes of men. Nothing is without significance. But man, not knowing the higher level of inner meaning, looks out upon a moving panorama of events and sees no meaning to life. There is always a level of meaning determining events and their essential relationship to our lives.

Here is a story that will enable us to seize the good in things seeming evil; to withhold judgment, and to act aright amid unsolved problems.

Just a few years ago, our country was shocked by a seeming injustice in our midst. The story was told on radio and television, as well as in the newspapers. You may recall the incident. The body of a young American soldier killed in Korea was returned to his home for burial. Just before the service, his wife was asked a routine question: Was her husband a Caucasian? When she replied that he was an Indian, burial was refused. This refusal was in accordance with the laws of that community, but it aroused the entire nation. We felt incensed that anyone who had been killed in the service of his country should be denied burial anywhere in his country. The story reached the attention of the President of the United States, and he offered burial with full military honors in Arlington National Cemetery. After the service, the wife told reporters that her husband had always dreamed of dying a hero, and having a hero's burial service with full military honors.

When, we in America, had to explain why progressive, intelligent people like ourselves, not only enacted but supported such laws in our great land of the free and the brave, we were hard put for an explanation. We, as observers, had seen only "what" happened, and "how" it happened. We failed to see "why" it happened.

That burial had to be refused if that lad was to realize his dream. We tried to explain the drama in terms of the lower level of "how" it happened, which explanation could not satisfy the one who had asked "why" it happened.

The true answer, viewed from the level of higher meaning, would be such a reversal of our common habits of thinking that it would be instantly rejected. The truth is that future states are causative of present facts-the Indian boy dreaming of a hero's death, with full military honors, was like Lady Macbeth transported "beyond this ignorant present", and could "feel now the future in the instant."

"... and by it he being dead yet speaketh."

—Hebrews 11:4

CHAPTER 45

THE GAME OF LIFE

"I can easier teach twenty what were good to be done, than be one of the twenty to follow mine own teaching."

—Shakespeare

With this confession off my mind, I will now teach you how to play the game of life. Life is a game and, like all games, it has its aims and its rules.

In the little games that men concoct, such as cricket, tennis, baseball, football, and so on, the rules may be changed from time to time. After the changes are agreed upon, man must learn the new rules and play the game within the framework of the accepted rules.

However, in the game of life, the rules cannot be changed or broken. Only within the framework of its universal and everlastingly fixed rules can the game of life be played.

The game of life is played on the playing field of the mind. In playing a game, the first thing we ask is, "What is its aim and purpose?" and the second, "What are the rules governing the game?" In the game of life, our chief aim is towards increasing awareness an awareness of things of greater significance; and our second aim is towards achieving our goals, realizing our desires.

As to our desires, the rules reach only so far as to indicate the way in which we should go to realize them, but the desires themselves must be the individual's own concern. The rules governing the game of life are simple, but it takes a lifetime of practice to use them wisely. Here is one of the rules:

The Game of Life

"As he thinketh in his heart, so is he."
—Proverbs 23:7

Thinking is usually believed to be a function entirely untrammeled and free, without any rules to constrain it. But that is not true. Thinking moves by its own processes in a bounded territory, with definite paths and patterns.

"Thinking follows the tracks laid down in one's own inner conversations."

All of us can realize our objectives by the wise use of mind and speech. Most of us are totally unaware of the mental activity which goes on within us. But to play the game of life successfully, we must become aware of our every mental activity, for this activity, in the form of inner conversations, is the cause of the outer phenomena of our life.

" . . . every idle word that man shall speak, they shall give account thereof in the day of judgment. For by thy words thou shalt be justified, and by thy words thou shalt be condemned."
—Matthew 12:36, 37

The law of the Word cannot be broken.

". . . A bone of him shall not be broken."
—John 19:36

The law of the Word never overlooks an inner word nor makes the smallest allowance for our ignorance of its power. It fashions life about us as we, by our inner conversations, fashion life within ourselves. This is done to reveal to us our position on the playing field of life. There is no opponent in the game of life; there is only the goal.

Not long ago, I was discussing this with a successful and philanthropic business man. He told me a thought provoking story about himself.

He said, "You know, Neville, I first learned about goals in life when I was fourteen, and it was on the playing field at school. I was good at track and had had a fine day, but there was one more race to run and I had stiff competition in one other boy. I was determined to beat him. I beat him, it is true, but, while I was keeping my eye on him, a third boy, who was considered no competition at all, won the race.

"That experience taught me a lesson I have used throughout my life. When people ask me about my success, I must say, that I believe it is because I have never made 'making money' my goal: 'My goal is the wise, productive use of money'."

This man's inner conversations are based on the premise that he already has money, his constant inner question: the proper use of it. The inner conversations of the man struggling to "get" money only prove his lack of money. In his ignorance of the power of the word, he is building barriers in the way of the attainment of his goal; he has his eye on the competition rather than on the goal itself.

> "The fault, dear Brutus, is not in our stars, But in ourselves, that we are underlings."
>
> —*Julius Caesar*: Act 1, Scene II

The Game of Life

As "the worlds were framed by the Word of God", so we as "imitators of God as dear children" create the conditions and circumstances of our lives by our all-powerful human inner words. Without practice, the most profound knowledge of the game would produce no desired results. "To him that knoweth to do good-that is, knoweth the rules -and doeth it not, to him it is sin". In other words, he will miss his mark and fail to realize his goal.

In the parable of the Talents, the Master's condemnation of the servant who neglected to use his gift is clear and unmistakable, and having discovered one of the rules of the game of life, we risk failure by ignoring it. The talent not used, like the limb not exercised, slumbers and finally atrophies. We must be "doers of the Word, and not hearers only". Since thinking follows the tracks laid down in one's own inner conversations, not only can we see where we are going on the playing field of life by observing our inner conversations, but also, we can determine where we will go by controlling and directing our inner talking.

What would you think and say and do were you already the one you want to be? Begin to think and say and do this inwardly. You are told that "there is a God in heaven that revealeth secrets," and, you must always remember that heaven is within you; and to make it crystal clear who God is, where He is, and what His secrets are, Daniel continues, "Thy dream, and the visions of thy head are these". They reveal the tracks to which you are tied, and point the direction in which you are going.

This is what one woman did to turn the tracks to which she had been unhappily tied in the direction in which she wanted to go. For two years, she had kept herself estranged from the three people she loved most. She had had a quarrel with her daughter-in-law, who ordered her from her home. For those two years, she had not seen or heard from her son, her daughter-in-law or her grandson, though she had sent her grandson numerous gifts in the meantime. Every time she thought of her family, which was daily, she carried on a mental conversation with her daughter-in-law, blaming her for the quarrel and accusing her of being selfish.

Upon hearing a lecture of mine one night-it was this very lecture on the game of life and how to play it -she suddenly realized she was the cause of the prolonged silence and that she, and she alone, must do something about it. Recognizing that her goal was to have the former loving relationship, she set herself the task of completely changing her inner talking.

That very night, in her imagination, she constructed two loving, tender letters written to her, one from her daughter-in-law and the other from her grandson. In her imagination, she read them over and over again until she fell asleep in the joyful mood of having received the letters. She repeated this imaginary act each night for eight nights. On the morning of the ninth day, she received one envelope containing two letters, one from her daughter-in-law, one from her grandson. They were loving, tender letters inviting her to visit them, almost replicas of those she had constructed mentally. By using her imagination consciously and lovingly, she had turned the tracks to which she was tied, in the direction she wanted to go, towards a happy family reunion.

A change of attitude is a change of position on the playing field of life. The game of life is not being played out there in what is called space and time; the real moves in the game of life take place within, on the playing field of the mind.

"Losing thy soul, thy soul Again to find; Rendering toward that goal Thy separate mind."

—Laurence Housman

CHAPTER 46

"TIME, TIMES, AND A HALF"

*"I can easier teach twenty what were good to be
done, than be one of the twenty to follow mine
own teaching."*

—Shakespeare

*"And one said to the man clothed in linen,
which was upon the waters of the river, How long
shall it be to the end of these wonders?" linen, which
was upon the waters of the river, when he held up
his right hand and his left hand unto heaven, and
swear by him that liveth forever that it shall be for
a time, times, and an half."*

—Daniel 12:6,7

At one of my lectures given in Los Angeles on the subject
of the hidden meaning behind the stories of the Bible, someone asked me to interpret the above quotation from the Book
of Daniel. After I confessed I did not know the meaning of
that particular passage, a lady in the audience said to herself,
"If the mind behaves according to the assumption with which
it starts, then I will find the true answer to that question and
tell it to Neville." And this is what she told me.

"Last night the question was asked: 'What is the meaning
of time, times, and an half as recorded in Daniel 12:7?'
Before going to sleep last night I said to myself, 'Now there is
a simple answer to this question, so I will assume that I know

it and while I am sleeping my greater self will find the answer and reveal it to my lesser self in dream or vision.'

"Around five A.M. I awakened. It was too early to rise, so remaining in bed I quickly fell into that half dreamy state between waking and sleeping, and while in that state a picture came into my mind of an old lady. She was sitting in a rocking chair and rocking back and forth, back and forth. Then a voice which sounded like your voice said to me: 'Do it over and over and over again until it takes on the tones of reality.'

"I jumped out of bed and re-read the Twelfth Chapter of Daniel, and this is the intuitive answer I received. Taking the sixth and seventh verses, for they constituted last night's question, I felt that if the garments with which Biblical characters are clothed correspond to their level of consciousness, as you teach, then linen must represent a very high level of consciousness indeed, for the 'man clothed in linen' was standing 'upon the waters of the river' and if, as you teach, water symbolizes a high level of psychological truth, then the individual who could walk upon it must truly represent an exalted state of consciousness. I therefore felt that what he had to say must indeed be very significant. Now the question asked of him was 'How long shall it be to the end of these wonders?' And his answer was, 'A time, times, and an half.' Remembering my vision of the old lady rocking back and forth, and your voice telling me to 'do it over and over and over again until it takes on the tones of reality', and remembering that this vision and your instruction came to me in response to my assumption that I knew the answer, I intuitively felt that the question asked the 'man clothed in linen' meant how long shall it be until the wonderful dreams that I am dreaming become a reality. And his answer is, 'Do it over and over and over again until it takes on the tones of reality. A time means to perform the imaginary action which implies the fulfillment of the wish. Times mean to repeat the imaginary action over and over again. Half means the moment of falling asleep while performing the imaginary action, for such a moment usually arrives before the pre-determined action is completed and, therefore, can be said to be a half, or part, of a time."

To get such inner understanding of the Scriptures by the simple assumption that she did know the answer, was a wonderful experience for this woman. However, to know the true meaning of time, times, and an half, she must apply her understanding in her daily life. We are never at a loss in an opportunity to test this understanding, either for ourselves or for another.

A number of years ago, a widow living in the same apartment house as we, came to see me about her cat. The cat was her constant companion and dear to her heart. He was, how-ever, eight years old, very ill and in great pain. He had not eaten for days and would not move from under her bed. Two veterinarians had seen the cat and advised the woman that the cat could not be cured, and that he should be put to sleep immediately. I suggested that that night, before retiring, she create in her imagination some action that would indicate the cat was its former healthy self. I advised her to do it over and over again until it took on the tones of reality.

This, she promised to do. However, either from lack of faith in my advice or from lack of faith in her own ability to carry out the imaginary action, she asked her niece to spend the night with her. This request was made so that if the cat were not well by morning, the niece could take it to the vet-erinarian's and she, the owner, would not have to face such a dreaded task herself. That night, she settled herself in an easy chair and began to imagine the cat was romping beside her, scratching at the furniture and doing many things she would not normally have allowed. Each time she found that her mind had wandered from its predetermined task to see a normal, healthy, frisky cat, she brought her attention back to the room and started her imaginary action over again. This she did over and over again until, finally, in a feeling of relief, she dropped off to sleep, still seated in her chair.

At about four o'clock in the morning, she was awakened by the cry of her cat. He was standing by her chair. After attracting her attention, he led her to the kitchen where he begged for food. She fixed him a little warm milk which he quickly drank, and cried for more.

That cat lived comfortably for five more years, when, without pain or illness, he died naturally in his sleep.

"How long shall it be to the end of these wonders?
A time, times, and an half. In a dream in a vision of the night, when deep sleep falleth upon men, in slumberings upon the bed; Then he openeth the ears of men, and sealeth their instructions."

—Job 33:15,16

CHAPTER 47

BE YE WISE AS SERPENTS

". . . be ye therefore wise as serpents, and harmless as doves."
—Matthew 10:16

The serpent's ability to form its skin by ossifying a portion of itself, and its skill in shedding each skin as it outgrew it, caused man to regard this reptile as a symbol of the power of endless growth and self-reproduction. Man is told, therefore, to be "wise as the serpent" and learn how to shed his skin his environment-which is his solidified self; man must learn how to "loose him, and let him go". . . how to "put off the old man" . . . how to die to the old and yet know, like the serpent, that he "shall not surely die".

Man has not learned as yet that all that is outside his physical body is also a part of himself, that his world and all the conditions of his life are but the out-picturing of his state of consciousness. When he knows this truth, he will stop the futile struggle of self-contention and, like the serpent, let the old go and grow a new environment.

> "Man is immortal; therefore he must die endlessly. For life is a creative idea; it can only find itself in changing forms."
> —Tagore

Be Ye Wise as Serpents

In ancient times, serpents were also associated with the guardianship of treasure or wealth. The injunction to be "wise as serpents" is the advice to man to awaken the power of his subtle body—his imagination—that he, like the serpent, may grow and outgrow, die and yet not die, for from such deaths and resurrections alone, shedding the old and putting on the new, shall come fulfillment of his dreams and the finding of his treasures. As "the serpent was more subtle than any beast of the field which the Lord God had made" . . . Genesis 3 :1— even so, imagination is more subtle than any creature of the heavens which the Lord God had created. Imagination is the creature that:

"... was made subject to vanity, not willingly, but by reason of him who hath subjected the same in hope. . .

For we are saved by hope: but hope that is seen is not hope: for what a man seeth, why doth he yet hope for? But if we hope for that we see not, then do we with patience wait for it."

—Romans 8:20, 24, 25

Although the outer, or "natural", man of the senses is interlocked with his environment, the inner, or spiritual, man of imagination is not thus interlocked. If the interlocking were complete, the charge to be "wise as serpents" would be in vain. Were we completely interlocked with our environment, we could not withdraw our attention from the evidence of the senses and feel ourselves into the situation of our fulfilled

319

desire, in hope that that unseen state would solidify as our new environment. But:

> "There is a natural body,
> and there is a spiritual body."
>
> —I. Corinthians 15:44

The spiritual body of imagination is not interlocked with man's environment. The spiritual body can withdraw from the outer man of sense and environment and imagine itself to be what it wants to be. And if it remains faithful to the vision, imagination will build for man a new environment in which to live. This is what is meant by the statement:

> ". . . I go to prepare a place for you.
> And if I go and prepare a place for you,
> I will come again, and receive you unto
> myself; that where I am, *there* ye may
> be also."
>
> —John 14:2,3

The place that is prepared for you need not be a place in space. It can be health, wealth, companionship, anything that you desire in this world. Now, how is the place prepared?

You must first construct as life-like a representation as possible of what you would see and hear and do if you were physically present and physically moving about in that "place". Then, with your physical body immobilized, you must imagine that you are actually in that "place" and are seeing and hearing and doing all that you would see and hear and do if you were there physically. This you must do over and over

Be Ye Wise as Serpents

again until it takes on the tones of reality. When it feels natural, the "place" has been prepared as the new environment for your outer or physical self. Now you may open your physical eyes and return to your former state. The "place" is prepared, and where you have been in imagination, there you shall be in the body also.

How this imagined state is realized physically is not the concern of you, the natural or outer man. The spiritual body, on its return from the imagined state to its former physical state, created an invisible bridge of incident to link the two states. Although the curious feeling that you were actually there and that the state was real is gone, as soon as you open your eyes upon the old familiar environment, nevertheless, you are haunted with the sense of a double identity with the knowledge that "there is a natural body, and there is a spiritual body." When you, the natural man, have had this experience you will go automatically across the bridge of events which leads to the physical realization of your invisibly prepared place.

This concept, that man is dual and that the inner man of imagination can dwell in future states and return to the present moment with a bridge of events to link the two clashes violently, with the widely accepted view about the human personality and the cause and nature of phenomena. Such a concept demands a revolution in current ideas about the human personality, and about space, time and matter. The concept that man, consciously or unconsciously, determines the conditions of life by imagining himself into these mental states, leads to the conclusion that this supposedly solid world is a construction of Mind—a concept which, at first, common sense rejects. However, we should remember that most of the concepts which common sense at first rejected, man was afterward forced to accept. These never-ending reversals of judgment which experience has forced upon man led Professor Whitehead to write: "Heaven knows what seeming nonsense may not tomorrow be demonstrated truth".

The creative power in man sleeps and needs to be awakened.

> ## "Awake thou that sleepest, and arise from the dead."
> —Ephesians 5:14

Wake from the sleep that tells you the outer world is the cause of the conditions of your life. Rise from the dead past and create a new environment.

> ## "Know ye not that ye are the temple of God, and that the Spirit of God dwelleth in you?"
> —I. Corinthians 3:16

The Spirit of God in you is your imagination, but it sleeps and needs to be awakened, in order to lift you off the bar of the senses where you have so long lain stranded.

The boundless possibilities open to you as you become "wise as serpents" is beyond measure. You will select the ideal conditions you want to experience and the ideal environment you want to live in. Experiencing these states in imagination until they have sensory vividness, you will externalize them as surely as the serpent now externalizes its skin.

After you have outgrown them, then, you will cast them off as easily as "snakes shed their skin." The more abundant

Be Ye Wise as Serpents

life—the whole purpose of Creation—cannot be saved through death and resurrection.

God desired form, so He became man; and it is not enough for us to recognize His spirit at work in creation, we must see His work in form and say that it is good, even though we outgrow the form, forever and ever.

"He leads Through widening chambers of delight to where Throbs rapture near *an end that aye recedes*, Because His touch is Infinite and lends *A yonder to all ends*."

* * *

"And, I, if I be lifted up from the earth, will draw all men unto me."
—John 12:32

If I be lifted up from the evidence of the senses to the state of consciousness I desire to realize and remain in that state until it feels natural, I will form that state around me and all men will see it. But how to persuade man this is true that imaginative life is the only living; that assuming the feeling of the wish fulfilled is the way to the more abundant life and not the compensation of the escapist—that is the problem. To see as "through widening chambers of delight" what living in the realms of imagination means, to appreciate and enjoy the world, one must live imaginatively; one must dream and occupy his dream, then grow and outgrow the dream, forever and ever. The unimaginative man, who will not lose his life on one

323

level that he may find it on a higher level, is nothing but a Lot's wife—a pillar of self-satisfied salt. On the other hand, those who refuse form as being unspiritual and who reject incarnation as separate from God are ignorant of the great mystery: "Great is the mystery, God was manifest in the flesh".

Your life expresses one thing, and one thing only, your state of consciousness. Everything is dependent upon that. As you, through the medium of imagination, assume a state of consciousness, that state begins to clothe itself in form. It solidifies around you as the serpent's skin ossifies around it. But you must be faithful to the state. You must not go from state to state, but, rather, wait patiently in the one invisible state until it takes on form and becomes an objective fact. Patience is necessary, but patience will be easy after your first success in shedding the old and growing the new, for we are able to wait according as we have been rewarded by understanding in the past. Understanding is the secret of patience. What natural joy and spontaneous delight lie in seeing the world—not with, but as Blake says—through the eye! Imagine that you are seeing what you want to see, and remain faithful to your vision. Your imagination will make for itself a corresponding form in which to live.

All things are made by imagination's power. Nothing begins except in the imagination of man. "From within out" is the law of the universe. "As within, so without." Man turns outward in his search for truth, but the essential thing is to look within.

"Truth is within ourselves; it
takes no rise From outward things,
what e'er you may believe.
There is an inmost center in us all,
Where truth abides in fullness and to
know, Rather consist in opening out a
way Whence the imprisoned splendor
may escape, Than in effecting entry for
a light Supposed to be without."

—Browning: "Paracelsus"

I think you will be interested in an instance of how a
young woman shed the skin of resentment and put on a far
different kind of skin. The parents of this woman had separated when she was six years old and she had lived with her
mother. She rarely saw her father. But once a year he sent her
a five dollar check for Christmas. Following her marriage, he
did increase the Christmas gift to ten dollars.

After one of my lectures, she was dwelling on my statement that man's suspicion of another is only a measure of his
own deceitfulness, and she recognized that she had been har-
boring a resentment towards her father for years. That night
she resolved to let go her resentment and put a fond reaction
in its place. In her imagination, she felt she was embracing her
father in the warmest way. She did it over and over again until
she caught the spirit of her imaginary act, and then she fell
asleep in a very contented mood.

The following day she happened to pass through the fur
department of one of our large stores in California. For some
time she had been toying with the idea of having a new fur
scarf, but felt she could not afford it. This time her eye was

caught by a stone marten scarf, and she picked it up and tried it on. After feeling it and seeing herself in it, reluctantly she took off the scarf and returned it to the salesman, telling herself she really could not afford it. As she was leaving the department, she stopped and thought, "Neville tells us we can have whatever we desire if we will only capture the feeling of already having it." In her imagination, she put the scarf back on, felt the reality of it, and went about her shopping, all the while enjoying the imagined wearing of it.

This young woman never associated these two imaginary acts. In fact, she had almost forgotten what she had done until, a few weeks later, on Mother's Day, the doorbell rang unexpectedly. There was her father. As she embraced him, she remembered her first imaginary action. As she opened the package he had brought her—the first gift in these many years —she remembered her second imaginary action, for the box contained a beautiful stone marten scarf.

> "Ye are gods; and all of you
> are children of the most High."
> —Psalms 82:6

> ". . . be ye therefore wise as
> serpents, and harmless as doves."
> —Matthew 10:16

CHAPTER 48

THE WATER AND
THE BLOOD

". . . Except a man be born again he cannot see the kingdom of God."
—John 3:3

"But one of the soldiers with a spear pierced his side, and forthwith came there out blood and water."
—John 19:34

"This is he that came by water and blood, even Jesus Christ; not by water only, but by water and blood."
—I. John 5:6

According to the Gospel and the Epistle of John, not only must man be "born again" but he must be "born again" of water and blood. These two inward experiences are linked with two outward rites of baptism and communion. But the two outward rites baptism to symbolize birth by water, and the wine of communion to symbolize acceptance of the blood of the Savior, cannot produce the real birth or radical transformation of the individual, which is promised to man. The outward use of water and wine cannot bring about the desired change of mind. We must, therefore, look for the hidden meaning behind the symbols of water and blood.

The Bible uses many images to symbolize Truth, but the images used symbolize Truth on different levels of meaning. On the lowest level, the image used is stone. For example:

" . . . a great stone was upon the well's mouth. And thither were all the flocks gathered: and they rolled the stone from the well's mouth, and watered the sheep. . ."

—Genesis 29:2, 3

" . . . they sank into the bottom as a stone."

—Exodus 15:5

When a stone blocks the well, it means that people have taken these great symbolical revelations of Truth literally. When someone rolls the stone away, it means that an individual has discovered beneath the allegory or parable its psychological life germ, or meaning. This hidden meaning which lies behind the literal words is symbolized by water. It is this water, in the form of psychological Truth, that he then offers to humanity.

"The flock of my pasture, are men."

—Ezekiel 34:31

The literal-minded man who refuses the "cup of water"— psychological Truth-offered him, "sinks into the bottom as a stone". He remains on the level where he sees everything in pure objectivity, without any subjective relationship. He may keep all the Commandments—written on stone—literally, and yet break them psychologically all day long. He may, for example, not literally steal the property of another, and yet see the other in want. To see another in want, is to rob him of his birthright as a child of God. For we are all "children of the Most High."

"And if children, then heirs; heirs of God, and joint-heirs with Christ. . ."
—Romans 8:17

To know what to do about a seeming misfortune is to have the "cup of water" —the psychological Truth -that could save the situation. But such knowledge is not enough. Man must not only "fill the water pots of stone with water" —that is, discover the psychological truth behind the obvious fact, but he must turn the water—the psychological truth into wine. This he does by living a life according to the truth which he has discovered. Only by such use of the truth can he "taste the water that was made wine . . ." —John 2:9.

A man's birthright is to be Jesus. He is born to "save his people from their sins". . . Matthew: 1: 21. But the salvation of a man is "not by water only, but by water and blood".

To know what to do to save yourself or another is not enough; you must do it. Knowledge of what to do is water; doing it is blood. "This is he that came not by water only, but by water and blood." The whole of this mystery is in the conscious, active use of imagination to appropriate that particular state of consciousness that would save you or another from the present limitation. Outward ceremonies cannot accomplish this.

> ". . . there shall meet you a man bearing a pitcher of
> water: follow him. And wheresoever he shall go in, say ye
> to the good man of the house, The Master saith, Where is

The Water and The Blood

the guest-chamber, where I shall eat the passover with
my disciples? And he will show you a large upper
room furnished and prepared: there make ready for us."
—Mark 14:13, 14, 15

Whatever you desire is already "furnished and prepared".
Your imagination can put you in touch inwardly with that state
of consciousness. If you imagine that you are already the one
you want to be, you are following the "man bearing a pitcher
of water". If you remain in that state, you have entered the
guest-chamber—passover—and committed your spirit into
the Hands of God—your consciousness.

A man's state of consciousness is his demand on the
Infinite Store House of God, and, like the law of commerce, a
demand creates a supply. To change the supply, you change the
demand—your state of consciousness. What you desire to be,
that you must feel you already are. Your state of consciousness
creates the conditions of your life, rather than the conditions
create your state of consciousness. To know this Truth, is to
have the "water of life".

But your Savior-the solution of your problem- cannot be
manifested by such knowledge only. It can be realized only as
such knowledge is applied. Only as you assume the feeling of
your wish fulfilled, and continue therein, is your "side
pierced; from whence cometh blood and water". In this manner only is Jesus the solution of your problem—realized.

"For thou must know that in the government of thy
mind thou art thine own lord and master, that there will
rise up no fire in the circle or whole circumference of thy
body and spirit, unless thou awakest it thyself."
—Jacob Boehme

330

The Water and The Blood

God is your consciousness. His promises are conditional. Unless the demand—your state of consciousness—is changed, the supply—the present conditions of your life— remain as they are. "As we forgive"—as we change our mind—the Law is automatic. Your state of consciousness is the spring of action, the directing force, and that which creates the supply.

> "If that nation, against whom I have pronounced, turn from their evil, I will repent of the evil that I thought to do unto them. And at what instant I shall speak concerning a nation, and concerning a kingdom, to build and to plant it; If it do evil in my sight, that it obey not my voice, then I will repent of the good, wherewith I said I would benefit them."
>
> —Jeremiah 18:8,9,10

This statement of Jeremiah suggests that a commitment is involved if the individual or nation would realize the goal—a commitment to certain fixed attitudes of mind. The feeling of the wish fulfilled is a necessary condition in man's search for the goal.

The story I am about to tell you shows that man is what the observer has the capacity to see in him; that what he is seen to be is a direct index to the observer's state of consciousness. This story is, also, a challenge to us all to "shed our blood"—use our imagination lovingly on behalf of another.

There is no day that passes that does not afford us the opportunity to transform a life by the "shedding of our blood".

"Without the shedding of blood
there is no remission."

—Hebrews 9:22

One night in New York City I was able to unveil the mystery of the "water and the blood" to a school teacher. I had quoted the above statement from Hebrews 9:22, and went on to explain that the realization that we have no hope save in ourselves is the discovery that God is within us—that this discovery causes the dark caverns of the skull to grow luminous, and we know that: "The spirit of man is the candle of the Lord"—'Proverbs 20:27'—and that this realization is the light to guide us safely over the earth.

"His candle shined upon my head
and by his light I walked through
darkness."

—Job 29:3

However, we must not look upon this radiant light of the head as God, for man is the image of God.

"God appears, and God is Light,
To those poor souls who dwell in
Night; But does a Human Form display
To those who dwell in realms of Day."

—Blake

But this must be experienced to be known. There is no other way, and no other man's experience can be a substitute for our own.

332

The Water and The Blood

I told the teacher that her change of attitude in regard to another would produce a corresponding change in the other; that such knowledge was the true meaning of the water mentioned in I. John 5:6, but that such knowledge alone was not enough to produce the re-birth desired: that such re-birth could only come to pass by "water and blood", or the application of this truth. Knowledge of what to do is the water of life, but doing it is the blood of the Savior. In other words, a little knowledge, if carried out in action is more profitable than much knowledge which we neglect to carry out in action.

As I talked, one student kept impinging upon the teacher's mind. But this, thought she, would be a too difficult case on which to test the truth of what I was telling her concerning the mystery of rebirth. All knew, teachers and students alike, that this particular student was incorrigible.

The outer facts of her case were these: The teachers, including the Principal and school Psychiatrist, had sat in judgment on the student just a few days before. They had come to the unanimous decision that the girl, for the good of the school, must be expelled upon reaching her sixteenth birthday. She was rude, crude, unethical and used most vile language. The date for dismissal was but a month away.

As she rode home that night, the teacher kept wondering if she could really change her mind about the girl, and if so, would the student undergo a change of behavior because she herself had undergone a change of attitude?

The only way to find out would be to try. This would be quite an undertaking for it meant assuming full responsiblity for the incarnation of the new values in the student. Did she dare to assume so great a power-such creative, God-like power? This meant a complete reversal of man's normal attitude towards life from "I will love him, if he first loves me", to "He loves me, because I first loved him." This was too much like playing God.

"We love him, because he first loved us."

—I. John 4:19

But no matter how she tried to argue against it, the feeling persisted that my interpretation gave meaning to the mystery of re-birth by "water and blood".

The teacher decided to accept the challenge. And this is what she did. She brought the child's face before her mind's eye and saw her smile. She listened and imagined she heard the girl say "Good morning". This was something the student had never done since coming to that school. The teacher imagined the very best about the girl, and then listened and looked as though she heard and saw all that she would hear and see after these things should be. The teacher did this over and over again until she persuaded herself it was true, and fell asleep.

The very next morning, the student entered her classroom and smilingly said, "Good morning". The teacher was so surprised she almost did not respond, and, by her own confession, all through the day she looked for signs of the girl returning to her former behavior. However, the girl continued in the transformed state. By the end of the week, the change was noted by all; a second staff meeting was called and the decision of expulsion was revoked. As the child remained friendly and gracious, the teacher has had to ask herself, "Where was the bad child in the first place?"

"For Mercy, Pity, Peace, and
Love Is God, our Father dear,
And Mercy, Pity, Peace, and Love
Is man, His child and care."
(The Divine Image)

—Blake

Transformation is in principle always possible, for the transformed being lives in us, and it is only a question of becoming conscious of it. The teacher had to experience this transformation to know the mystery of "blood and water"; there was no other way, and no man's experience could have been a substitute for her own.

"We have redemption through his blood."

—Ephesians 1:7

Without the decision to change her mind in regard to the child, and the imaginative power to carry it out, the teacher could never have redeemed the student. None can know of the redemptive power of imagination who has not "shed his blood", and tasted the cup of experience.

"Once read thy own breast right, And thou hast done with fears! Man gets no other light, Search he a thousand years."

—Matthew Arnold

CHAPTER 49

A MYSTICAL VIEW

*"And with many such parables spake he the
word unto them, as they were able to hear it.
But without a parable spake he not unto them:
and when they were alone, he expounded all
things to his disciples."*
—Mark 4:33,34

This collection of parables which is called the Bible is a
revelation of Truth expressed in symbolism to reveal the Laws
and purposes of the Mind of man. As we become aware of
deeper meanings in the parables than those which are usually
assigned to them, we are apprehending them mystically.

For example, let us take a mystical view of the advice
given to the disciples in Matthew 10:10. We read that as the
disciples were ready to teach and practice the great laws of
Mind which had been revealed to them, they were told not to
provide shoes for their journey. A disciple is one who disci-
plines his Mind that he may consciously function and act on
ever higher and higher levels of consciousness. The shoe was
chosen as a symbol of vicarious atonement or the spirit of
"let-me-do-it-for-you", because the shoe protects its wearer
and shields him from impurities by taking them upon itself.
The aim of the disciple is always to lead himself and others
from the bondage of dependency into the liberty of the Sons
of God. Hence the advice, take no shoes. Accept no intermediary between yourself and God. Turn from all who
would offer to do for you what you should, and could, do far
better yourself.

A Mystical View

"Earth's crammed with Heaven,
And every common bush afire with
God, But only he who sees takes off
his shoes."

—Elizabeth Barrett Browning

"Verily I say unto you, Inasmuch as
ye have done it unto one of the least
of these my brethren, ye have done
it unto me."

—Matthew 25:40

Every time you exercise your imagination on behalf of another, be it good, bad or indifferent, you have literally done that to Christ, for Christ is awakened Human Imagination. Through the wise and loving use of imagination, man clothes and feeds Christ, and through the ignorant and fearful misuse of imagination, man disrobes and scourges Christ.

"Let none of you imagine evil in your hearts against his neighbor"—Zechariah 8:17, is sound but negative advice. A man may stop misusing his imagination on the advice of a friend; he may be negatively served by the experience of others and learn what not to imagine, but that is not enough. Such lack of use of the creative power of imagination could never clothe and feed Christ. The purple robe of the Son of God is woven, not by not imagining evil, but by imagining the good; by the active, voluntary and loving use of imagination.

"Whatsoever things are of good report; if there be any virtue, and if there be any praise, think on these things."

—Philippians 4:8

"King Solomon made himself a chariot of the wood of Lebanon. He made the pillars thereof of silver, the bottom thereof of gold, the covering of it of purple, the midst thereof being paved with love. . ."

—Song of Solomon 3:9, 10

The first thing we notice is "King Solomon made himself". That is what every man must eventually do - make himself a chariot of the wood of Lebanon. By chariot, the writer of this allegory means Mind, in which stands the spirit of Wisdom—Solomon—controlling the four functions of Mind that he may build a world of Love and Truth.

"And Joseph made ready his chariot and went up to meet Israel his father." "What tributaries follow him to Rome to grace in captive bonds his chariot wheels?" If man does not make himself a chariot of the wood of Lebanon, then his will be like Queen Mab's: "She is the fairies' midwife; . . . her chariot is an empty hazelnut."

The wood of Lebanon was the mystic's symbol of incorruptibility. To a mystic, it is obvious what King Solomon made himself. Silver typified knowledge, gold symbolized wisdom, and purple—a mixture of red and blue—clothed or covered the incorruptible Mind with the red of Love and the blue of Truth.

A Mystical View

"And they clothed him with purple."
—Mark 15:17

Incarnate, incorruptible four—fold wisdom, clothed in purple —Love and Truth—the purpose of man's experience on earth.

"Love is the sage's stone;
It takes gold from the clod;
It turns naught into aught,
Transforms me into God."
—Angelus Silesius